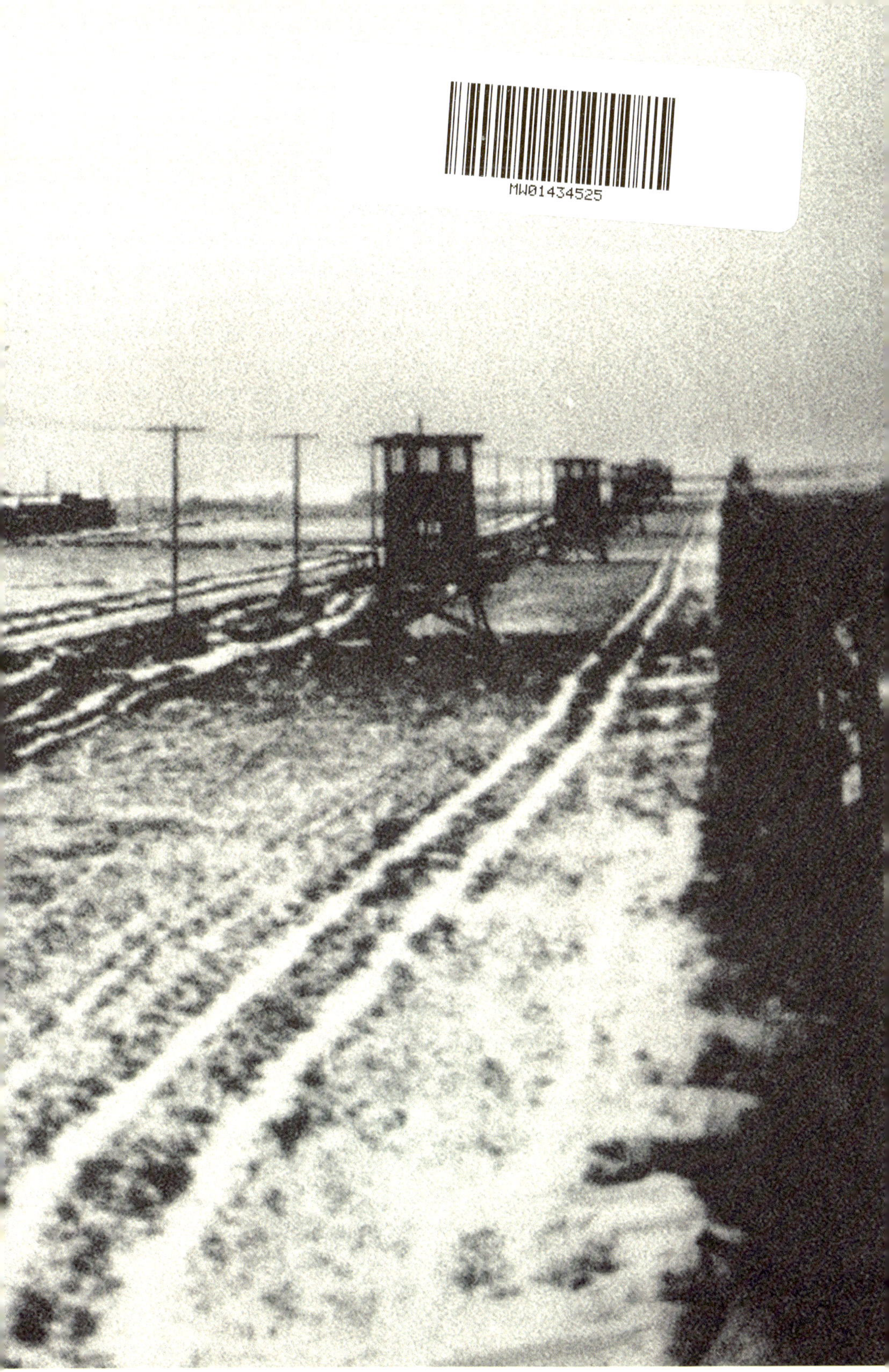

Hanged in Medicine Hat

Hanged in Medicine Hat

MURDERS IN A
NAZI PRISONER-OF-WAR CAMP,
AND THE DISTURBING TRUE STORY
OF CANADA'S LAST MASS EXECUTION

NATHAN M. GREENFIELD

sh.
SUTHERLAND
HOUSE
TORONTO, 2022

Sutherland House
416 Moore Ave., Suite 205
Toronto, ON M4G 1C9

Copyright © 2022 by Nathan M. Greenfield

All rights reserved, including the right to reproduce this book or portions thereof in any form whatsoever. For information on rights and permissions or to request a special discount for bulk purchases, please contact Sutherland House at info@sutherlandhousebooks.com

Sutherland House and logo are registered trademarks of The Sutherland House Inc.

First edition, October 2022

If you are interested in inviting one of our authors to a live event or media appearance, please contact sranasinghe@sutherlandhousebooks.com and visit our website at sutherlandhousebooks.com for more information about our authors and their schedules.

We acknowledge the support of the Government of Canada.

Manufactured in China
Cover designed by Lena Yang

Library and Archives Canada Cataloguing in Publication
Title: Hanged in Medicine Hat : murders in a Nazi prisoner-of-war camp, and the disturbing true story of Canada's last mass execution / Nathan M. Greenfield.
Names: Greenfield, Nathan M., 1958- author.
Identifiers: Canadiana 20220245142 | ISBN 9781989555804 (hardcover)
Subjects: LCSH: Serial murders—Alberta—Medicine Hat. | LCSH: Trials (Murder)—Alberta—Medicine Hat. | LCSH: Hanging—Alberta—Medicine Hat. | LCSH: Nazis—Alberta—Medicine Hat. | LCSH: World War, 1939-1945—Prisoners and prisons, Canadian.
Classification: LCC HV6535.C33 M43 2022 | DDC 364.152/30971234—dc23

ISBN 978-1-989555-80-4

To Micheline, who also didn't anticipate a global pandemic, but who has been there for me through the hundreds of days we call, "March 27, 2020"

And

Finn Daniel Max Greenfield, my second grandchild, who has restarted the clock of December 9, our birthdays

and

Irving A. Greenfield, my father, who taught me the power of the written word, and who has been gone these last two years.

Contents

Preface		ix
Prologue		xii
CHAPTER ONE	The Establishment of POW Camps in Canada and the Transfer of the Captured Afrika Corpsmen to Canada 1941–1942	1
CHAPTER TWO	Life in Canadian POW Camps 1942–1945	9
CHAPTER THREE	The Murder of August Plaszek July 22, 1943	28
CHAPTER FOUR	The Investigation into the Murder of August Plaszek July 24, 1943 to September 16, 1944	37
CHAPTER FIVE	The Investigation into the Murder of Dr. Karl Lehmann September 11, 1944 to April 8, 1945	55

CHAPTER SIX	From the German Surrender to the Plaszek Murder Trials May 8, 1945 to March 6, 1946	77
CHAPTER SEVEN	*Rex v. Werner Schwalb* February 25 to March 5, 1946	102
CHAPTER EIGHT	*Rex v. Adolf Kratz* March 7 to March 16, 1946	127
CHAPTER NINE	The Appeals in the Plaszek Murder Trials, *Rex v. Johannas Wittinger,* and the Execution of Adolf Kratz April to June 1946	140
CHAPTER TEN	The Lehmann Murder Trials June 24 to July 2, 1946	151
CHAPTER ELEVEN	Lehmann Appeals and Pleas for Clemency September 6 to December 17, 1946	190
CHAPTER TWELVE	The Executions of Bruno Perzenowski, Heinrich Busch, Walter Wolf, and Willy Müeller December 18, 1946	202
	Epilogue: Executing Justice	205
	Acknowledgments	219
	Notes	221
	Bibliography	243

Preface

FIFTEEN YEARS AGO, WHILE researching the book that became *The Damned: The Canadians at the Battle of Hong Kong and the POW Experience, 1941–1945* (2010), I had the great privilege to get to know George MacDonell, Jean-Paul Dallain, Bill MacWhirter, and Phil Doddridge. Along with almost 2,000 other men of C Force, they were taken prisoner by the Japanese on Christmas Day, 1942. They shared with me their stories of battle against the Imperial Japanese Army, military defeat, the emotional storms of being captured, and the horrors inflicted on them by their captors. More than half a century later, I could tell from their pained expressions that the beatings they witnessed and endured were difficult to talk about. Torture and the effects of malnutrition were never far from their minds or bodies. Being forced to play the role of a slave labourer in mines and shipyards was pain in a different, deeper, key.

That pain was shared and understood by men from their father's war who were captured by Imperial Germany. Some of the almost 4,000 Canadians caught by Kaiser Wilhelm's armies, as I tell in *The Reckoning: Canadian Prisoners of War in the Great War* (2016), were essentially slave labour in German mines. Unlike MacDonell's comrades, in camps in Japan and Hong Kong, the so-called "guests of the Kaiser" stood some chance of making it to neutral ground—Holland, Denmark, Switzerland—if they escaped. A POW on the run in Europe could hope to blend in with the local population (some spoke sufficient German or French). This was impossible for POWs in Japanese camps. Escape would have meant travelling at night and steering by the stars.

Whether held by the Kaiser or Hitler, POWs in Europe required luck and trust to evade capture and escape. Ian MacDonald was one of the dozens of men (out of 10,000) I wrote about in *The Forgotten: Canadian POWs, Escapers and Evaders in Europe, 1939–45* (2013). Shot down in 1942, he trusted his life to the famed Comet Line, a resistance organization in occupied France and Belgium, only to be betrayed by the last man in the "circuit" who led him not into Spain but into the hands of the Gestapo. Sergeant Major Lucien Dumais, who survived Dieppe, was more fortunate. After jumping from a moving train, he connected with an escape line that arranged for him to be picked up from a French beach.

There were many differences in the treatment of POWs in Germany, Japan, and Canada. In Germany some went hungry while in Japan they were starved; in Canada, the German POWs were so well fed they put on weight. Germany pressured men to work while Japan forced them at the point of a bayonet or the threat of a beating. In Canada, the German POWs were offered work outside the POW camp that earned the same wages paid to local labourers. In all three countries, some prisoners maintained discipline; others fell to pieces. But all possessed a certain understanding of what it meant to be a prisoner of war, under the thumb of an enemy administration yet expected to remain loyal to a distant land and military leadership.

Save for the thirty-two Canadians captured during the Korean war, the Canadians who lived behind Japanese and German barbed wire in

PREFACE

the World Wars are the only soldiers who could appreciate the circumstances endured by the men in this book. They would have understood the isolation, the fears, the longings, and most importantly the actions of German prisoners of war stashed by the thousands in camps stretching from Hull, Quebec, to Fort Henry in Kingston, Ontario, to the setting of our story, Camp 132 in Medicine Hat, Alberta. What would they have made of the murders by men wearing the uniforms of the Wehrmacht and Luftwaffe of two of their own? It's difficult to say for certain, but their perspective would undoubtedly have been different than that of the court officials and jurors who conducted the questionable murder trials that led to the mass hanging of four German soldiers in Medicine Hat in 1946.

Ottawa, Ontario
March, 2022

Prologue

"A summary of what I learned the day I skipped an afternoon at school to go to the German trial"

—Joyce Reesor

ON EITHER THURSDAY, MARCH 7, 1946, or the following day, Joyce Reesor stood before the forbidding J.T. Cuyler, principal of Medicine Hat High School, awaiting her punishment for being truant earlier in the week. The usual punishment for such a crime was a week's detention, but the sixteen-year-old Reesor was not a typical troublemaker. She was a good student with a clean record, and a member of the school's female glee club, the "Victory Girls." The shortest of the six girls, she was vivacious, and the focal point of the club's photograph. Her good standing weighed in her favour with Principal Cuyler, as did the unique reason she had skipped school. Instead of suspending her, he sentenced Reesor to write an essay on what she learned that Wednesday, watching the conclusion of the first of six of the most unique murder trials in Canadian history.

PROLOGUE

Like most "Hatters," as the denizens of Medicine Hat, Alberta, call themselves, Reesor knew the open secrets about prisoner-of-war Camp No. 132 on the eastern fringe of the small prairie city. In 1943, one prisoner had been murdered by other inmates of the camp, followed by another murder a year later. These crimes were not reported in the press during the war. But heavy censorship did nothing to stop the Hatters from talking.

Reesor perhaps had a stronger interest in Camp 132 than did most students. She and the five other Victory Girls, and the club's director, Reesor's mother Dorothy, were the only women known to have visited the "other side of the wire."[1] On the evening of December 20, 1943, the girls performed a Christmas concert in the camp's theatre. They sang twenty songs, including Vera Lynn's 1941 standard, "When They Sound the Last 'All Clear'," which likely meant something different to the German POWs captured in Britain after being shot down than it did to the Canadian men who had survived the trench bombardments during the Great War and now supervised Camp 132 as Veterans Guardsman, but it was appreciated all around. Another number, "The Sailor with the Navy Blue Eyes" had surprisingly suggestive lyrics, especially for a girl's high-school glee club in the mid-1940s: "Who's got girls in every port/ hanging around like flies." Dorothy Reesor likely chose it knowing that the prisoners keenly felt their isolation. The same could be said for Joyce's solo, "They're Either Too Young or Too Old," which had been sung by Bette Davis in the 1943 film *Thank Your Lucky Stars*. It laments the fact that all the eligible men are in the army. Naturally, the concert also featured that year's hit, "I'll Be Home for Christmas," expressing the fervent wish of every prisoner in attendance.

But for a small timing error, Reesor, her mother, and the other Victory Girls would not have had any close contact with the POWs. Either the club arrived in the space set aside as its dressing room a little early, or it had taken the prisoner detailed to clean the room a few moments longer than expected. Or perhaps he had lingered, hoping to give himself the Christmas gift of proximity to young women. "As we were entering the dressing room," Reesor said, "we saw a good-looking man, a POW, sweeping the area." The Veterans Guardsman escorting the girls stepped up and yelled, "Get out of here, you baby killer." With the horrors of Auschwitz and Treblinka not yet revealed, the epithet referenced atrocities in Belgium from the guard's war, possibly before the prisoner was born.[2]

That Reesor noticed the prisoner was a "good looking man" fits with other memories Hatters had of the POWs, who were quite visible. Some worked on local farms, and imprisoned senior non-commissioned officers (NCOs) and the one German officer in the camp, Captain Dr. Maximillian Nolte, were allowed walking tours of the city. Many of the POWs were elite troops. Several thousand of the camp's 12,500 inmates belonged to Field Marshall Erwin Rommel's famed Afrika Korps: they were young, strong, disciplined, confident, and, by all accounts, a handsome bunch. The young women were impressed, as was the author Barry Broadfoot, himself a soldier at the time. He recalled seeing about forty German POWs working outdoors. "[E]very bloody one was a giant, six-foot-two.... All fair-haired, blue-eyed, thighs like hams, and tanned like Charles Atlas, Mr. World, and we thought 'Christ, who *are* these guys." A guard told Broadfoot the men had belonged to "the Eighth Army, Rommel's supermen, Hitler's elite, and they'd been captured in North Africa.... Here were these supermen, and I do mean supermen, and they looked at us as if we were common clay."[3]

Impressive as the Nazis seemed, Medicine Hat mothers deemed them less of a threat than the Norwegian airmen training in another part of town at the British Commonwealth Service Flying Training School. These allies were "so attractive that parents tried to hide their daughters from them," Reesor recalls.[4]

The Second World War was over and Camp 132 almost empty by the time Reesor attended the Medicine Hat murder trial. For years, newspapers had been filled with stories about great battles: the Fall of France, the Battle of Britain, Pearl Harbor, the Fall of Hong Kong, Stalingrad, D-Day, Okinawa, and the dropping of atomic bombs. Now they were filled with accounts of war crimes trials.

British Prime Minister Winston Churchill, U.S. President Franklin D. Roosevelt, and Soviet Premier Joseph Stalin had agreed at their Yalta conference to prosecute prominent members of the Nazi's political, military, judicial, and economic leadership. Out of this gossamer and, partly, from the spirit of the Convention Relative to the Treatment of Prisoners of War, Geneva, July 27, 1929, (the Geneva Convention), international lawyers wove a war crimes code that undergirded the International Criminal Court that sat in Nuremberg, and other courts that would sit elsewhere. Brushing away the complaint that this was "victor's justice," the court settled on four counts: conspiracy, crimes against peace, war crimes, and crimes against humanity. In total, thirty-two men, including Hitler's deputy Rudolph Hess and Reichsmarshall Hermann Göring, were tried in Nuremberg. Twelve, including Hess, were executed. Göring spared himself the noose by biting down on a cyanide capsule the night before his scheduled execution.

Other war crimes news hit closer to home. In December 1945, Canadians read about the trial of SS Brigadeführer Kurt Meyer, who was accused of killing forty-one Canadians captured on June 7 and 8, 1945, following D-Day. He was found guilty and sentenced to death, although his sentence was later commuted to life in prison.

The trials in Medicine Hat, population 13,500, incorporated for less than four decades and 7,500 kilometres from Berlin, were different from those high-profile affairs in that they involved Nazified German servicemen murdering other German servicemen. The courtroom drama Joyce Reesor witnessed concerned POW Sergeant Warner Schwalb, accused of killing fellow POW Private August Plaszek in Camp 132. Although Reesor's family had a history of involvement in public affairs—her father, William Colby Reesor was sheriff of the court, and among her forebears was the Honourable William McDougall, a father of Canada's confederation—the trial was not discussed at home.[5] Joyce followed the proceedings in the pages of the *Medicine Hat News,* which was now free, in peacetime, to report them. The headlines compelled her interest: "Nazi Prisoners on Trial"; "Not a Kangaroo Court: Plaszek One of Four Called for Questioning Before [German] Camp Officials"; "Had Blood on His Hands: Witness Tells of Seeing Schwalb After Plaszek Found Hanging in Hall."[6] These stories, and others explaining Canada's requirements under the Geneva Convention, informed the assignment she wrote for Principal Cuyler following her attendance in court.

The high schooler deftly turned her offence around in "A Day in Court: A Penalty Essay," noting how "fortunate" she was to spend four hours in the courtroom. With a bit of cheek, she told Cuyler that she "learned more of [the] Canadian justice and court procedure, than any class-room or text-book could teach me in a month."[7] She declined to tell how she gained access to the court. Had she done so, her father's authority would have hovered over the essay; he had arranged her seat in the crowded courtroom. She is careful not to name him in her only reference to him: "The court-room was hushed as the six-man jury filed in and the Sheriff called the roll."

The girl who had once sung Christmas Carols for the man on trial for his life "sat enthralled for almost four hours as Chief Justice W. R. Howson elaborated to the jury the facts of the case and the law as written in the Criminal Code of Canada." She was struck by how Howson "stressed over and over again that if there was the slightest fragment of a reasonable doubt as to the man's innocence, a verdict of 'not guilty' must be the final conclusion."

In those four hours, Reesor learned to parse the difference between murder and manslaughter. "Murder is cold and calculating," while manslaughter is enacted under an "insult.... before the attacker has regained his self-control." The sentence for murder was death and for manslaughter, life imprisonment. She recognized the importance of what might have seemed obscure points of law, undiscussed in the newspapers: the controversy over whether the defendant Schwalb should even be tried in a civil court. Given that he was a soldier, should he have faced a military tribunal instead? This would become a key question at Alberta's Appeals Court and, indeed, for the federal cabinet.

As a seasoned thriller writer might have done, Joyce built tension in her account using one sentence paragraphs: "The jury, however, after thirty-five minutes of careful deliberating, returned to a breathless court-room."

Followed by: "Even the ticking of the clock seemed exaggerated as the selected foreman of the jury rose, and delivered the verdict: 'We find the accused guilty of murder.'"

She fairly placed the reader in the courtroom: "The silence was electric. The low monotone of the interpreter could be heard as he translated into German the dreaded statement."

Joyce skillfully reported on two levels of consciousness. "What could Schwalb be thinking?" she wondered, even as she told us, "The judge spoke solemnly, but for the first time that afternoon I tried to exclude his words from my thoughts. I could not see the face of the prisoner—what emotion was betrayed there when his interpreter translated into his own tongue: 'and you shall be hanged by the neck until you are dead, and may the Lord have mercy on your soul.'"

With the verdict still ringing in her ears, Reesor left the stately Medicine Hat court house. It differed from most Canadian court houses, foregoing the traditional Neoclassical formula in favour of an ornate, red-brick Beaux-Art Classicist façade with many recessing and projecting elements, arched windows, and second-storey pilasters. Had she looked to her left, to the east, she would have seen the town's water tower, at the top of which, early in the war, a teenaged boy had painted a swastika. The unflappable townsfolk took years to paint it over and, in the meantime, it had allowed the POWs, who came to see Camp 132 as a "little town in Germany," to enjoy the sight of the Nazi emblem taking pride of place in Medicine Hat's skyline. Given that the populations of the camp and the Hat were roughly equal, the swastika almost made sense.

Reesor's route took her west down 1st Street SE, a block south was 2nd Street SE, the Hat's main shopping district. Anchored by the general post office, 2nd Street SE boasted both the Monarch and Roxy movie theatres, which were playing *Confidential Agent* (starring Charles Boyer and Lauren Bacall) and *The Crystal Ball* (starring Ray Milland and Paulette Goddard). Three blocks further, she turned left on Division, which separates the town's streets into east and west. One more block and she turned right onto 2nd Street SW, which is cut out of a hill. Access to houses on her left was via steps going up and on the right by steps going down. On either side, the two-storey brick houses were fronted with porches, some screened and used only in summer, some with windows that allowed three seasons of enjoyment; the winters were so frigid that porches could not even serve as mud rooms. After crossing 1st Ave SW, she passed an open lot on the north side of the street and turned right down a few steps to her front door.

Reesor's family had been in Medicine Hat since not long after the town was founded in the 1880s. Her paternal grandfather had been a rancher in Walsh, Alberta, forty-eight kilometres south of Medicine Hat on the border with Saskatchewan. The family moved to Medicine Hat when her father, William, was a child. Because of his tuberculosis, William did not work steadily during the 1930s; he became the sheriff of the court in the early 1940s. Joyce's maternal grandfather was English and had been wounded several times in the Great War. He visited Medicine Hat after the armistice, returned to England to marry, and came back with his bride to run a hardware store in another nearby town.

Like so many other cities across Canada, Medicine Hat owed its founding to the Canadian Pacific Railway, and its name to indigenous peoples. The Blackfoot, Cree, and Assiniboine had all hunted in the area for several hundred years, and gathered at the future townsite where the hills sloped gently to the winding South Saskatchewan River. "Medicine Hat" comes from the Blackfoot word "*Saamis,*" which refers to the eagle tail-feather headdress worn by medicine men. One legend that the German POWs would have enjoyed—many of them devoured German author

Karl May's westerns, which were also favoured by their führer—holds that a Cree medicine man lost his headdress in the South Saskatchewan while retreating from a great battle with the Blackfoot.

In 1883, the Canadian Pacific Railway reached the area, halfway between Winnipeg, in the middle of the continent, and Vancouver, on the west coast. As a divisional point for the railroad, Medicine Hat hosted coaling facilities, repair shops, a passenger station, and the water tower familiar to Joyce Reesor. It was incorporated as a city in 1906 and dubbed the "Pittsburgh of the West" when such a term denoted industrial strength. Thanks to an abundance of gas, coal, clay, and sand, the Hat sprouted brick and glass works as well as pottery factories. It also became a major entrepôt for crops and livestock. Of the 10,000 residents who lived in the city in 1940, most traced their heritage to the British Isles, with Germans comprising the largest minority. Among the latter was Army Intelligence officer, sergeant James "Jim" Papsdorf, who authenticated the translation during Schwalb's trial.

Canada's southern prairies had been unusually wet in the last decades of the nineteenth century and the first decades of the twentieth, conditions that encouraged the Canadian government to adopt a policy of agricultural settlement. When the region reverted to more typical dry and barren conditions in the 1930s, Medicine Hat became a dust bowl of the sort John Steinbeck wrote about in *The Grapes of Wrath* and Americans and Canadians saw on the big screen in the 1940 movie of the same name starring Henry Fonda. Joyce Reesor and her cohort at Medicine Hat High School remembered these Great Depression years primarily for the dust storms. "There being no irrigation between Lethbridge [170 kilometres west] and Medicine Hat, when the strong winds blew, they would just blow the dust into town," recalls James

Keating, who grew up in the city and would marry Joyce in 1951. "Then the tumble weeds would roll in."[8]

Of one storm in July 1937, the *Medicine Hat News* wrote, "Another terrible dust storm passed over this district… with a high velocity wind sweeping all before it and drying the land beyond description." The paper added a sentence that was as much an imploration as it was news: "The country is so very much in need of rain."[9]

The Hat's winter cold was as harsh as its summer heat. Bright sunshine in January belied an average low temperature of −14 °C (6.6 °F). At times, locals would be treated to the worst of both worlds: a dust storm on April 4, 1939 was followed in swift succession by two inches of snow. As a lonely, unforgiving outpost, 1,260 kilometres across the Rocky Mountains from tidewater, Medicine Hat struck Canada's military leaders and mandarins as an ideal place to store 12,500 captured Nazis for the duration of World War Two.

Opened early in 1943 and representing a sizeable increase in employment and economic activity for the city, Camp 132 was welcomed by Hatters. That the prisoners were available for farm labour and the occasional hockey game only made their presence more welcome. The locals treated the captives with courtesy, and their manners were reciprocated. The existence of Camp 132 was as positive an experience as could be expected for both sides, except for the shocking killings of Private August Plaszek in 1943 and Sergeant Dr. Karl Lehmann a year later.

After police, Royal Canadian Mounted Police (RCMP), and military intelligence had spent thousands of hours investigating the killings, prosecutors filed their "Information and Complaint" in 1945. The document laid charges of murder against seven POWs, three for killing Plaszek, and four for killing Lehmann. Yet questions remained. Did the authorities indeed, "get their men?" Or had they accused too many men? Should they have been tried in civilian court? Indeed, since they were soldiers claiming they had enforced military law, had they even committed a crime? Was Canada committing a grave injustice by prosecuting POWs for actions that may have been within their rights to commit?

Decades later, Reesor still pondered these questions. The one thing of which she was certain: "I came face to face with history."

CHAPTER 1

The Establishment of POW Camps in Canada and the Transfer of the Captured Afrika Corpsmen to Canada

1941–1942

On 25 November, 1941, almost two years into the Second World War, Private August Plaszek was captured by New Zealand forces near the storied fortress of Tobruk on the Libyan coast. By then, the German attack on Poland that had started the war in September 1939 had been obscured by the smoke of the Blitzkrieg, the six-week campaign that ended with the Fall of France in June 1940, and left the Nazis in control of almost all Western Europe. Then came the Blitz, the 242-day bombing of London, Coventry, Birmingham, Liverpool, Manchester, and other towns and cities across Britain, and the associated air battles. More than 1,497 RAF airmen were killed in the Blitz, along with 43,500 civilians, and another 139,000 wounded. But the redoubtable Royal Air Force checked the Luftwaffe. And, without mastery of the skies—which was needed to seize control of the English Channel—in mid-September 1940 Hitler called off the planned invasion of Britain known as Operation Sea Lion, and turned east. Ten months later, he hurled three army groups totaling more than 3.8 million men against his erstwhile ally, Joseph Stalin's Russia.

Within weeks, scouts for Hitler's Army Group Centre could see the onion dome of the Kremlin in the distance and, closer, the westernmost entrance to the Moscow metro. The winter soon set in, however, and the Wehrmacht would advance no further. Behind it lay a devastated landscape. Hitler's army had suffered more than a million casualties and Stalin's almost four million. Since Soviet Russia had not signed the Geneva Convention, neither Germany nor Russia considered itself bound by its terms. Accordingly, the Germans allowed millions of captured Soviet POWs to die of exposure and malnutrition; those who were transported to camps in eastern Europe were often worked to death. The Russians treated Germans who fell into their hands in the same manner.

Moscow might have been taken had Hitler not answered an SOS from Benito Mussolini in January 1941. The Italian dictator's forces in North Africa had been routed by the British at the First Battle of Al Alamein and were being chased back towards Tripoli. Hitler sent General Rommel and the newly formed Afrika Korps in support. For almost two years, Afrika Korps, led by the "Desert Fox," and General Bernard Montgomery's Desert Rats slugged it out in the sands of what Prime Minister Winston Churchill referred to as the Western Desert.

In October 1941, to bolster Rommel, the Germans despatched the 361st Afrika Regiment, which included Plaszek and hundreds of other men of whom the Afrika Korps wanted no part, even though most had experience fighting in the desert. Plaszek *et al* had been members of the French Foreign Legion before the fall of France. Seeing how the wind was blowing after the Wehrmacht reached Paris, they proactively requested repatriation to Germany rather than await a forced repatriation. Goebbels declared that serving in the Afrika Korps would rehabilitate these men in the eyes of Germany.

The soldiers already breathing dust and sand thought differently. For them, the fact that these men had adopted the Legio Patria Nostra (The Legion is our homeland) when joining the French Foreign Legion signalled their lack of fidelity to the fatherland and Völk. And if they had broken their bond with the Legion, how could they be trusted to now uphold the personal bond between German men in uniform and their führer?

August Plaszek, the balding diminutive private known to his family by his middle name, Männe, which means "strong man," did not serve long in the field. He was captured two days after a savage battle in which New Zealand's 25th Battalion suffered its nation's heaviest casualties in a single day's fighting since the start of the war: 100 dead, some 125 wounded, and another 100 captured.[1] Plaszek was among the 250 men left behind when his battalion collapsed under pressure from two platoons belonging to New Zealand's 18th Battalion. The prisoner-of-war description form notes Plaszek's fair complexion, slightly baggy eyes, poor bite, two small scars, and that he had been a farmer and had a "farmer appearance." (It does not, for some reason, mention Plaszek was all but bald.) He had left a wife and child at home in Germany.

The Germans' beat-up uniforms and lack of food were early indications of the supply problems that would ultimately doom Rommel's expeditionary force. It surrendered in May 1943, serving up a new cohort of POWs, including Sergeant Dr. Karl Lehmann, who was captured at the Gambolia Airfield near Tunis, Tunisia. The one-time university professor, overweight (five-feet-eight inches and 192 pounds) with a receding hairline, good teeth, and a round, double chin, was a translator for the Luftwaffe, responsible for interrogating downed Allied airmen. In addition to German, he spoke English, French, and Italian.

Given Hitler's orders to hold every inch of North Africa and Nazism's idea of the Teutonic Superman, capitulation, difficult for any soldier, was perhaps even more so for Germans than it had been for the Canadians who surrendered at Dieppe in August 1942 or at Hong Kong eight months earlier. Whether the man wore Luftwaffe blue and was captured on a British field, as did two of the true-believing Nazis charged with murdering Lehmann in Camp 132, or he was one of Rommel's desperately thirsty and dusty men, raising hands in supplication was a profoundly emasculating act. Those who claimed to be Übermenschen expected that they would be the ones with their fingers on triggers, saying "*Für Sie ist Krieg zu Ende*"—"For you the war is over."

Unlike the Soviets, Britain, which had signed the Geneva Convention, treated German POWs in accord with the Geneva Convention, as, in fact, for the most part, the Germans treated British, Canadian, Australian, New Zealand, South African, and American POWs. The British provided medical care when needed, as well as food and water and housing in tents. Leaving the captives in the desert, however, was impractical, as was housing them in the United Kingdom, which imported most of its food and thus was at the mercy of the U-boat war on British shipping. Nor did densely populated Britain have the empty space where camps housing tens of thousands of POWs could be constructed, especially given the need for huge bases and training grounds once American soldiers began pouring into Britain in 1942. Accordingly, the British sent the POWs to Canada or South Africa.

Routes to Canada varied. Most of the prisoners saw the Suez Canal (Rommel's ultimate goal) on ships to South Africa where they were held until another ship was available to take them to Halifax or New York. On May 22, 1942, Plaszek and thousands more of Rommel's men arrived in New York harbour aboard RMS *Queen Elizabeth*. They were incredulous at seeing the city's skyscrapers still standing, contrary to what they had read and heard in Goebbels's media reports.[2] Expecting to be herded into cattle cars, as were Russian, British, and Canadian troops who fell into German hands, the POWs instead found Canadian Veterans Guardsmen ushering them onto a Canadian Pacific train where they sat in regular seats. About a day later, having crossed New York State and parts of Pennsylvania and Ohio, they entered Canada at Sarnia, Ontario, which lacked the impressive view that a later group of POWs enjoyed as their train crossed the bridge at Niagara Falls. One captured U-boat officer remembered being struck by the amount of food, meat, sandwiches, apples, and bananas distributed on the train to Canada, and the young people he saw in the cities, towns, and villages his train passed on its way across the Dominion. "They all looked so happy and carefree—totally unlike anything I'd been used to, with the military training and background I'd had."[3] That the Canadian guards on the train carried rifles with fixed bayonets apparently had faded from his memory.

By the time the prisoners arrived in Canada, diplomats in Ottawa and London had been arguing over the placement of POWs for more than two years. Among the strongest voices in Ottawa inclined to accept them was Under-Secretary of State for External Affairs, Oscar Douglas Skelton. He believed Canada's participation in the war should be governed by a policy of "limited liability."[4] This less-than-robust stance was designed to provide material support to the Allies while keeping the need for Canadian troops low enough that the country did not need to conscript soldiers, which would have been highly unpopular in Quebec.

On June 7, 1940, Skelton convinced Prime Minister Mackenzie King to take, at Britain's request, the 7,000 men then in British POW camps.

While the transfer out of Britain of POWs to Canada made both strategic and logistic sense, doing so created unique legal problems, especially as the number of prisoners increased. Under the Geneva Convention, a prisoner of war is the responsibility of the detaining power, or government, that captured him. For Canada, this raised two issues, the first financial, the second touching on Canadian sovereignty.

Since the detaining power, Britain, was financially liable for the support of prisoners, Canada insisted that it be reimbursed after the war for the cost of maintaining the prisoners. In January 1942, King wrote to Vincent Massey, Canada's High Commissioner to Great Britain, telling him that accepting 4,000 Nazis captured in North Africa would "exhaust the capacity of the existing system of camps" in Canada and that "Canadian authorities are considering plans for such units [new camps] to take 10,000 prisoners of war each."[5] Two months later, King instructed Massey to approach the British for permission to start building the camps. In this case, permission meant securing Britain's agreement to pay the cost, almost $2.2 million dollars (or roughly four times the cost of building a corvette for the Royal Canadian Navy) for each camp, one at Medicine Hat, another at Lethbridge, and a third at Ozada, Alberta, which ended up being temporary.[6]

Sovereignty was a thornier issue. Only nine years earlier, the Statute of Westminster recognized Canadian sovereignty and, thus, control over its foreign policy. Nevertheless, as George Warner of the British Foreign Office explained to those he saw as mere colonials, notwithstanding the statute, Britain was the detaining power, and Canada was merely the "holding power," a term which does not exist in the Geneva Convention.

It followed in Warner's mind that Canada's regulations pertaining to prisoners and the running of POW camps had to be identical to Britain's. Some of the regulations dealt with prisoner's pay. Geneva mandated that POWs be paid at the rate of their rank (in the Wehrmacht) and for work, including farm labour. By the end of the war, thousands of POWs had worked on Canadian farms, many around Medicine Hat. At the start of the war, Britain had negotiated an agreement with Germany that POWs would be paid at the rate of 15 RM to 1£. London feared that if the pay rate was calculated from Reichsmarks to Canadian dollars, Berlin would expect to deal directly with Canada on other POW matters, weakening Britain's hand when negotiating with Germany through the International Committee of the Red Cross. In October 1940, Britain agreed that the pound would be converted to Canadian dollars before being credited to the POWs' accounts.

Another regulatory issue flagged by Warner was resolved by an all-too-predictable compromise between Britain's inclination to centralize authority and the desire of the dominion governments of Canada and Australia for a seat at the table in matters that concerned their soldiers. Accordingly, Canada and Australia delegated to Britain the responsibility to speak on international issues pertaining to POWs while at the same time establishing an InterGovernmental Prisoner of War Committee, a subcommittee of which was charged with reconciling differences over interpretations of the Geneva Convention. The subcommittee rarely met.

One other area of jurisdiction ripe for conflict lay within the prisoner of war camps themselves. Obviously, the camps were on Canadian soil, and the POWs were captives of the detaining power, Canada on behalf of Great Britain. But the Geneva Convention and international law recognized that prisoners of war exercised a certain amount of sovereignty over life in POW camps, electing their own leadership, maintaining order to their standards, and planning their own activities. The resulting tension between Canadian oversight and German camp leadership, and uncertainty about whose authority and laws applied under certain circumstances—in the aftermath of a murder, for instance—would become particularly relevant in Medicine Hat's Camp 132.

CHAPTER 2

Life in Canadian POW Camps[1]

1942–1945

THE PRISONERS OF WAR who had endured the dust of Africa and the monotony of the trans-Atlantic voyage were astounded at the distance they found themselves travelling across Canada as well as by the country's natural beauty. Though only a tent-camp, Ozada, today a ghost town in the foothills of the Rockies, had its charms, recalled the Luftwaffe anti-aircraft gunner Gottfried Dukes. "I shall always remember the lush green of the meadows and the lovely mountains shimmering blue in the distance. And also, this wonderful smell of pine wood and prairie flowers.... I was so much reminded of my home country and I liked this place on the spot." Dukes was equally impressed by the snow that piled up six months later and the "mysterious patterns in the sky of the Aurora Borealis zigzagging across the starlit sky."[2]

A year later, Dukes' comrades in Camp 40 in Farnham, Quebec, 60 kilometres south east of Montreal, took a more military view of winter: they tunnelled through a snow bank pushed up against the camp's barbed wire so they could cut it without being seen. A similar trick in Ozada would have led only to vast winter wilderness.

Medicine Hat was almost as remote as Ozada, an important geographical requirement for a large POW camp. The nearest urban centre, Calgary, was 300 kilometres away and had fewer than 100,000 people. The flat layout of the 123-acre camp meant that guards in sixteen towers had clear sight lines to fire on prisoners if necessary. The Canadian Pacific rail lines were the primary routes in and out of the city. Patrols of boxcars ensured that a POW who managed to get past the double-wired fence would not be able to board a train. Escape on foot was almost impossible, for a "person unfamiliar with the region could easily become disoriented and perish from heat exhaustion during the summer and hypothermia during the winter," wrote Robin W. Stotz, who wrote his doctoral thesis on the POW camps on the prairies. A stolen car might get a prisoner as far as Calgary but, again, there was no reliable route to tidewater, apart from rail.

Luftwaffe men knew that if they were shot down and picked up by the British they would likely be transferred to their dominions. They joked amongst themselves about ending the war chopping wood in Canada. But even as the airmen and the veterans of the Afrika Korps enjoyed their train journeys west, they feared what would happen once they reached their destinations. They had been told that the commandants of Canada's POW camps were "Jewish and would treat the German prisoners harshly."[4] Accordingly, many of them were surprised at the benign regimen of the Canadian camps.

Daily life began at 6 a.m., with lights out at 10 p.m. At Medicine Hat, as many as 12,000 men were divided among 36 barracks. There were three seatings in the six mess halls, lasting a half hour each for breakfast, lunch, and dinner. Unlike the Germans, who mostly ignored Geneva's requirement to provide food comparable to nearby garrisoned troops and counted Allied prisoners' Red Cross parcels as part of their rations, Canada followed Geneva and provided 3,500 calories per day, including ten ounces of beef per week, ten ounces of bread and biscuits per day, and two ounces of prunes once a week, resulting in POWs gaining an average of twelve pounds (5.5 kilograms) in ten months, according to one report. Since their food was prepared by the POWs themselves and some of them had professional chef's training, their meals were often better than those served in the camp's staff mess. This mostly chagrined the Canadians, although Carmen Jackson, who patrolled Ozada in 1942, recalled the Christmas dinner the German cooks shared with him "as the best Christmas dinner I ever had."[6]

The barracks at Medicine Hat each housed 350 men sleeping on double bunks. Eighteen huts were dedicated to classrooms. There was a detention barrack, two recreations halls (officially denominated East and West), a dental hut, and a well-equipped hospital staffed by German doctors and orderlies. At a time when a large number of Canadian homes, especially farm houses on the prairies, did not have running hot water, the camps had showers with hot water available twenty-four hours a day. Canada supplied the men with shaving kits. Each camp, moreover, had a well-stocked canteen where prisoners could purchase luxury items at local market prices. The POW camp in Petawawa, Ontario, for example, sold bottles of Coca Cola for 5 cents, two bars of Palmolive Soap were 15 cents, and a dozen eggs for 30 cents. When available, the canteens also sold fresh fruits and vegetables.[7]

In a quixotic attempt to stamp out the illegal stills, prisoners were allowed to purchase six pints of beer per month, each pint costing 25 cents. But obtaining something stronger was seldom a problem.

As in the campy 1960s TV situation comedy *Hogan's Heroes*, most camps had at least one still, which amateur brew masters used to turn sugar and raisins lifted from the kitchens into booze with a higher alcohol content. In most camps, the copper tubing needed to make a still was stolen from toilet plumbing. Inmates at Camp 30 in Bowmanville, Ontario, got their tubing from a guard who was reminded "that his officers would not react too favourably to the news that he had been drinking with the prisoners." There was so much illegal liquor around Bowmanville, recalled one POW, "that the camp atmosphere became more and more like that of an exclusive country club."[8]

Under Geneva, prisoners had the right to wear uniforms and their badge of rank. Hence, the good people of Medicine Hat saw POWs on supervised walks in town wearing Luftwaffe blue, army field grey, Afrika Korps tan, and even the Hugo Boss-designed black of the Waffen SS, complete with *Totenkopf* (Death's Head) pins and lightning bolt collar badges. In colder weather, these uniforms were obscured by winter great coats supplied by Canada, for which the POWs were grateful, although they strongly objected to the fourteen-inch red circle that looked and felt like a target sewn on the back of each one. The prisoners teased their guards that they couldn't shoot a man without the circle's assistance, but its existence "produced a stigma amongst the prisoners."[9]

The first currency in the camps were tickets debited to the POW's pay account. Prisoners earned 50 cents-a-day working outside the wire on farms or lumber camps approved by the Federal Department of Labour, or by selling handicraft items such as ships in bottles and jewelry boxes at farmer's markets. But the prisoners could also exchange their earnings for homemade tokens that were accepted by the canteen.[10] It wasn't long before a POW camp inversion of Gresham's Law kicked in and "good money," tokens with an exchange value in a real market, drove out "bad money," the tickets issued by the POW administration. There is no case of German POWs using cigarettes from Red Cross parcels for currency as was common in the POW camps in Germany. POWs in Canada were able to purchase cigarettes at their camp's canteen.

Prisoners could use funds held in trust accounts by the Canadian government to purchase items from a special Eaton's Catalogue. Married men and those with sweethearts sent stockings and lingerie back to Germany through neutral Turkey. As per Geneva, officers were allowed seven letters or postcards home each month while other ranks could send six letters or postcards. Neither the parcels from Eaton's nor the letters or postcards required postage. Prisoners had to pay for airmail letters and telegrams, however. There was no limit on the number of letters or parcels a POW could receive.

Parcels typically contained extra clothing, shaving equipment, and fruit cakes. As was the case in German POW camps, in order to ensure that canned food sent from home did not contain prohibited items (and that the can was not later used, for example, to make an air duct for an escape tunnel), the contents of each can were dumped into a prisoner's bowl. Bottles marked "Hair Oil" were often found to contain brandy, schnapps, and home made wine.

The numbers of letters and postcards handled by Canadian and German censors was staggering. On December 10, 1943, for example, eight carloads of letters arrived in Lethbridge, where the censors were located. Secret messages formed by "underlining of phrases, words or letters or use of question marks; veiled and obscure language in music [music notation], spelling of words backwards, and by chess problems or mathematical formulae; the use of drawings to conceal messages in shorthand, Morse or other codes," were either inked or cut out.[11] Any of these might be transmitting valuable military information that the POWs could have learned while travelling across country. At the request of the U.S. Federal Bureau of Investigation, every letter sent from the United

States or South America to a POW in Canada was read with special attention to South American names. FBI director J. Edgar Hoover feared that South America harboured many Nazi sympathizers. Clothing, too, was examined to ensure that none of the hems or linings hid secret messages. For their part, censors in Germany destroyed any references to how the war was developing, and any words praising the POWs' treatment in Canada.

Knowing that their letters would be censored, families and friends focused on personal news. Almost every first letter or card from a family member or friend begins with a variant of this card August Plaszek received from a friend he called Liesel in June 1943: "At last after a long wait, I received a sign of life from you a few days ago."[12] In another letter a month later, Liesel promises him a picture and, as many letters do, tells him that someone else, in this case, a certain Agnes, had received her letter and replied. This cataloguing of letters, also done with numbers or the date on the POW's letter or card, was one way both POW and his loved ones and friends organized themselves into what could seem like a conversation.[13]

In his letter to Agnes, Plaszek told her he could not take part in sports because of a wound. He also asked if she had ever seen *Frischer Wind aus Kanada* (*Fresh Wind from Canada*), a 1935 German comedy, presumably because it would give her some idea of his current circumstances.

A topic of frequent complaint in the cards and letters is the length of time it takes for them to be delivered. Plaszek's niece "Puppa" begins her early August 1943 letter by writing, "This morning I received another card from you. Indeed, the card was only eight weeks on the way, so I think it was forwarded very quickly."[14]

Sometimes the correspondence never arrived at all. Adolph Kratz, who would be accused of killing Plaszek, wrote a letter to Frauline

Margo Evertz in the first days of 1943. The censor noticed the writer had "erased all over his card and smeared the writing somewhat," which might have been some sort of code. The letter was withheld on grounds of "Interference with Stationery."[15]

Censors also took an interest in the personal lives of correspondents. One dwelt on Plaszek's wound, and another reported on Karl Lehmann's private family dramas. The latter's letters to and from Fräuelein Else Riegert demonstrated the "intimate" nature of Lehmann's relationship to her. The censors noted: "Her correspondence has shown her to be a rather uneducated person of a different social class from the P/W. His mother disapproves of the relationship between them and even informed the girl that the P/W was engaged to someone else. P/W's comment on this was that it related to a former time long past."[16]

While incoming mail was a balm for the prisoners, it was also a means by which the camp's POW leadership exerted power over inmates. By summer of 1943, at the latest, the men inside the wire at Medicine Hat lived under a simulacrum of Nazi Germany. They elected their own leadership, but like the German election of July 1932 in which violence and intimidation contributed to Hitler's rise, the voters did not have an entirely free hand. A contingent of hard core Nazis dominated the camp and held sway over rank-and-file POWs. The camp's thirty-six hut leaders were each elected with Nazi support. These thirty-six then delegated six individuals, one for each of six barracks, to elect the camp leader.

One of the main responsibilities the camp leadership had was handling incoming letters; once in the camp, they were given to the NCOs chosen by the leadership and not the prisoners themselves. This made it "possible to keep out news from Germany which would have an adverse effect (from the Party point of view) on the prisoners of war," notes a Canadian Army report. Letters to Germany were also given to the

NCOs, who monitored the POWs' views and determined who was a loyal Nazi soldier and who wasn't. Those who were caught writing defeatist or anti-Nazi words might have their mail withheld. The psychological value of letters from the *Heimat*[17] to POWs in a strange land, surrounded by sworn enemies, cannot be overstated, and the Nazis exploited it ruthlessly. "Holding back a prisoner's mail is probably more effective than beatings as means of making the prisoners of war a 'loyal' Nazi," wrote an Allied military intelligence official in 1944.[18]

Not that the camp Nazis were averse to beatings or other forms of torture. The insufficiently loyal were also brought before courts of inquiry, and bloodied and bruised out of sight of prison guards. Some were threatened that their recalcitrance would be communicated to Nazi authorities in Germany, putting their families in danger. Among other measures applied to men who made the mistake of being free with their thoughts in correspondence were the squeezing of testicles, the application of electric wires to testicles, and the insertion of pins under fingernails and toenails. While on guard duty at night at Ozada, Carmen Jackson heard "the screams of prisoners being beaten by other prisoners."[19]

Welcome as they were, letters from home could never quite dispel what French sociologist Jean Cazeneuve in 1945 called the feeling of "social alienation" that comes with breaking all links with home. In fact, mail from home could increase a POW's feelings of alienation, and not just because of the German equivalent of the "Dear John" letter. On December 19, 1942, for example, POW Gottfried Dukes received twenty-two letters, some more than a year old and some only two months old. Glad as he was to receive them, the letters generated intense suffering because the "prisoner realizes that life in his home country continues without him... his absence has been filled by other people, and... someone else is doing his job. For many prisoners, this sense of social abandonment results in a sort of internal death."[20]

In an interview in the 1980s, Ernest Guter, who had been a prisoner in Quebec, pointed to an important difference between criminal prisoners, who know when their sentences will end, and a prisoner of war: "It is hell on earth mentally to wake up in the middle of the night... and to say to yourself, 'I'll never get out here,' 'This war is not going to end in my lifetime,' and 'They'll keep me here for life.' That feeling was the worst of internment."[21]

Another POW is recorded in an intelligence file as saying, "One slowly declines here morally. One has days that one would like to take one's own life. Nobody can imagine what it means to be five years behind barbed wire."[22]

The strain broke some men, the most obvious sign being a POW Camp version of the 1,000-yard stare that had been noted on the Western Front in the previous war. Other signs, as a war diarist of one camp wrote, were making "many tempests in the compound teacup."[23] Aware that bored prisoners suffered from what one French POW in the First World War called *le cafard*, the cockroach of disgrace that "crawled round in the brain, round and round and round," and the tension of constantly eating and living with the same men day after day, week after week, month after month, year after year, Canadian authorities did what they could to fight barbed-wire sickness.[24]

Work was one salve. At Medicine Hat, hundreds of prisoners were employed as tailors, barbers, postal clerks, and orderlies in the camp's hospital. Farming and forestry may have been back breaking work, but hundreds of POWs volunteered to do both, which, of course, meant they could get out of the camp and also be paid for their labour.

Education was another answer. In a letter to a family member, Lehmann, the former professor, reported that he was teaching French and Spanish to other POWs, that he had been named an authorized examiner for forthcoming matriculation exams, and that he read or played chess in his spare time.

Medicine Hat had six huts containing classrooms where the men could take courses, the credits of which were to be accepted in Germany after the war. English classes were given by teachers belonging to the Medicine Hat District School Board, as well as POWs like Lehmann who held university degrees. System-wide, some 3,000 prisoners took 88 courses, including, "Canada and Its People," "Canadian Indians," "New France," and "Wilfred Laurier and his Times." Two others must have raised eyebrows among the Nazified bureaucrats back in Berlin who were briefed on educational activities by the Red Cross: "Development of Self-Government" and "Canadian Political Parties."[25]

Books and other materials were donated by Canadian and American universities and colleges as well as by the Red Cross and the YMCA. The Camp 132 library contained 4,600 books. One POW's diary lists more than thirty-five books he read, including works by Shakespeare, John Galsworthy, and the bard of the British Empire, Rudyard Kipling. Franz-Karl Stanzel, who survived the sinking of U-331 in the Mediterranean in 1942 and spent almost three years in a series of Canadian POW camps, did not recall there being a single Canadian author on any syllabus.

Medicine Hat could not boast of musicians with the skill of John Newmark, who was a POW in Quebec and, after the war, returned to Canada to live. He performed with the famed contralto, Maureen Forrester. Still, the camp had enough trained musicians to fill two orchestras: one of twenty-five men and the other of fifty-six. Although no playlists survive, it's reasonable to assume that scores by the likes of Felix Mendelssohn and Gustav Mahler, both of whom were Jewish, never graced the camp's music stands. Works by composers favoured by the

Nazis, such as Richard Strauss, and, especially, Richard Wagner (Hitler's favourite composer), almost certainly did.

The POWs produced live theatre and variety shows, the production of which entailed not only rehearsals but the time-consuming painting of backdrops and costume making. As was the case with Canadian and other Allied prisoners of war in Germany, the theatre, which required men to dress up as women, entailed some visual and gestural gender-bending. These actors' experiences would have been very similar to those of Dieppe survivor Robert Prouse, who wore a grass skirt and bra to portray a South Seas woman in theatricals. The costume, he recalled, elicited "a lot of good-natured 'cat-calls' from the audience, along with a few lewd suggestions."[26]

Any consideration of sexual activity in the POW camps must begin by recognizing that while Plaszek and Lehmann were in early middle age, the majority of the men in the camps were in their twenties and, thus, in their physical prime. Unlike the Canadians in Japanese POW camps who were close to starving, the German POWs were healthy and well-fed. Naturally, they remained libidinous.

The unnatural all-male environment of a POW camp took a psychological toll. Explained Mario Duliani, interned in France as a civilian enemy alien during the war, in his memoir *La ville sans femme*: "This is the city without women…. We speak of them in the morning, in the afternoon, in the evening…. Of those we loved, of those we still love, of those we hope to love. And this irritates, fatigues, riles us." In each barracks, there are "scraps of newspapers and magazines that show naked, or almost naked women in lascivious poses. The photos have been cut from *Esquire*… by comrades bursting with sexual urges. Through this ingenious iconography, the absent woman remains ever present."

For some, the proverbial cold shower and masturbation sufficed. Siegfried Jansch, who was held at Fort Henry in Kingston, Ontario, hit on another idea. He wrote Canadian authorities demanding they "bring girls into the camp so that the prisoners could satisfy their instincts."[27] His letter never found its intended audience: smuggled out of camp in an empty cigarette package, it was discovered by guards.

One-way prisoners coped with physical loneliness was by dancing. Camp 132 had two dance bands, one of fourteen and one of twenty players. Despite the Nazi cultural paladins who dubbed jazz "N***** Music," the soldiers had a taste for it (as, indeed, did the many youth back in Germany). The bands almost certainly played the Charleston and the Lindy Hop, the latter named for famed aviator Charles Lindbergh, whose dalliance with Nazism led Hermann Göring, commander of the Luftwaffe, to present him with the Commander Cross of the Order of the German Eagle in 1938.

By far, the activities that took up the most time in camp were athletics, which, for the Germans, had a decidedly ideological character since the POWs were technically still men at war and were instructed to keep "their bodies in perfect condition for the time when the fatherland would again require them."[28] In August 1943, barely a month after August Plaszek's murder, acting camp leader, Regimental Sergeant Major Richard Elstermann told the prisoners at Medicine Hat that "only a healthy body could maintain a healthy spirit [which] was in particular measure a law of the younger generation of National Socialist Germany."[29]

Under the guidance of athletic leaders like Staff Sergeant Walter Wolf, (who would become a key figure in the Lehmann murder), more than 1,000 POWs were divided into ninety soccer teams. Soccer was so important in Camp 132 that retrieving a soccer ball was the only acceptable reason for prisoners to approach the barbed-wire perimeter of the facility. Otherwise, an inner wire strung about one foot off the ground kept them ten feet from the fence. The soccer players waved white cloths as they crossed into the forbidden zone, signalling to the tower guards not to shoot.

More than 1,100 men at Camp 132 played handball, soccer, and tennis, while hundreds of others took part in boxing, calisthenics, wrestling, and even gymnastics.[30] YMCA donations of ice skates—twenty-four per 1,000 prisoners in 1942 alone—could not keep pace with demand once ice hockey became popular among the prisoners.

To accommodate their athletic activities, the POWs built themselves a stadium with a three-tiered embankment for spectators. It was on the west side of the camp and was called the Rhine, after the river that marks the traditional border between France and Germany. A similar-sized building used for camp performances was dubbed Weichsel, the German word for the Vistula River. This was bold of the prisoners: the Vistula is only a German river if Germany is allowed to incorporate hundreds of kilometres of Poland. Canada, of course, followed Britain into war in 1939 after Britain (and France) honoured their promise to protect Poland against Nazi aggression. Still, Weichsel was permitted to stand as the building's name. The street signs were also in German, another touch that made the camp seem almost like "A small island of Germany," as Stotz put it.[31]

* * *

Notwithstanding all of its activities and amenities, Camp 132 was a prison, and the POWs shared those German-named streets with a special detail of the Veterans Guard known as scouts. The scouts worked inside the wire, technically called the "enclosure." They were unarmed, for three reasons. Absent firearms, a mob of prisoners could not seize a scout and acquire his weapon. Not carrying a gun "relay[ed] a message of trust" between the camp leadership and the POWs.[32] Finally, that the scouts had no weapons showed confidence in the firepower of the armed men in the watch towers.

The scouts had several tasks, beginning with counting prisoners. For the fun of it, and to register contempt for these tedious reminders of their captor's power over them, POWs often disrupted roll calls. Three scouts would count two ranks of thirty to forty prisoners at a time, watching out for men moving mischievously from line to line, or giving false names or POW numbers. Counts held within the POWs barracks, which the prisoners considered an invasion of privacy, required an extra scout to watch the door.

The scouts were also alert to signs of tunnelling or other activities preparatory to escaping, such as men covertly gathering at certain points in the camp. Searches of the barracks were usually conducted during outdoor roll calls. Scouts were after such illicit articles as real money, civilian outerwear, anything resembling a weapon including large pocket knives and scissors (nail scissors were allowed), tools suitable for use in escape or sabotage, compasses, maps, cameras, field glasses, spirits and alcohol, telephones or radio apparatuses, books not bearing the censorship stamp, and books with the cover destroyed which could be used for codes, as well as A.W. Faber pencils.[33]

Although formally enjoined from speaking with prisoners, the human reality of being inside the enclosure day after day meant that some scouts got to know their charges. According to Carmen Jackson, a guard at Medicine Hat in 1943, some scouts even counted a few prisoners as friends. Usually, conversations were on general topics such as sports and the weather. Other times, a POW would warn a scout that a particular prisoner was in danger, prompting his being taken into protective custody. The scouts also provided a window into the camp's Zeitgeist, as demonstrated by reports of how the camp's morale would ebb or flow depending on how the war was unfolding from the German point-of-view.

News of the war came from four sources. The most immediate was the camp's clandestine radios, which could tune into German shortwave broadcasts. One of the radios in Medicine Hat was hidden in a ship model, and an antenna was found threaded through a laundry line. Stenographers monitored broadcasts, and in order to ensure the accuracy of the news and/or orders they took down, no message was considered official until heard on two different radio frequencies at different times. Despite this time lag, POWs often heard of outside events before Canadians. In August 1942, *Calgary Herald* journalist Fred Kennedy and his photographer arrived at Ozada to cover the POWs' transfer to Lethbridge. He was surprised to hear them jocularly saying, "Canadian *kaput*," and "How do you like Dieppe?" in reference to the very recent Allied setback in Northern France.[34]

Almost as immediate as radio news were Canadian newspapers and magazines, which were translated by men like Lehmann, the former professor. Despite the best efforts of Canadian mail censors who used ink and scissors to obscure or remove banned war news from publications, messages slipped through. Still other messages reached prisoners through Red Cross parcels sent from home. Sausages and cakes were cut open to ensure they did not contain documents or escape materials, and tins of food were opened for the same reason, but if the sender was ingenious enough to hide the message in a walnut or in chewing gum packaging, it had a reasonable chance of reaching its target. The last sources of news were recently captured POWs or transfers from another camps.

The largest single group of POWs in Canada were members of the Afrika Korps, many of its members reputed to be among the more fanatical Nazis. They rejected any news that contradicted what they heard on the shortwave radios or elsewise from Germany. Their own defeat, more recent reports of how a battered Britain fought on, or what they saw about America and Canada being untouched by the war, could not dent their faith. While in Ozada, prior to their transfer to Medicine Hat, many of these men "planted flowers outside their tents to make the camp look presentable for when Hitler arrived" in southern Alberta.[35]

These hopes survived the move to the Hat, and were reinforced by smuggled German news clippings that "consistently heralded German victories." Long after U-boats had been withdrawn from the North Atlantic, these sources and shortwave broadcasts would claim that hundreds of Allied ships were being sunk and that "the British Isles was being virtually bombed off the map."[36]

After being captured on D-Day, Willi Breitenbach arrived in Medicine Hat in 1944. "Do you think we're going to lose the war?" he was asked by the older POWs. He answered, "Yes," adding that anyone would "if you'd seen the invasion force." His frankness was repaid by fists and night attacks which POWs attributed to the *"heiliger Geist,"* because, like the Holy Ghost, the perpetrators were never seen.[37]

It was important to members of Afrika Korps and ranking German officers in Canadian camps that their fellow prisoners maintain their morale. This was sometimes accomplished rather spectacularly, as in a riot that broke out in Bowmanville camp in October 1942. Its genesis was Germany's discovery of a number of its soldiers who had been shot with their hands behind their back. When Britain refused to provide assurances that no more violations of the laws of war would occur, Germany decided to shackle the Allied survivors of the Dieppe raid it was keeping in Stalag VIII-B in Lamsdorf, Germany. Canada retaliated by attempting to put manacles on German prisoners in Bowmanville, and the fight was on.

What *Time* dubbed the "Battle of Bowmanville" lasted three days. Determined to avoid the humiliation of shackles—they were military men, not criminals—the Germans imaginatively armed themselves with bags of pepper, sand-filled bottles, jam jars, and table legs; they barricaded themselves in barracks with walls of mattresses.

Many of the POWs were quickly brought under the control of the Veterans Guard but a hundred or more held out in the mess hall and beat off the first attempt to evict them. Eventually commando trainees from nearby Kingston were shipped in to cut a hole in the roof, crash through windows, and break down the camp door with a long wooden pole. The POWs fought hard but were eventually subdued by the guards who had helmets, riot sticks, tear gas, and a fire hose. Eighty German officers and twenty Canadian soldiers required medical care. One POW was bayonetted, another shot, and a guard had his skull fractured by a jam jar.

When the dust had settled at Bowmanville, the POWs were assembled in a field opposite the Canadian guards and troops. The Canadian commanding officer said, "Well, it was a good fight, men. Now three cheers for our German opponents. Hip, Hip, Hooray!" A German general, formerly of Rommel's army, reciprocated, saying to his men: "You must agree, it was a wonderful fight. Three cheers for the Canadians. Hip, hip, horray!"[38]

* * *

In the aftermath of Bowmanville, seven German medical personnel were transferred to Camp 132 in Medicine Hat. These were Nazi hardliners who brought with them an order from Lieutenant General Schmidt, the senior German general in Canada, that the camp leadership establish a "Gestapo" or secret police force that he charged with ensuring "all the soldiers of the camp behaved as exemplary Nazis."[39]

Heeding these orders in the summer of 1944, the Camp 132 Gestapo in Medicine Hat instituted a reign of terror against homosexuals. While Section 175 of the German criminal code (dating to 1871) outlawed oral and anal intercourse, and the Nazi's 1935 amendment to the code outlawed any sexual activity between men, definitions of homosexuality in POW camps were rather fluid and tolerant, writes historian Chris Madsen. In some Quebec camps, a live-and-let-live attitude prevailed, with one or two areas "entirely 'reserved' for gay activities."[40] Not so in Medicine Hat. Its new Gestapo decided to make an example of a POW named Hermann Hutt, who had confided his homosexual activities to a POW who turned out to be a mole.

Following a court of honour, Hutt and another POW also found to be guilty of violating Section 175 were paraded in front of 800 POWs in the recreation hall for a "degrading ceremony." Hutt's shoulder braids and stars were ripped from his uniform. Worse was to come, Hutt realized as the men filed out of the hall. Four inmates known for their violence stayed behind. Hutt's appeal to POW camp leader Wilhelm Wendt brought the curt response that he "should have contemplated these things before" breaking the law and, in the Gestapo's eyes, dishonouring the Germany army.[41]

The four men forced Hutt to return to his barracks, where they were joined by eight other men in beating him with sticks, ropes, and fists. When Hutt tried to crawl away, a POW stepped on him. This same POW stopped Hutt from crawling under the bed by sitting on him. When the hut leader arrived and tried to stop the beating, another assailant made their endgame clear: "He isn't dead yet."[42] The hut leader again ordered the men to stop, which, after a few more moments, they did.

The doctors at the camp's hospital refused to treat Hutt. Indeed, Dr. Nolte, the chief medical officer and the only German officer in the

An aerial view of Medicine Hat on the banks of the South Saskatchewan River in the Canadian badlands, circa 1940.

Downtown Medicine Hat in the 1940s.

Joyce Reesor, third from the right, and the Victory Girls.

German prisoners of war pose in uniform in Camp 132, Medicine Hat (photograph by Luke Fandrich).

The prisoner-of-war hockey team at Camp 132 (Library and Archives Canada).

Drawings from a Medicine Hat POW's scrapbook depicting the well-kept barracks, life within the living quarters, and a POW variety show.

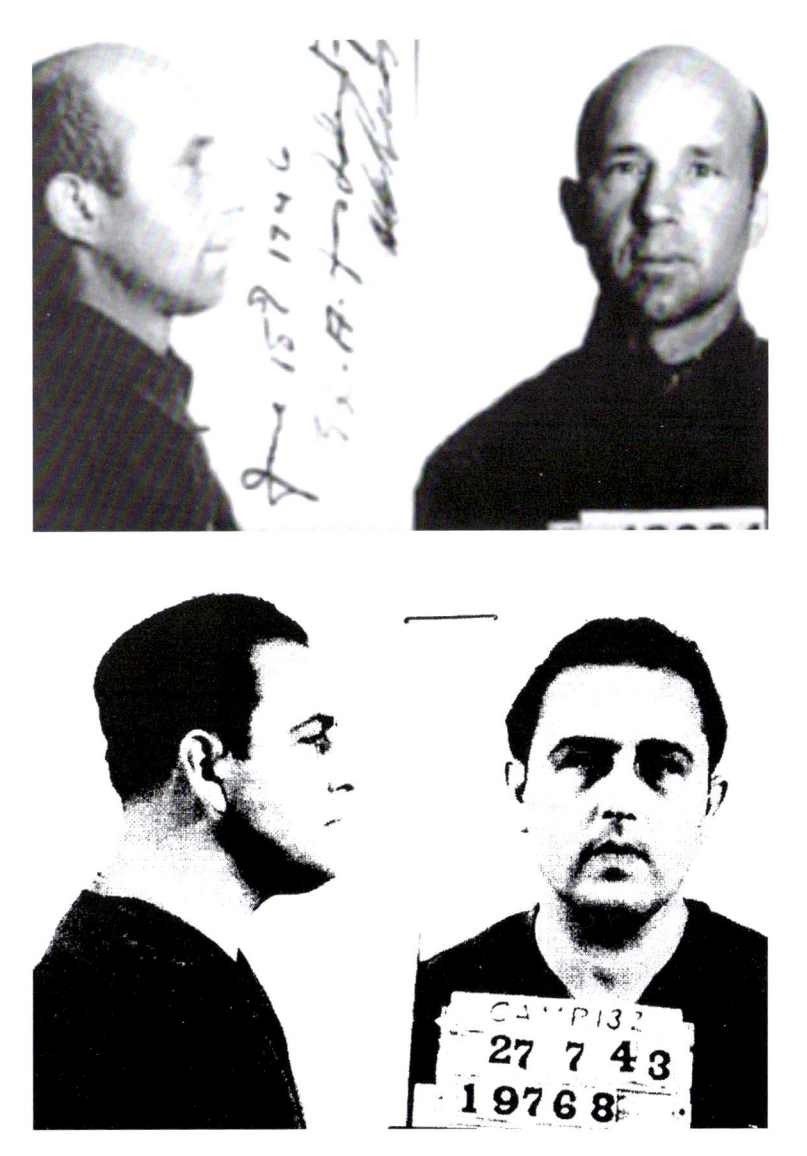

The victims: Private August Plaszek (top) and Sergeant Dr. Karl Lehman, both suspected by POW leadership of insufficient loyalty to the Third Reich.

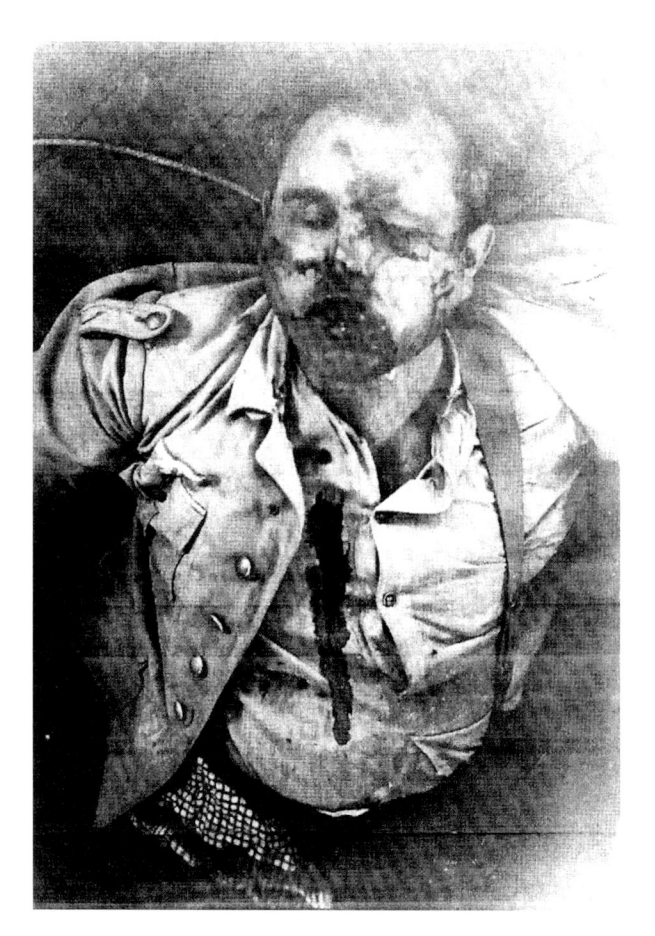

Lehman's body as found by investigators.

Clockwise from top left: Werner Schwalb, hanged for the murder of August Plaszek; Willi Müeller, Bruno Perzenowski, Walter Wolf, and Heinrich Busch, hanged for the murder of Karl Lemann.

Accused of Murder

Shown here are two of the four Nazi prisoners of war charged with murdering a fellow captive, Cpl. Karl Lehmann, at the Medicine Hat prisoner of war camp on Sept. 10, 1944. At left is Staff Sgt.-Major Bruno Perzenowski while at right is Sgt Willi Mueller, both former members of the German air force. R.C.M.P. took extreme precautions to prevent cameramen from getting pictures of prisoners but two of the alleged murderers were caught.

—Photos by Everett Studios; Herald Engraving.

Perzenowski (left) and Müeller as they appeared on the front page of the Lethbridge Herald during their trial. (Photo by Everett Studios.)

The gravestone of Bruno Perzenowski (misspelled) and Werner Schwalb, buried along with all other German POWs who died in Canada in Kitchener, Ontario. (Courtesy of CBC.)

enclosure, approved of the "admonitions" meted out to the likes of Hutt. He called the beating of another POW a week later "a marvellous piece of work."[43]

Although Hutt received no medical treatment, he was allowed to remain in the hospital the fifteen days it took before he could walk again. As soon as possible on leaving the hospital, he approached a scout and asked to be taken into protective custody. He was examined by Canadian doctors who said that his injuries could result in permanent disabilities. A Canadian military court of inquiry struck by Colonel R. O. Bull, who had been assigned by the department of national defence as commandant of Camp 132,[44] ordered that the POWs who beat Hutt be charged and tried. None of the 800 men who witnessed the degrading ceremony, or those who had witnessed the beating, would testify at the trial. Nolte and the other doctors, the victim's hut leader, and camp leader Wendt all denied knowing anything of the incident.[45]

Despite the lack of co-operation, Hutt's assailants were tried. Their defence attorney used the victim's status as a "homosexualist" against him. It was a mitigating factor in the assault, he claimed, while also expecting the trial judge to understand that a man with a "perverted mind" could not be a trustworthy witness to his own beating. The court nevertheless found the assailants guilty.[46]

While the Hutt incident resulted in no loss of life and a measure of justice, it was scarcely the only outrage perpetrated by the Camp 132 Gestapo, and not all of them were to be discovered and prosecuted so satisfactorily.

CHAPTER 3

The Murder of August Plaszek

July 22, 1943

"One More Dead Heine, More or Less"
—RCMP Constable George Krause's Report (October 12, 1943)

AROUND 5 P.M. ON July 22, 1943, Private Reginald Back of the Veterans Guard saw a man waving a white cloth and running toward the warning wire of Camp 132. But no soccer ball had bounced out of bounds. No one was playing soccer when Back looked down from his perch in Tower No. 7. Rather, he saw that the man waving the white cloth was being chased by hundreds of angry, shouting inmates. Once the desperate POW crossed the warning wire, his pursuers halted, knowing that without white flags they risked being shot. To ensure that the mob respected the boundary, Back ostentatiously aimed his rifle.[1]

The chore of sorting out what had prompted Private Christian Schulz to run for his life in the camp that day fell to a tall man with spectacles perched on his beaked nose, RCMP Corporal Reginald Arthur Bull (no relation to Commandant R.O. Bull, in charge of Camp 132). Raised as a Quaker and a veteran of two decades with the Mounties, the RCMP constable was so well-regarded in Medicine Hat that the city would make him chief of its municipal police force after the war (a position he held until 1967). He interviewed the camp's staff and a number of POWs, some of whom asked for "protection" in return for their co-operation, and pieced together the story.

One of those taken into protection was POW Corporal Bernhard Kafka, who told the RCMP that he and August Plaszek "had been among a number of Legionnaires who gathered almost daily in a hollow on the east side of the enclosure, and a rumour had circulated that they had been plotting against the camp leadership with the support of Canadian officers," something Kafka utterly denied.[3] Constable Bull learned that the POW's acting camp leader, Richard Elstermann, (temporarily replacing Wendt), had initiated an investigation into those "rumours and alleged written reports" of anti-Nazi activities by former French Foreign Legionnaires at Camp 132.[2]

Elstermann authorized First Lieutenant Hans Justus Schnorrenpfeil, a lawyer before the war, to interview two POWs to see what they knew of the rumours. That very evening, Schnorrenpfeil reported back to Elstermann, Captain Dr. Maximillian Nolte, the camp's medical officer, and six block leaders, all of whom were strong Nazis. Elstermann ordered a "court of honour" to investigate three former Legionnaires in addition to Schulz: Max Weidaner, Alfons Burkhart, and August Plaszek.

On the hot afternoon of July 22, Regimental Sergeant Major Wilhelm Weidemann led Private Weidaner, the first man to be questioned, into hut A-Z. Weidaner was nervous, thinking of a soldier who had been murdered in the South African transit camp he had visited on his way to

Canada, and others in Medicine Hat who had been beaten at night on suspicious of "being less than enthusiastic about the Nazi leaders."[4]

Elstermann's inquiry was not precisely a kangaroo court; indeed, it was structured close to both the German and French systems of civil law.[5] In hut A-Z, questions were asked by either Weidemann or Schnorrenpfeil, while Elstermann listened. Another trusted Nazi typed up a transcript. Behind a half-wall, three block leaders listened to the interrogations.

"Did you make any remarks that for Germany the war is already lost?" Weidaner was asked. "*Nien*," he answered. That seemed clear enough, although Weidaner thought his answer might have had more weight had he not already admitted to translating Canadian newspapers. On the question of Germany's military prospects, Weidaner said with clear-eyed military reasoning that "it would be more difficult for Germany to win the war" having made an enemy of Russia (which a few months earlier had triumphed over Field Marshall Friedrich von Paulus's army at Stalingrad).[6] Knowing that his interrogators would think these words skated close to the defeatism his inquisitors associated with the Legionnaires, Weidaner underscored that while he was a member of the Afrika Korps, he had never been in the French Foreign Legion. And towards the end of his interview, he metaphorically pulled rank, reminding his questioners that he had earned both an Iron Cross first class and an Iron Cross second class. Moreover, he had been a trusted member of Rommel's electronic eavesdropping unit. How could *they* accuse him of treason? The gambit worked, and Weidaner was allowed to return to barracks.

Schulz was not so fortunate. Told he was to be examined, he asked why. Weidemann answered ominously: "You will soon find out." These words rang in the former Legionnaire's ears as he entered the hut and saw Elstermann and the others. At the end of his hour-long session, Schulz was declared to have contradicted himself a number of times.

Elstermann ordered Weidemann to hold Schulz in an adjacent hut for "two or three days."[7]

Fearing he would be beaten or killed (as had happened to men in a similar situation in the Lethbridge POW camp, a fact that was well known), Schulz broke away from his escort as he exited the hut and ran for his life. After a few strides toward the nearest guard tower, his slippers flew off his feet. Most of the way he ran barefoot over rocky ground.

The hundreds of men who took off after Schulz didn't have to know that a court of honour was in session to begin the chase. All clearly understood what a man running from a block leader towards the wire meant. When he reached his destination, Schulz stepped over the wire and the chase stopped as Private Back raised his rifle in the tower. Schulz crouched low to protect himself from rocks thrown by some of the prisoners.

Private Back called the guard room at 5:20 p.m. and waited for scouts to arrive on the scene. Sensing that the "turbulent" crowd of a couple hundred men was about to rush the wire, he fired a warning shot over their heads. Within ten minutes, nine scouts, led by Lieutenant William A. Dawe had arrived to escort Schulz away. The POW mob followed threateningly along the warning wire.[8]

The scouts couldn't get Schulz to the camp entrance without taking him back through the mob, so they walked him to an edge of the enclosure, outside of which was a detention yard. The prisoner was given boots so he could climb over the fence to the safety of the yard. Enraged by what they were seeing, the Germans rushed toward Dawe, with one saying, "Sir, this man is a traitor. We are soldiers and we wish to deal with this man ourselves. Give him up to us and we will disperse."[9] Although backed by the armed guards in the towers, Dawe and his men were unarmed, making his response all the more impressive: "I have no authority or desire to deal with a mob." He asked to see acting camp leader Elstermann.[10]

In the confused moments that followed, several scouts muscled their way through the mass of prisoners to the gate, leaving the scene. Dawe and another guard proceeded to the camp leader's orderly room where they found themselves effectively prisoners of the hundreds of Germans milling outside.

Meanwhile, a staff car carrying camp Commandant Bull and some of his men made its way into camp, as did an armed party of fifty men with fixed bayonets. The POWs could surmise that each of the men had been given live ammunition. With Lieutenant L.C. Thornton-Prehn translating, Bull ordered the mob outside the Camp Leader's orderly room to disperse so that the Canadians inside could leave. The mob didn't budge. Instead, referring obliquely to the Geneva Convention's rules about POW camps and, especially, the perseverance of the command structure of a POW's army, "one German prisoner replied to the effect that this was their camp and they would do as they liked."[11]

The Canadian guards had gone to the orderly room to meet Elstermann, but the acting camp leader wasn't there. He was busy overseeing the interrogation of his third suspect, Lance Corporal Alfons Burkhart. Perhaps simply to demonstrate his authority, Elstermann continued this interview for ten minutes after being notified that he was wanted by Canadian officials in the orderly room. Just before the deadline that Bull had set for the camp to be placed in detention if the Canadians were not released, Elstermann arrived at the orderly room standoff and ordered the Germans to disperse. He and two other POWs led the Canadian guards and Bull's party to the camp gate where they were met by another small force of scouts that had entered the enclosure.

As the Bull party was dispersing, another disturbance broke out in the camp. From their vantage points on Towers 7 and 4 respectively, Private Back and Sergeant Frederic C. Byers struggled to make out which of the prisoners was being dragged backward away from them, and the faces of the two men who were doing the dragging.

The victim was the bald former farmer August Plaszek, who as the fourth of the POW suspects had been waiting at hut A-Z for his turn before the court of honour. Byers could see Plaszek being kicked and hear him "hollering for help," and he noted that one of the men doing the dragging had a pronounced "swagger," (this would become an important point in both the investigation and subsequent trial).[12]

The tower guards could see Plaszek being taken toward the west recreation hall. Private Back called the guard room asking for scouts to return to the enclosure, make their way to the recreation hall, and free the man. Byers also called the guard room with the same request. In an effort to deter the four men manhandling Plaszek, Back called the sentries in Tower No. 6 and ordered them to fire shots over the men's heads, but for reasons unknown, the men in this tower did not follow Back's orders. After ten minutes, with no sign of the scouts re-entering the enclosure, Back called the guard room again. By this time, he "felt the man would be dead because of the delay."[13]

The first senior POW to hear of what happened to Plaszek after he was dragged to the recreation hall appears to have been Dr. Nolte. Through the open window of his hospital, he heard someone yell that "they had hanged a man," he later told the RCMP. He immediately left the hospital, and, in the company of three other POWs, rushed to the recreation hall where between 80 and 120 men were milling about. Nolte saw "a body hanging by the west wall." The rope had been passed around the victim's neck twice and drawn so tight it cut into his flesh by about an inch. After pushing his way through the crowd, Nolte felt for a pulse but "found no sign of life" and ordered Plaszek's body to be cut down.[14]

A prisoner produced a piece of a razor blade that served as a knife and the corpse was released. Soon after placing a shirt over the dead man's face, Nolte heard a man outside the hall shout, "There must be a third one," meaning another target beyond Schulz and Plaszek.[15] The crowd gathered around the recreation hall heard the same. Nolte rushed out of the hall toward the shouting.

The shout had also been heard by Schnorrenpfeil, who was still interrogating the court of honour's third suspect, Burkhart. Soon the room in which he was interrogating was surrounded with forty or fifty men shouting, "Get the traitors out—there is one more."[16] Schnorrenpfeil opened a window and told the men to disperse. Instead, the mob called for Burkhart and forced the door. Mistaking Schnorrenpfeil for Burkhart, who had wisely hidden behind the door, some prisoners began punching Schnorrenpfeil while others wanted to drag him away. Before this could happen, the man in charge of the block's post office, who knew Schnorrenpfeil, interposed himself between the frightened lawyer and the baying prisoners. A moment later, Nolte arrived and vouched for Schnorrenpfeil.

As Nolte lowered the temperature in the hut, a staff car containing Canadian Army officer Thornton-Prehn, three scouts, and Elstermann attempted to reach the recreation hall. The mass of men mingling outside prevented them from getting within 50 yards of the hall. They got out of the car and, following Thornton-Prehn's order, Elstermann told the men to disperse. It is not clear whether they did so or simply allowed the Canadians and Elstermann to reach the hall. Nor is it clear who was first into the hall and, thus, first to see Plaszek's body. It was a horrible sight. He had been beaten about the head before he was hanged. Said Royal

Army Medical Korps Captain W. F. Hall: "[The] face of the deceased was very swollen—the tongue was sticking out slightly and there was blood from the nostrils and mouth and also from the back of the head."[17]

Later that evening, Elstermann had an announcement read out saying that Plaszek and Schulz "had expressed themselves as enemies of the German State and had sought support for their ideas for the purpose of organizing internal opposition." A second statement made a few hours later added that "there was no truth to the rumour that a list of forty names of Legionnaires and other anti-Nazis had been compiled." It failed to calm the nerves of former Legionnaires.[18]

At minutes after midnight on July 23, a telegram arrived at National Defence Headquarters in Ottawa saying, "POW MC042024 Plaszek August was Hanged by his Comrade at approx 1800 hours this evening STOP Court of Inquiry commencing tomorrow." By the end of the day, Colonel H.W. Streight, the director of the Prisoners of War office had sent a number of similar telegrams, including one to the Swiss Consul in Montreal, one to the Swiss Legation in London, and one to Prisoners of War Information Bureau in London.

Although Plaszek's body was moved to a funeral home in Medicine Hat for autopsy and embalming at a cost of $75, the Canadian government managed to keep the fact that a man had been murdered within Medicine Hat's city limits out of the papers. The killing was nevertheless an open secret in town. Hatters like twenty-two-year-old Howard Millen, ineligible to serve in the armed forces due to a bout of rheumatic fever as a child, knew a great deal about it. Not long before Schulz ran toward the wire, Millen was waiting while POWs unloaded soda pop from a truck he'd driven into the camp. A few moments later, Millen saw what looked to him like 1,000 men gathering in the enclosure. Guards shouted at him to climb into his truck and drive out of camp immediately. "The next day, we found out Plaszek had been murdered," he recalled.[19] Millen would later learn much more when he served as a juror in one of the Plaszek murder trials.

On July 26, under fair skies, August Männe Plaszek, a diminutive man who had looked like a farmer, was buried in Medicine Hat's Hillside Cemetery. Since his POW identification form listed him as Roman Catholic, Rev. Father McKay officiated, while Captain R.R. Macgregor, M.C., led the burial party of twenty-three, including two buglers who played the "Last Post." At 10:15 a.m., Macgregor gave the order to "present arms" and Plaszek's body was lowered into the ground some 7,000 kilometres from where he was born in Germany, and about the same distance from his wife and child.

CHAPTER 4

The Investigation into the Murder of August Plaszek

July 24, 1943 to September 16, 1944

I<small>N THE DAYS AFTER</small> Plaszek's killing, as the nation read headlines like "Palermo Falls: Canadians Press on" and "Germans Pressing the New British Line," the RCMP, in co-operation with Canadian Army Intelligence and National Defence, opened a court of inquiry. It was unusual for a civilian police force to investigate a crime in a POW camp, but it made some sense in Medicine Hat simply because the RCMP had considerable investigative expertise and the military authorities did not.

RCMP Corporal A.R. Bull took the lead. He had the *corpus delecti*, the means, motive, and opportunity for Plaszek's murder. What he did not have was first-hand evidence of who committed it. Among the first men he interrogated was Captain Dr. Maximillian Nolte who, in addition to telling Corporal Bull where he was and what he was doing around 6 p.m. the previous evening, tried to shape the narrative of the disturbance.

Giving "every evidence of co-operation," Nolte told Bull that in his opinion, "the hanging was not in any way planned but it was rather a spontaneous outburst" led by persons unknown.[1]

As the Nolte interview suggests, the early hours of the court of inquiry were not especially productive. Bull quickly learned that he was up against what amounted to an *omertá*, the code of silence that protected the Sicilian mafia, enforced by the Nazi element in Camp 132. POW Walter Aberle put it to the inquiry succinctly: "If they had told me [about the murderer] I would not give this information as I am a good German."[2]

Fortunately for the Canadians, the *omertá* was not airtight. Perhaps because of the savageness of the crime and the Canadians' clear-headed response, the Nazi leadership was thrown partially back on its heels in the wake of the killing. Having squelched one rumour about a list of forty anti-Nazi Legionnaires, on July 24 Elstermann circulated another, "that the three POWs questioned were Communists, heading a plot to kill six of the leading POWs [meaning block leaders] in the enclosure."[3] It had two effects Elstermann did not foresee. First, it prompted several POWs to ask for Canadian protection. Equally important, it undermined Nolte's claim that the hanging was spontaneous.

At the end of July, ex-Legionnaire Bernhard Kafka was caught trying to escape, as he intended. This gave him the opportunity to request Canadian protection.[4] The day before he had heard a POW staff sergeant say that all Legionnaires should be hung "before they could run over to the Tommy," meaning, betray their fellow prisoners to the Canadians.[5]

Kafka helped Corporal Bull's inquiry sort out the camp's factions. On one side were moderates, supporters of camp leader Wilhelm Wendt, who was hospitalized due to a nervous breakdown prompted by hardline opposition to his rule. (Elstermann was his temporary replacement.) Wendt believed his job was to get along with Canadian authorities so as to wring the best deal he could for the POWs. On the other side was the strong Nazi clique, elements of which had previously caused trouble at the Lethbridge camp. Kafka said that Corporal Ernst Gurbat, leader of Camp 132's education organization, was one of the "principals among the fanatical element." He reported that the Nazi clique placed spies among the Legionnaires and branded men who volunteered to work outside the camp as "traitors," irrespective of the fact that Germany and Britain had negotiated work terms and pay rates.[6]

Another POW who also requested protection took the court of inquiry in another direction entirely. He said a prisoner named Felmeden told a group of men in hut B-6 that "the one who hung Plaszek is a master; he must have done it often." Felmeden mimed the actions of hanging a man. Felmeden's actions, his known associates, and his strenuously pro-Nazi views suggested both ability and motive.[8]

Still another prisoner pointed the RCMP in the direction of POW Johannes Woithe, who had described to his hut mates how Plaszek had been caught and had pleaded for his life, saying, "'I haven't done anything.' Then, one man hit Plaszek on the head with a stone and he became unconscious." Plaszek was subsequently dragged into the hall and hanged.[9]

When the RCMP brought in Woithe himself, they tried to soften him up by putting him in protective custody for the night. But he denied to the RCMP knowing anything about Plaszek's murder. And Woithe kept his silence among the POWs with whom he was placed overnight.

By mid-September, Corporal Bull believed he was getting somewhere. He recorded his belief that his "investigation is now reaching a climax."[10] Yet, three days later, interviews with two prisoners from whom he expected crucial co-operation, twenty-five-year-old POW Paul Kazmirzak and twenty-three-year-old Leo Cisa, quashed the RCMP investigator's hopes.

Kasmierczak's statement that he "was not at all interested" and did not know "anything about who killed" Plaszek, conflicted directly with what another prisoner reported him saying the day after the murder: "He had seen Private Kratz strike Plaszek."[11]

Kazmierczak also claimed to be unaware of the noise made while Plaszek was being pulled toward the recreation hall. This was not credible: he lived in a hut only a few yards from where Plaszek died. Kazmierczak's testimony and behaviour would be key elements in the trials to come.

Similarly dubious claims were made by POW Cisa, a Pole who had been drafted into the German Army. Although he had been taken into protective custody and was cited by other prisoners as an eye witness to the killing, Cisa said he had not looked at the dead man. The battlefield stretcher bearer claimed the sight of blood made him ill, and that he did not know it was Plaszek. He insisted that he had not "describe[d] to anyone how Plaszek was killed and if they say I did it is a lie."[12] Corporal Bull didn't believe him but there was nothing he could do about it.

Based on what these POWs said, the RCMP investigator concluded that witnesses from Camp 132 were "under the domination of the Nazi element." Its power was so strong that "it is useless to continue the investigation under the present circumstances," Bull concluded on September 20.[13]

* * *

That the camp had closed ranks did not mean peace had returned to it. Former Legionnaire Hugo Stolte, for one, was uneasy.[14] In conversations with the RCMP, he had implicated Private Adolf Kratz, also mentioned by Kasmierczak, in the killings. In the minutes after Schulz's escape, Stolte had heard Kratz say, "Now we have hanged one of those swine; they [presumably all the Legionnaires] should be hanged," in a boastful manner that convinced Stolte "that he had personally taken part in the hanging," Stolte told Canadian authorities.[15]

A few days later, a POW buttressed what Stolte had told the Canadians. Although he could not say Kratz was "present at the hanging" (meaning participating in it), the POW insisted that he had heard him say "he would have liked to have eaten [Plaszek's] testicles."[17]

Another former Legionnaire, Lorenz Kasmirzak (no relation to Paul Kazmirzak), told the RCMP he heard a man say to Kratz, "You took a main part in this," to which Kratz replied: "Yes, it was my duty. All the swine should hang."[18]

No doubt prompted by tower-guard Byers' observation that the man leading those pulling Plaszek toward the recreation hall walked with a "swagger," Bull asked Kasmirzak if there was "anything peculiar about the walk of Kratz?" Kasmirzak said "No." In his follow up, Bull used the word "swagger," which elicited a more useful response: "[Kratz] goes in for boxing and when he walks, he walks heavily and as if he wants to show that he is a strongman. He has a nickname which expresses the thought that he pretends to be stronger than he is."[19]

Kratz figured prominently in at least one other interview. POW Adam Jansen, who identified him from pictures the RCMP presented, reported that Kratz had said, "I helped hang that pig" and that "Nobody from the 361s Regiment [i.e., former Legionnaires] is allowed in my room anymore."[20]

* * *

Aware that the POWs' statements had "established [only] that there was a murder committed at a certain place at a certain time" but that they had "avoid[ed] any direct evidence against any particular person," RCMP placed its own eyes and ears in the enclosure in late August.[21]

Since the POWs would have immediately recognized RCMP Constable George G. Krause's name as being German and, might well have suspected he spoke the language (as did many who lived on the Canadian prairies), Krause was disguised as a Canadian Army Engineer named Sapper King, whose ostensible job inside the wire was repairing lighting and sewage lines. Krause had learned German at home from his bilingual (English/German) parents. His English was polished at a public school in Leduc, Alberta, while his German was refined at the local German Baptist Church established in 1927, where every Sunday there was an hour devoted to reading and writing German. As the fictitious Sapper King, he spoke only English in the camp.

Like all civilian workmen, Krause was accompanied by a scout as he went about his duties in the enclosure. He overheard prisoners talking about the prohibition on speaking about the killing and about the strength of the Nazi leadership in the camp. Although instructed to follow the non-fraternization rule, he one day managed a short discussion with two POWs working in a kitchen. He learned nothing new about the recent violence because both men denied seeing anything, "saying they were too busy to inquire as to who actually had done the deed." Both said the "matter would be dealt with after the war."[22]

Kraus as "Sapper King" observed the Gestapo's surveillance system in action, which mostly involved German NCO's listening in on all the prisoner conversations they possibly could. To ensure that they were not being overheard, POWs who wanted to speak in confidence regularly looked backward to "watch for the arrival of their own N.C.O.s;" the POWs called this the *Deutscher Spaziergang* or German Walk.[23] Kraus heard arguments about the war, including excuses for the defeat in Russia that ranged from the cold weather to the overwhelming amount of Soviet equipment to the Germans' poor clothing and food. All of this information was likely gleaned from clandestine news sheets prepared from German shortwave broadcasts. A few POWs, thinking the workman did not speak German, were brave enough to aver to each other that "attacking the Soviet Union was poor strategy." However, these men also believed that the Germans were superior fighters and "might be able to hold out for an indefinite period of time at their own borders."[24]

Prisoner perceptions of the war were shaped by the camp leadership's efforts to maintain Nazi morale. News stories about German setbacks were clipped out of Canadian newspapers before they were distributed in the camp. To counter official announcements such as the resignation of Mussolini (July 26, 1943), Elstermann circulated fictitious information among the POWs. Seven weeks later, when Italy switched sides, the prisoners, after some initial confusion, professed relief at being "rid of a liability and resentment over having been betrayed." One wag said to a Canadian officer, "Well, I see you have new allies. You are welcome to them. They have always been a burden to us." Censors found letters replete with phrases like "cowardly swine" and "dogs," in reference to the Italians, with one man writing, "a heavy blow, but this cannot shatter my faith in the Führer."[25]

During the United States' bloody but successful attack on Salerno, Italy, word spread in camp "that the Germans had taken 10,000 prisoners." Krause estimated that 60 percent of the POWs felt that Germany could not win the war, but that the majority remained "loyal Nazis." In what must have been welcome news to the department of national defence, he heard nothing about tunnelling. Indeed, he'd heard "it would be useless to try [to escape], as the distance and mode of travel would make it nearly impossible to reach Germany."[26] This differed with reports from POW camps elsewhere in the country. Between April and late August of 1943, the department had dealt with ten escapes from Southern Quebec alone.

In September of that year, Krause's ultimate superior, RCMP commissioner Clifford Harvison, discovered a 300-metre-long tunnel beneath the Bowmanville POW camp that he declared "a masterpiece of engineering." It was reinforced by beams, ventilated, and lit by a string of lights that tapped into the camp's power supply. To throw off scouts looking and listening for tunnelling, several ninety-metre decoy tunnels were dug. The planned mass break out was to be followed by a dash out of Ontario and across most of Quebec to the Baie des Chaleurs (between the southern shore of the Gaspe and New Brunswick) where the men were to be picked up by a waiting U-boat.[27] It came a cropper when a prisoner digging to fill a flower box pushed his shovel into the ground and the earth gave way. Moments later, with rifles at the ready, a guard said to the tunnellers, "Well, well. Where do you think you are going?"[28]

* * *

The court of inquiry continued its operations into autumn without much success. Private Severin Fries, another prisoner who'd requested protection from the Canadians, felt safe enough to provide the RCMP with a haunting image of the last time he'd seen his friend, Plaszek. As Fries walked to dinner on the day of the killing, he saw Plaszek listening to "another man who was playing a harmonica" under the hot prairie sky.[29]

What Fries had heard from a POW named 'Gizza or Zizza'—in fact, Cisa—was more germane to the investigation. Cisa, the stretcher bearer with the weak stomach, was reportedly sick all the time and could not eat because of what he had seen at the hanging. Said Fries: "He told me how they had tied Plaszek up and then lifted him up about two feet and pulled him down quickly [to break his neck]."[30]

The investigators' work was occasionally aided by information from Canada's censors. In mid-November, they redirected (to the director of the prisoners-of-war office) a letter written by POW Walter Kohle to his wife in Darmstadt, Germany. "Last Saturday we had our second funeral procession," he said, noting that one man had died as a result of wounds suffered in battle and another had died of cancer. In parenthesis he added, "the third deceased had become tired of his Germanism and for this reason was given a little help to his death." These words indicated that the man was killed deliberately and not in some spontaneous outburst.[32]

In order to keep information flowing, the Canadian authorities did what they could to assuage the apprehension of those co-operating witnesses it kept in protective custody. The witnesses feared they had become, as Corporal Bull wrote in mid-September with a nod toward a famous short story by the American writer, Edward Everett Hale, "more or less [men] without a country."[33] As quickly as possible, the witnesses were sent away to work on farms in Alberta and Ontario. A large cohort of men who had indicated that they would talk if they were removed from Camp 132 were among the 420 men sent to a camp in Riding Mountain, Manitoba, which the RCMP believed to be 80 percent anti-Nazi (it was not).

In mid-December, RCMP Corporal Bull visited the men he had stowed on farms for further interviews. At least in the case of Stolte, Bull found that the change of venue was apparently having the desired effect. "I notice a change in his demeanour since he was at Medicine Hat," he said, noting that he should be interviewed again at a later date. Bull's report ends with an excerpt of a letter POW H. Sauerzweig wrote to his parents on 26 October. The cryptic lines put him on the RCMP's radar:

> I have been so busy that I had no time to write. I will tell you later what I have done. You will be surprised that I have done something like that. I would never have thought that I could have done anything like that. Unfortunately, I cannot give you any details but these will be settled orally.[34]

The investigation slowed over the Christmas holiday season, which was a difficult time of year for POWs, perhaps even more so for the men who worked on farms and could see Canadian family members gathering and sharing happy times. The complicated routine that saw letters from a family in Germany go first to neutral Turkey, then to Portugal before finally arriving in Canada, combined with the time it took censors to clear letters, meant that unless a wife, sweetheart, or parent wrote a Christmas letter in early September, it probably arrived well after the holidays. Within Camp 132, huts were decorated with Christmas trees and tin foil from cigarettes, and hearty rounds of "Stille Nacht" and "O Tannenbaum" helped the POWs observe the holiday. But nothing, not Christmas greetings from their führer, not the turkey dinner with all the trimmings—not even the performance by Joyce Reesor's glee club—could fill the void these men shared with millions of POWs in Canada, the United States, Germany, Poland, Russia, and across the Japanese empire.[35]

In the new year, RCMP Superintendent E.G. Frere, then the commander of "A" Division in Ottawa, interviewed several prisoners who had been placed on farms near Ottawa. Corporal Peter Fergen, who had been captured at El Alamein, told this senior RCMP official that he had come to the conclusion in late July 1943 that "the murder of the French Legionnaire had been planned and that it was forthwith a murder." He also mentioned that he had stopped to visit a friend, Willie Werner, in his hut. Werner had wanted to know if the staff doctor, Nolte, pushed himself into the crowd and stabbed Plaszek in the back before disappearing into the crowd.[36]

Almost every RCMP interview produced rumours or "hearsay" evidence. Yet, Frere's analysis of Fergen's testimony is one of the few times an RCMP officer underscores this fact. By doing so, the investigator signalled that he did not believe the accusations against Nolte. Showing his familiarity with Corporal Bull's reports, as well as Bull's high opinion of Nolte, Frere notes that he questioned Fergen closely about the alleged stabbing. Frere reports that Werner "was very definite that Dr. Nolte had stabbed Plaszek."[37] Werner's story, we know, is incorrect. And the superintendent clearly sided with those RCMP officers inclined to doubt it as well.

In Frere's interview with Fritz Dornseif, who was at a farm in Richmond, Ontario, the investigation came back around to Kratz, the man who wanted to eat Plaszek's testicles. On the day of the killing, said Dornseif, Kratz came into their hut after supper and rolled onto his bed. He had a hard-boiled egg in his hand and, as he began to eat it, said, "it still tastes good." Once he was finished, he said, "A while ago we had a little fun. We hanged that pig."[38]

Dornseif recalled Kratz adding, "I just kicked Plaszek in his guts and hit him with a stone on the head."[39] These words were too much for their POW bunkmate, W. Zehpfund, who motioned to Kratz to remain silent. Ignoring him, Kratz continued, "There are many more French Legionnaires to be hanged." Once Kratz was finished, Zehpfund said, "Even if I get ten years, I won't talk." Frere had already heard from two other POWs that Zehpfund was "a real Nazi" and someone who "will not talk unless treated in the Nazi manner," presumably meaning being given the Hitler salute and finishing with "Heil Hitler."[40]

While the rest of Dornseif's testimony was hearsay, including a statement by yet another POW that "I would never have believed that Kratz could be so brutal.... I saw how he cut Plaszek's face in two places with his knife," Frere does not mention this evidentiary limitation.[41] Nor does he find it necessary to note that the autopsy put paid to what two POWs told him about the stabbing of Plaszek.[42] The autopsy also showed that some of the blood on Plaszek's face came from the blow to his head that ripped open part of his scalp and not, as per Dornseif's story, from a cut to his face with a knife.

While Bull was pleased with what he was getting from some of the prisoners on farms, his hopes for those sent to Riding Mountain camp had turned sour. "It is apparent," the RCMP officer wrote, "that the same terroristic measures are being continued by the Nazi[s] at Riding Mountain as at Medicine Hat."[43]

Not long before, Canadian authorities had considered Riding Mountain to be at the lighter end of the spectrum of the PERHUDA system for classifying POWs by their allegiance to Nazism. Developed in 1942 by Americans' Joint Psychological Warfare Committee, PERHUDA was an acronym for the seven subject areas on which prisoners were interrogated.[44] Their answers segregated them into categories of Blacks (Nazis), Greys (no strong leanings), and Whites (anti-Nazi). Corporal Bull wanted to re-interview some of the men he'd sent to Riding Mountain but realized that the Nazis in the camp would likely recognize him, thus endangering the men he wanted to interview. To protect the interviewees, Bull had them transferred in February to the less Nazified POW Camp 32 in Hull, Quebec.

Despite the setbacks and the continued power of the Gestapo in Medicine Hat, Bull's informants had given him some reason for optimism. While the "Nazi propaganda in the camp convinces some that there is still the possibility that Germany will win the war," they felt that when the mass of the POWs "finally realize that Germany is beaten, they will be willing to give information" about the murder.[45]

* * *

Around the time of D-Day, in June 1944, Allied officials, knowing that tens of thousands more Germans would be added to camps with active Gestapos in Britain and across Canada and the United States, sought to develop a psychological understanding of Nazified soldiers in order to develop a denazification program. In Canada, these efforts were overseen by the department of external affair's new Psychological Warfare Committee and the department of national defence's Military Intelligence 7 (MI7) unit. Save for the PERHUDA classification system, how much the RCMP and military intelligence officers assigned to investigate the Plaszek killing knew of the psych-ops reports produced by these committees is unclear.

After extensively interviewing the captured Deputy Führer Rudolph Hess in England, British military psychologist Dr. Henry Dicks had assessed the Nazi mind in Freudian terms: "Nazis or near Nazis were likely to be men of markedly pre-genital or immature personality structure." He concluded that "a hasty re-education program aimed at adults whose personality had already acquired irreversible, pathological traits" would fail.[46] If Corporal Bull had read Dr. Dicks' work, parts would have rung true, given his experiences with Gestapo leadership and terrorized prisoners in Medicine Hat and Riding Mountain.

The Nazi re-education plan developed in Canada owed less to Freud and more to the American educator John Dewey. Simply put, Dewey argued against rote learning in education and in favour of learning by doing. Rather than memorizing the times tables, children should be led to discover the powers of multiplication. The top-hatted diplomats who met in Geneva did not place into their famous convention the requirement that POWs choose their own leadership in the camps because of Dewey's philosophy. Yet, under the influence of Dewey-inspired officials, including University of Chicago philosopher Dr. Thomas V. Smith, both Canadian and American officials came to view elections for POW camp leadership as opportunities for the prisoners to learn democratic habits of thought by performing them.

That Nazi cliques bent the elections to their will was regrettable, perhaps even predictable. Yet in the realpolitik world of operating POW camps, allowing prisoners to vote abided by the letter and spirit of the Geneva Convention (in hopes that Germany would, too). Further, allowing the soldiers to largely control the world within the wire was considered a price worth paying to help keep order. As one historian of American POW camps wrote, "instead of disrupting the prisoner-of-war program, the Nazi-dominated camps, in fact, were usually models of efficiency."[47]

If they couldn't control the outcome of the elections, one thing camp authorities could directly influence was the official flow of outside information into camps. Part of this flow consisted of library books and films. Some films came from Germany, which had an agreement to exchange films with Britain, Canada, and the United States. These were allowed only if their content was far from political. The selection of films produced in Allied nations came close to breaching the Convention's implied injunction against subjecting POWs to propaganda. *Abe Lincoln in Illinois* and Cecil B. DeMille's epic about Jesus, *King of Kings*, were screened in American POW camps (and probably in Canada) despite their obvious political and religious messages. Shakespeare, whose *Julius Caesar*, *Macbeth*, *Richard II*, and *Richard III*, could be seen as meditations on the causes and costs of tyranny, had been banned by the Nazis, yet his plays were available in POW libraries. So, too, were works by such authors as John Steinbeck and Thomas Mann (then in exile in the United States), alongside those of Jewish writers such as Franz Kafka and Stephan Zweig, all of whom were banned in Nazi Germany.

Less fraught so far as Geneva was concerned, but perhaps more useful from the re-educator's point-of-view, were newspapers and magazines. Following Dewey, the re-educators believed that showering the POWs with factual information (or what passed for factual in wartime) would encourage them to form their own anti-Nazi opinions. This became easier after the invasion of Italy in September 1943. Camps were inundated with headlines such as "Bomb Nazis Out of Monte Cassino Monastery." News of bombing raids also drove home the point: "Burning Augsburg Hit Hard Last Night," "U.S. Bombers Attack Berlin in Force."[48] These were accompanied by words and maps depicting the relentless Russian advance and, after D-Day, the Canadian, British, and American battles in Normandy and, after that, the Germans' retreat from France. Altogether, the stream of bad news (from the German point of view) was seen as a sort of psychological counterpart to the Allied strategic bombing campaign. That campaign, aimed at major German cities, was intended not simply to destroy industrial plants and undermine the efficiency of the Nazi's workforce but to produce among the German people a psychological shock that might "break up well-established attitudes and behaviour patterns so that new influences can operate."[49]

Historians of the strategic bombing campaign have shown that German military production remained strong until early 1945. Moreover, while propaganda minister Joseph Goebbels knew that grousing had become more common, Germany's home front did not collapse in World

War Two as it had in World War One.[50] In other words, the Allies strategic-bombing campaign failed to achieve its primary psychological aim. Nor was the avalanche of bad news into POW camps having much effect. The reign of the camp Gestapos was largely undisturbed and prisoners were not noticeably more amenable to informing on their fellows. Rather, Lieutenant General Schmidt, the most senior German general held in Canada, had ordered that POWs continue to view themselves as German soldiers and refuse to support the detaining powers.[51] This order was smuggled into Camp 132 inside the cover of a book carried by a transferee from Lethbridge to Medicine Hat.

Still, in mid-June, three POWs violated their top general's order. Each man, fearing for his life, had independently asked for protection. Moreover, all three told Bull they had heard that a Corporal Johannes Wittinger had hanged Plaszek.

One of these accusers, Corporal Karl Diabiase, was of Italian descent and both "anti-Nazi and anti-German." (He had been compelled to join the Wehrmacht because he was living in Austria when Germany absorbed it in the Anschluss of March 1938.) As an "anti-Nazi" POW, Diabiase was transferred for his own safety away from Medicine Hat to Riding Mountain camp, but the Gestapo was there too. He told Bull he had heard about Wittinger's role in the killing from a prisoner named Schnackenberg. But it soon got around camp that Schnackenberg was talking and he was warned that he "had better be careful what he talked [about] or else he too would be dealt with." Perhaps because of this threat, Schnackenberg tried to escape from a work party. The RCMP quickly recaptured him and put him in the camp hospital. Rather than take protection, he decided to return to camp, concerned for the safety of his family in Germany.[52]

The statement by another accuser, Private Oswald Schmidt, also shows that even as the tide of war turned against Germany, the majority of POWs remained wary of committing themselves. Because of this, Bull was still hearing a lot of "second-hand" stories. Schmidt said his source, a POW named Fritz Schmidbauer, "will not reveal this information [himself] to Canadian authorities until he was certain that Germany had lost the war, as he is afraid that his children and wife in Germany will be persecuted."[53] The more talkative Schmidt says he was told "You should have seen how Plaszek acted when he was stoned and shown the rope," and "Wittinger had actively helped to kill Plaszek."[54] Another POW, Joseph Siersczak, told Bull that he had heard that Wittinger had said, "Well, I have calmed my anger and helped to kill an anti-Nazi."[55]

Both Siersczak and Schmidt had been moved under protection to work on farms near Vauxhall, Alberta. It seemed Bull's prediction—that placing POWs beyond the easy reach of the Gestapo would produce new leads—was at last bearing some fruit. Two more prisoners, both former Legionnaires, identified a staff sergeant named Werner Schwalb as a culprit. After playing his part as a gunner in a Panzer tank during the Blitz through France in 1940, earning an Iron Cross First Class, Schwalb had been sent to Afrika Corps where he was an infantryman before being captured in mid-January 1942 in Egypt. Bull's sources said Schwalb had beaten and hanged the "half dead man," Plaszek. Also implicated was the same POW others had named earlier—Wittinger—who was seen coming back from the scene of the hanging with "blood on his hands."[56]

It was abundantly clear to Corporal Bull through the summer of 1944 that the Gestapo still had a strong grip over most of the men in the Medicine Hat and Riding Mountain POW camps. Almost all of the prisoners had closed ranks, determined to keep a lid on what they viewed as their internal camp business. Nevertheless, the investigator was slowly making progress. He had been told by diverse sources that Plaszek had been hanged by someone who was a master at hanging. A number of prisoners had implicated the swaggering Private Adolf Kratz, and several more had fingered the bloody-handed Corporal Johannes Wittinger, and Staff Sergeant Werner Schwalb. Kratz, Wittinger, and Schwalb had all arrived in North America on the same ship as did August Plaszek in 1942.

As the investigation of Plaszek's murder advanced into its second year, Colonel Streight, director of the Prisoners of War office, wrote to the director of censorship on September 16, 1944. Streight wrote that an article on the POWs in Medicine Hat prepared by the *Lethbridge Herald* and submitted to the censor just over a month earlier should not be cleared for publication. Streight's decision had the support of the director of military intelligence and the commissioner of the RCMP. The reason for the censorship was the article's "reference to the hanging" of Plaszek.

Streight did not inform his colleague of a telegram he had received five days earlier informing him of another "Hanging in Medicine Hat."

CHAPTER 5

The Investigation into the Murder of Dr. Karl Lehmann

September 11, 1944 to April 8, 1945

"What would you do if you were in a German prison camp with 10,000 men under similar circumstances to us, and you found out one of your comrades to be a traitor?"

—POW Staff Sergeant Baron Jurgen von Manteuffel,
September 11, 1944

IT HARDLY MATTERS WHETHER the POWs learned about the attempt on their führer's life from the *Winnipeg Tribune* of July 21, 1944, which reported the failure of Operation Valkyrie, or from their hidden short-wave radios. The prisoners knew that the bloodletting had already begun. The first communique from Berlin announced that two of the attempted coup's leaders, Count Claus von Stauffenberg, who planted the bomb, and Colonel-General Ludwig Beck, the former chief of the German general staff, were "no longer among the living." The numbers—7,000 arrested, of whom almost 5,000 were executed—would come later and weren't needed for the Nazi cliques in Canadian camps to know what was expected of them once they'd heard Hitler say, "This time we will settle accounts in such a manner as we National Socialists are wont," a statement that recalled the "Night of the Long Knives," the bloody purge of the Nazi party in 1934.[1]

Hitler's order to "mercilessly eradicate" those who would stab Germany in the back radicalized the Gestapos in POW camps around the world.[2] Indeed, even before the assassination attempt, the flood of bad news from the front and, especially, stories of the carpet bombing of German towns and cities had caused the Gestapo's propaganda to become more "demagogical," spreading "more and more rumours about communistic activities" in the camp, as Georg Herdel, a former Waffen SS officer, later told the Canadians. Any "meeting by friends" was suspect. While Herdel admitted that the communist scare was a "chimera," he said it provided the "motive to look for traitors in [the] Medicine Hat camp." In their heightened zeal for Nazi purity, the Camp 132 Gestapo persecuted men who "according to their origin and their civilian occupations would be anything else but communists."[3]

On September 3, 1944, led by German Staff Sergeant Walter Wolf, the Gestapo audaciously arrested some fifty, mostly Austrian, POWs who had formed a secret club that met in a disused hut. The men were lined up with their arms behind their backs before being escorted from the theatre in the east recreation hall to another hut where they were held for several days and forbidden to speak. "When we wanted to go to the toilet, we were individually guarded and escorted by three *Unteroffiziers* (corporals)," one carrying a large stick, said one of the detainees. The entire action appears to have gone unnoticed by the scouts, despite the complications involved in supplying such a large number of men with food and accounting for them both in their huts and during the daily prisoner counts. While, in the end, all but four men were released unharmed, Wilhelm Wendt, now returned as camp leader and less moderate than before, reminded the prisoners that obedience was expected of good Germans. The four men, he said, had wanted the camp leadership out. They had been discovered and, he said, "they are going to be punished." Wendt also told the prisoners not to work for the Canadians: failure to follow this dictate would result in prison after the war.[4]

Further radicalizing the Gestapo in Camp 132 was the announcement a few days later that to make room for 800 to 900 men captured in Normandy, a like number of POWs were to be transferred to Lethbridge and Neys, Ontario. The Nazi clique did not need to know the details of the PERHUDA system to see that a large number of their supporters, "Blacks," were on the list of men about to be transferred.[5]

One name not on the list was the stout Dr. Karl Lehmann. Some men later told investigators that he did not have any enemies, and his position as a language teacher would suggest that he was in good standing with the camp leadership. But others said that Lehmann was not shy about challenging less educated men, which irritated them, and that he had been in the Gestapo's sights for some time.

There is no evidence that the camp Gestapo knew about Lehmann's pre-war career as a writer for left-wing journals, but they had other reasons to suspect him. At the transit camp in Oldham, England, where he and thousands of other men captured in Africa were kept before being shipped to Canada, Lehmann was seen as overly pessimistic about Germany's chances of winning the war. And on September 10, 1944, the very same day that Wendt reminded prisoners of the prohibition on listening to war news that originated outside the camp, Lehmann was believed to have been translating stories from the *Winnipeg Tribune* that reported "Canadians Push East After Caen Victory," and that Russian troops were less than 800 kilometres from Berlin.

In the eyes of Sergeant Robert Stoehr (a "Black"), Lehmann might have worn a uniform but he was "inwardly ... not a soldier, he never served on a battlefront—he was one of those who organized the educational and recreational activities of the army." Stoehr appears not to have known that as a translator Lehmann interrogated captured Allied soldiers and airmen. It especially offended Stoehr that the unmarried Lehmann "looked upon women as an object of pleasure" and not as pure vessels whose duty was to bear and raise the first true generation of Nazis.[6] Decent women did not excite or appeal to Lehmann, Stoehr said. Rather, he found pleasure in "visiting the Red Light districts in France where he could do with women on payment whatever he wished."[7]

For all these reasons, and because Lehmann had waited to be drafted rather than volunteering, and had "committed suicide by hanging himself," Stoehr later summed up Lehmann with the word "*feige*," which translates as "yellow" or "pusillanimous."[8]

Lehmann may have been overweight and reputed as a libertine, but he was no coward, as Canadian Army Intelligence knew, and the camp Gestapo suspected. He was one of the leaders of the Anti-Nazi group. And despite being "continuously watched" by the Gestapo for a period of months, he had been a regular informer. In mid-June, "he was brought out of the compound on the pretext of being required to give evidence to the board of inquiry [investigating August Plaszek's murder]." When he returned to the compound, his escorting guards threw up as much smoke as possible by saying "that he was taken out by mistake, that he was not required as a witness." While out of the compound, Lehmann had given "certain information of a secret nature." It was so sensitive that the RCMP report of September 18, 1944, does not allude to the details.

THE INVESTIGATION INTO THE MURDER OF DR. KARL LEHMANN

While out of the camp, demonstrating his mettle, Lehmann refused protective custody.[9]

On September 10, POWs being transferred out of Camp 132 were ordered to parade at 4 a.m. the following morning. This seems to have forced the Gestapo's hand, while also providing the opportunity to settle accounts with Lehmann. The immediate "charge" against him, according to four POWs interviewed weeks later, was that he had informed on fellow prisoners to Canadian authorities. Late that afternoon, a group of plotters assembled in hut DZ, which housed classrooms. Lehmann was summoned, ostensibly to sign language-proficiency certificates for some of the men being transferred out of Medicine Hat.

The first person to officially note that something was amiss with Lehmann was his hut-mate, POW Karl Gassner. Just after 3 a.m. on September 11, Gassner was awakened by reveille for the men leaving camp. He noticed that Lehmann was not in his bed and that one of the blankets remained folded while another appeared to have been thrown back on the bed. When the regular reveille sounded at 6:30 a.m. and Lehmann was still missing, the men in barracks considered the possibilities, one of which was that "he might be out drinking beer with friends," a theory that suggested a certain laxness in the camp's procedures.[10] A search by two POWs of the press room and other places Lehmann frequented turned up nothing. Lehmann's absence was then reported to the hut leader, who duly informed his section leader, who initiated a wider search. Meanwhile, almost a thousand POWs, including Lehmann's assailants, it would turn out, had boarded a train that took them away from the scene of the crime.

Rumours about Lehmann's disappearance spread quickly throughout the camp. They came as no surprise to the likes of Staff Sergeant (Baron) Jurgen von Manteuffel, who later that day rhetorically asked RCMP

Detective Corporal J.W. Stanton what Canadian POWs in Germany would do to a traitor in their midst.

Shortly after 8 a.m., prisoner Albert Schurr entered hut DZ. He was to meet a prisoner who was helping the naval mechanic study for university entrance exams back in Germany. "I entered and walked across the room over to a table in the rear, and I started looking through my books, then I glanced up and saw a man [who] appeared to be on his knees in the northwest corner of the room."[11]

Schurr immediately left the hut and, seeing three men he knew, including POW Joseph Angerstein, told them what he had seen. Together, the four returned to the hut and walked up to the crumpled body. All recognized the lifeless man as Lehmann. As curious prisoners began to congregate in the hut, Angerstein told them to leave; he then instructed Schurr to lock up the room while he went to inform camp leader Wendt. After locking the hut, Schurr returned the key to von Manteuffel's office; a few days earlier, Wendt had put von Manteuffel in charge of education and entertainment.

On being informed of the hanging by Angerstein, Wendt told him to alert Dr. Maximillian Nolte. But at the hospital, Angerstein was told that Schurr had already been there with the news. Schurr had then returned to hut DZ, where he was told to nail blankets over the windows. Later, Schurr would claim that when he saw Nolte and relayed news of the hanging, the doctor, unaccountably, had not gone immediately to examine the body.

Nolte did eventually see the body at around 9:45 a.m., nearly two hours after it was first discovered. Wendt had by then informed the Canadian camp security officer Major W. C. Pinkham that there had been a suicide in the enclosure and that it was POW Lehmann. Within an hour, a cursory examination of the body by Captain O'Donnell of the

Royal Canadian Army Medical Corps and Medicine Hat's city coroner determined that "death had resulted from foul play."

The RCMP was again called to Camp 132 to investigate a murder. The body remained where it was found until the next day when it was transported to a funeral home and an autopsy performed.

A new court of inquiry struck by the RCMP seemed to get an immediate break. A.J. Rayment learned that two POWs were seen boarding the train for Neys, the camp in Ontario, with home made bandages on their hands and arms. Both Rayment and camp commandant R.O. Bull surmised that the bandages covered wounds sustained while battering Lehmann's face to a pulp. Confusion over who had the authority to issue an order to detain the bandaged POWs and return them to camp, however, delayed the orders for several hours. By the time Rayment was granted authority, the two prisoners were no longer suspects. Lieutenant Thornton-Prehn, one of the Canadian officers who spoke German, had learned that they'd been wearing bandages for at least five days.

Again, Canada's censors furnished clues helpful to the investigation. On September 13, Private Karl Grabhandt, one of the POWs transferred to Neys, wrote a card promising a longer letter to follow in which he would tell his correspondent, Lisa, "the most important things," chiefly that "[d]uring the night when we left our camp somebody *hat mit Sailens-Touchter Hochzeit gafaiert*." The same misspelled German phrase appeared in a card written to his parents the day before. The words translate as, "somebody has celebrated his wedding with the daughter of a rope."[12]

By the time Grabhandt's card was translated in early October, the RCMP already knew from a September 25 interrogation of four POWs moved to Lethbridge that "prisoners from Camp 132 boasted of having 'executed' two fellow prisoners," Plaszek and Lehmann. In response, the Nazis at Lethbridge had 'apologized' for not yet having got around to that." The four POWs also told the RCMP that Lehmann was "accused of having given the Canadian authorities the names of Blacks."[13]

In his card, Grabhandt also asks Lisa how she looks upon his "'mute' and uninteresting writing." This describes the content of all letters adhering to rules of POWs correspondence but can also be read as an instruction to Lisa to read between the lines. After repeating that "somebody has celebrated his wedding with the daughter of a rope," Grabhandt mentions the men who were shipped out of Medicine Hat to new camps. He may have been signalling that the transferees were responsible for the "wedding."

The most intriguing part of Karl's letter, however, begins with the curious line, "You have probably also heard about a large forest fire in Ontario." There was no chance that the local papers in Naumburg-Saale, a small town 225 kilometres south west of Berlin, carried news of an Ontario forest fire, especially since there was no forest fire in Ontario at the time. "We got a taste of it here. For three days the air was so polluted that we could hardly distinguish day from night." Karl might have been referring to what he had heard about the effects of strategic bombing, or, perhaps more likely, to the atmosphere among the men after Lehmann's murder.[14]

It did not take the RCMP long to establish Lehmann's movements in the last few minutes before, in the words of the coroner's jury, he "came to his death."[15] Several POWs told the Canadians that Lehmann had been called from his hut early on the morning of September 11 on the pretext of retrieving from the lecture room books belonging to some of the POWs scheduled to leave camp. Once at the lecture hall, POW Robert Held said "he had been overpowered by men waiting for him, and had been killed as a traitor and hung up." Held prefaced his remarks by saying he had heard that Lehmann was "attempting to bring about an uprising in the camp against the Camp Leader" and that this had been discussed in camp the morning that Lehmann was found dead.[16]

As for the weapon with which Lehmann had been hung, Held saw four men cutting cord into six feet lengths the night before the crime was committed. Once cut, the lengths were tied together. Examining the shredded ends of the cord found next to Lehmann's corpse, the RCMP came to believe that the cord broke while the victim was being hung, necessitating a second hanging.

A routine check of the quarter-master stores showed that twenty-five feet of rope normally used to align broken limbs before plaster casts were applied had been signed out by Dr. Nolte, although the receipt had no date. The stores' rope was similar to the cord used to hang Lehmann. Nolte said that he'd used most of the rope to align a broken leg six months earlier, while the excess had been kept in a locked room in the hospital. He could not explain why it was no longer there. Nor could the orderly responsible for the hospital's supplies.

Just as this line of questioning appeared to be gaining ground, Nolte sent a message to investigators that a month earlier, one of the hospital's orderlies had used the rope to hang flower boxes in the hospital. A quick inspection revealed that a flower box there was indeed hanging by a quantity of rope. But Nolte's initial problem with the question did not go unnoticed by investigators, notwithstanding Corporal Bull's good opinion of the doctor.

*　*　*

On September 28, two weeks after Dr. Lehmann's body was found, camp commandant Colonel R.O. Bull ordered Lt. Colonel W. J. H. Elwood to carry out a search of the barracks. Knowing that the POWs would be upset at this invasion of their privacy—the Geneva Convention gave them more rights than criminal prisoners—Elwood's orders emphasized that "care is to be exercised by all ranks to disturb as little as reasonably possible the belongings of the P/W during the search." He further reminded his men that the "collection of souvenirs of any kind" was forbidden.[17]

The search began as scheduled at 9:15 a.m. when Elwood, seven guards, an interpreter, and German camp leader Wilhelm Wendt, who had been ordered to accompany the search, entered the orderly room and the hut in front of it. At the same time, one search party entered the camp hospital and another searched a second hut. Almost immediately, two large groups of POWs converged at the door to the orderly room. They were ordered back. Fifteen minutes later, while the room was being searched and after contraband documents had been found, several thousand prisoners surrounded the hut, some ripping screens from the windows and yelling "*Aus* (Out)!" and "*Schweinhund* (Pig dog)!"

Elwood reported that as Wendt tried to restrain the crowd, a group of six or eight POWs "burst into the spokesman's room at the rear of the building.... [and] were seen to pass several files and other articles to the waiting crowd outside." Wendt ordered them to withdraw, "which they did reluctantly." The crowd of POWs continued to mill about, "rabid with rage." At one point, Wendt threw up his hands and told the Canadians he could not be responsible for their safety. "The situation had become critical in the extreme." Recalling the moment, Elwood wrote that his unarmed party was "hopelessly outnumbered."[18]

Finally, a narrow corridor was opened through the POWs. Before following Wendt out of the mob, Elwood's men abandoned almost all of the documents they had seized. They were kicked and tripped as they passed through this gauntlet. One of the scouts did manage to hold onto a matchbox containing a number of documents written on tissue paper. These contained instructions on using codes and making invisible ink, and a directive to "turn in [i.e., send to Germany] all available news of use to the Fatherland."[19]

The two other search parties were also disrupted. POWs forcibly ejected the scouts sent to search Dr. Maximillian Nolte's hospital office. The second search team in another hut was held for ten minutes by enraged prisoners.

Commandant Bull reacted quickly to the manhandling of his guards by withdrawing all privileges from the prisoners, including newspapers and films. Further, he increased the number of roll calls and confined the POWs to their barracks after 8 p.m. Access to the canteen was restricted and the POWs were ordered to return the loud speaker that had been erected for their use on the sports field. Finally, Bull suspended walking parties outside the camp. Some weeks later, his point having been made, the commandant returned the camp to the regular number of roll calls and restored the POWs' privileges.

* * *

Army Intelligence had harboured doubts about Dr. Nolte even prior to Lehmann's death. Nolte had once persuaded a POW, then under protection of Canadian authorities, to return to the enclosure and guaranteed his safety in the hospital. The POW, K. Reiss, was subsequently "found dead with his wrists slashed." Nolte ruled it a suicide prompted by Reiss's "mental condition."[20] This allowed Reiss to receive a military funeral. Another POW mentioned it in a card he sent home: "A comrade was buried with full military honours. We all had a funeral parade."[21]

In another document dated the same day, October 16, 1944, army intelligence captain L. B. Yule writes that the "position and amount of influence exercised at this camp by Capt. Nolte… has always been something of an enigma, and it is felt that the position occupied by him in the internal administration might be greatly clarified if copies could be obtained of the German manuals referred to in the Orders for Camp Management of Camp 133 [Lethbridge], apparently issued by Lt. General Schmidt." Yet Yule also noted that while Nolte "has always appeared to be co-operative and helpful to camp authorities," a search of his quarters turned up a file that contained "references to the murdered [POW] Lehmann."[22]

Nolte wouldn't have been the first German physician to be classified as a Nazi. According to historian Judith M. Gansberg, the German medical corps at the Glennan General Hospital, part of the POW camp in Okmulgee, Oklahoma, was thoroughly Nazified. "Anyone complaining to an American physician was labelled 'queer' or psychotic by Nazi doctors and risked being locked up in the psychotic ward."[23]

It soon came to the attention of Canadian investigator Detective Corporal J.W. Stanton that Nolte and another German doctor, Maximillian Nietzsche, were believed to have been involved in several murders in prison camps in Africa. Lieutenant Thornton-Prehn had learned from other POWs and (unnamed) secret files that the circumstances of these murders were similar to those of Plaszek and Lehmann. As far as the RCMP was able to determine, no action was taken against either doctor while they were in custody in Africa, but this new information cast a darker light on Nolte's approval of the Gestapo's violent "admonitions," and his hospital's refusal to treat men beaten by the Gestapo.

Still more evidence against Nolte was discovered in early November 1944. A search of Sergeant Major Walter Wolf's possessions at the POW camp at Neys turned up a brown paper wrapping filled with musical notation paper addressed to Nolte. Between the lines of the music was German shorthand arranged to look like song lyrics. Turning the

THE INVESTIGATION INTO THE MURDER OF DR. KARL LEHMANN

shorthand into long hand and then translating it from German was a difficult task. The best efforts of the investigators produced this: "Perhaps it is possible for you [Nolte] to send us word whether Lehmann and Voes were really hanged. There is a rumour going around here?"[24]

The Canadians could not determine the identity of "Voes." Nor were they certain of a phrase that could be translated either as "Who was it?" or "Was it you?" The latter implied that the recipient of the paper "was the type who could commit murder, and the writer anxiously wishes to learn if he was [involved]."[25] Whether the message was written by Wolf to Nolte or Nolte to Wolf, it suggests that the medical doctor had no trouble, or was understood to have no trouble, setting aside his Hippocratic oath.

* * *

A series of telegrams and letters to and from various Canadian government departments, the Prisoner of War Information Bureau (PWIB) in London, the Swiss Consul in Montreal, and the Red Cross in Geneva, kept officials abreast of the investigation of Lehmann's murder. A few of these indicate the difficulty organizations had in exchanging information. Finding the telegram he received on Lehmann's death insufficiently precise, the Swiss Consul in Montreal on September 27 telegraphed Ottawa wanting to know the exact date of the death as well as the victim's next of kin (in the event of a POW's death, the Red Cross was responsible for notifying family). On October 10, the PWIB telegrammed their counterparts in Ottawa questioning what was said in "your cable of 6 October/Date of death of POW Lehmann Karl no clear/Repeat in Words Not Figures." The confusion of the PWIC was understandable. The telegram in question read "Lehmann Karl Found Dead 110830-8-Sep/Stop/Death may have occurred previous day."[26]

It wasn't just official communications that were suspect. In addition to the investigation of Lehmann's murder, a court of inquiry was launched to investigate the Canadian army's role in the circumstances surrounding his death. The three military officers comprising the court heard from thirteen scouts and other Veterans Guardsmen about the physical layout of the camp and procedures for its surveillance. Lance Corporal J.W. Stewart, who was on patrol inside the enclosure through the night of September 10–11, reported hearing no screams and seeing "nothing out of the ordinary" in the area of hut DZ.[27]

When he walked by the hall shortly after midnight, another patrol, Lieutenant M.W. English, saw "no sign of movement." What he assumed was a "farewell party between the block leaders of Block 'B' and some others" broke the rule of lights out at 10 p.m., but English was satisfied that it was "an innocent party.... I did not want to do anything which might interfere with the movement of the [POWs] several hours later."[28] He was satisfied that the party had "nothing to do with the death of Lehmann."[29]

While he couldn't name any of the assailants, security officer Major W.C. Pinkham, the first Canadian to hear of the hanging, gave testimony that demonstrated the limitations under which camp authorities were operating. "The strength of our scouts for this camp," he said, "has always been understrength."[30] That important, if infelicitous sentence, suggests that the Canadians deliberately supervised the camp with a light touch because they were short-handed. In order to have men ready to guard the POWs as they exited the camp early on the following morning, it had been necessary to withdraw some of the block patrols during the night. The Veterans Guard could not fill the gap: they, too, were under strength. Accordingly, there were parts of the camp unwatched for longer

THE INVESTIGATION INTO THE MURDER OF DR. KARL LEHMANN

than normal periods on the night in question, providing an opportunity for Lehmann's assailants.

The court of inquiry found that "military personnel carried out their duties efficiently and no negligence can be ascribed to any such personnel." While recognizing the limitations Pinkham's force was under, the court did not recommend increasing the number of Veterans Guardsmen or scouts. Recruiting more Veterans Guardsmen would only reduce the pool of manpower available to the Canadian army at a time when it needed more men in boots, and Ottawa, with memories of the conscription crisis of the First World War still fresh, was doing its best to avoid the politically unpalatable imposition of conscription, even though in the national referendum of April 1942 voters had released Prime Minister Mackenzie King from his no conscription pledge.

The court of inquiry also adopted Pinkham's recommendation that it would be "ill-advised [for the court] to attempt to gain evidence [from POWs] in this inquiry, because of the effect it might have on the investigation still going on by the RCMP."[31] Shortly after the conclusion of the court of inquiry, this decision was set aside by the Canadian Army's judge advocate general (JAG). Citing the "Special Agreement with German Government Arising out of the Prisoner of War and Sick and Wounded Conventions" signed by Britain and Germany in 1943, the JAG said POW evidence was "material" to the Lehmann case. Recognizing that it would be redundant to call POW witnesses after they had been interviewed by the RCMP, the JAG instructed the court of inquiry to reconvene so that its members could (officially) read the RCMP investigative reports and, more importantly from a legal point-of-view, include the reports as an exhibit. The court was also told to reconsider its findings in light of the additional material. After following the JAG's orders, the court of inquiry submitted a second report with no change to its findings. This was duly sent to the Red Cross and the Swiss Government, which sent it to Berlin.

* * *

The RCMP investigation of Lehmann's death followed a similar pattern to that of August Plaszek's. Lists of men to be interrogated were drawn up; a late September report contains the names of nineteen POWs. A search in Camp 130 in Seebe, Alberta turned up instructions for how POW courts should handle deserters and their punishments. On October 20, a severely beaten man crawled to the wire in Camp 132 and asked for protection, demonstrating that even after hundreds of Nazis were sent to other camps, the *Gestapo* still ruled in Medicine Hat's enclosure.

Nevertheless, some prisoners named others. POW Ewald Kruppa told the RCMP that Sergeant Richard Neil beat him with sticks while other men said, "Now we are going to hang him." Kruppa's offense was to be "not very fond of Hitler." He had previously identified himself to Canadians as an Evangelical and anti-Nazi.[32]

On 4 November, POW Baron Hans Helmel gave a Canadian officer a scrapbook or memoir that ran for nine single-spaced typed pages. It detailed the establishment of the Gestapo in Medicine Hat. Helmel sarcastically refers to Plaszek's murderers as men "whose eyes lit up with thirst for blood when this 'glorious deed' is mentioned." Breaking bones was among their favourite sadistic acts. The memoir repeats the story of Lehmann's last hours and records that on seeing Lehmann's body with a friend, Helmel said, "If *he* has committed suicide, I am a fool."[33]

Finding Helmel's account too dramatic, not to mention foolhardy, given the strength of the Gestapo in Medicine Hat, one RCMP officer cautioned that it should be taken with the proverbial grain of salt. But the similarities between Helmel's recounting of Walter Wolf's Gestapo-led mass arrest of almost fifty men and other versions of the same event gave RCMP reason to believe Helmel's words about how the Gestapo operated. Among the six "activist" Nazis named by Helmel were Wolf and Flight Sergeant Bruno Perzenowski. With regard to the latter, Helmel's friend POW Herbert Schwab, whose pre-war career as a public prosecutor taught him to recognize the "scent of a crime," had this to say: "[T]hese people are capable of anything."[34]

* * *

During the first week of February 1945, another of the Plaszek suspects, Staff Sergeant Warner Schwalb, caught the directorate of censorship's attention with a letter to his wife. Just as the POWs had metaphorically thumbed their noses at the guards after the failed raid on Dieppe, the Canadians must have seemed rather smug in early 1945. The long weeks of slugging through Normandy were just a memory, Paris had been liberated, and the Russians were already at the Oder, some 50 kilometres east of Berlin, where, on February 3, a bombing raid by 1,500 planes belonging to the United States Army Air Force dropped 2,000 tons of bombs. Exactly what set Schwalb off in his letter is unrecorded; his spleen, however, caught a censor's eye: "Here much has changed. Our guards are again showing their true faces, this I can only say, that people who lay their hands on the defenceless are 'devoid of honour.'"[36]

Another letter, this one anonymous, turned up in the Neys camp in mid-February. In addition to casting aspersions on various prisoners, it gave investigators advice on how to interrogate men who "have knowledge concerning the death of Dr. Lehmann." Every time "a prisoner of war leaves the enclosure he is accompanied by an interpreter," said the correspondent, "[which] causes the interrogations to be doomed before they even get started." This was probably not news to the Canadian investigators but it would have confirmed a serious flaw in their methods.[37]

While Joseph Stalin, Winston Churchill, and President Franklin D. Roosevelt were meeting in Yalta in early February to determine how to deal with the defeated Reich and the shape of post-war Europe, RCMP Corporal Bull continued interviewing POWs about Dr. Lehmann's murder in Medicine Hat. The most fruitful of these was with prisoner Robert Schufart, who told Bull that he not only agreed with Lehmann's political views but was close enough to him to kid him about being a communist. Around 10 p.m. on the night Lehmann was murdered, Schufart and several other men, including Staff Sergeant Jurgen von Manteuffel, left the camp's art studio and saw Walter Wolf. To Schufart's surprise, Wolf came up to him and said, "I would like to say good bye." Schufart wanted nothing to do with Wolf, knowing his camp Gestapo reputation, but felt it best to accept his proffered hand. He did, and noticed that Wolf was sweating. "He acted very queerly and had a peculiar look on his face."[38] Schufart was doubly shocked when Wolf slapped him on the shoulder and said goodbye.

Lehmann's friend admitted that he had no hard evidence to link Wolf to the killing. One detail Schufart did offer was that as Wolf walked away, he met up with a friend and—instead of walking toward their hut, as would have been expected at lights out—the two men "appeared to walk south towards the main gate... towards D-2 where Lehmann lived."[39]

RCMP were unsure what to make of Wolf's walk in the direction of Lehmann's barracks, given that he was not murdered there but in the education hut, several hours later. Also, Schufart's discussion of von Manteuffel illustrates some of the difficulties faced by Canadian investigators interrogating men who lived in a social environment in which comrades were both brothers and a danger to anyone demonstrably short on Nazi rectitude. According to Schufart, after the Hitler bomb plot, von Manteuffel's manner changed as "he put on a front of being a good Nazi." Schufart's evidence that this was a "front" was that they remained good friends. He was sure von Manteuffel "would not approve of the Nazi atrocities" in the POW camps.[40]

Corporal Bull noted that Schufart's opinion of von Manteuffel was contradicted by information obtained by an intelligence officer, which showed von Manteuffel to be a firm Nazi. That von Manteuffel remained friends with Schufart and another known anti-Nazi suggested to Bull that "Von Manteuffel may have been playing a double game and may have lent himself to the betrayal of Lehmann."[41]

Corporal Bull's interrogation of POW August Siegel in early March 1945 suggested that other POWs were not entirely clear themselves on their attitudes toward Nazis. "Siegel at first disclaimed affiliation with the Nazi Party and appeared quite open and straightforward," wrote Bull, "but as the interview progressed it became apparent that he is still imbued with the German ideology." The interview ended with Siegel saying, "I do not know the reason Dr. Lehmann was killed but he would not have been killed if he had been a good German. I am a good German and if I knew who killed him, I would not say so, as it would be against my character."[42] If Bull noticed the irony that the psychological defences provided to Siegel by Nazi ideology had outlasted the Nazi defences of the Reich, he did not record it. The *Calgary Herald*'s headline that day, March 27, 1945 read, Allied tanks "Raced Unchecked Over Open Plains."

In early April, Army intelligence got more imaginative in an attempt to loosen POW Heinrich Weiler's tongue, resorting to what amounted to an investigative *ruse de guerre*. Thinking that he might have written the anonymous letters found in Neys back in February, an intelligence officer suggested that Weiler be interviewed and that the interviewer should discreetly lead the discussion to the appearance of the letters. If at that point Weiler did not say who wrote them, he "should be asked point-blank" if he had written them. If Weiler denied authorship, the interviewer should be willing to confront him with the (completely fabricated) "fact that the handwriting on the letter had been identified as his."[43] Unfortunately, Weiler didn't take the bait.

* * *

At least for a few days after Hitler's death on April 30, 1945, POW camp officials were less concerned with murder investigations than with possible attacks by self-styled HARIKARI Clubs. A conspiracy named for the Japanese word for ritual suicide had been uncovered in Camp 40 in Grand Ligne, Quebec the previous October. The HARIKARI Club amounted to a land-based version of the Kamikaze attacks then plaguing the American navy in the Pacific. Upon hearing of Hitler's death or Germany's surrender, these POWs planned to rush the guard towers, break out of their camps, and head to the nearest factories, electrical distribution centres, military or civilian airports, and ammunition dumps where they would murder as many people as they could and damage as much property as possible. The POWs knew these would be suicide missions, but they appear to have imagined themselves as enacting a climactic moment of Norse mythology. In what may be the only document produced by any nation's military intelligence to reference an opera, the director of military intelligence refers to the last opera of Richard Wagner's famous *Der Ring des Nibelungen*. Hitler was entranced by Wagner's *Götterdämmerung* (*The Twilight of the Gods*), in which the gods kill each other in an orgy of violence and Valhalla burns to the ground.[44]

The RCMP and the army were relatively sure that they had squashed the nascent HARIKARI Club. Its known leaders had been sent to the POW camp in Seebe, Alberta late in 1944. Prisoners there could see that the guard towers were being reinforced, and that flood and search lighting were being improved, as were barbed-wire entanglements. They could not see that three platoons based in nearby Camp Farnham had been tapped to augment the Veterans Guard. The six new machine gun posts facing the camp spoke eloquently enough of Canadian might.

No record survives as to how the POWs in Medicine Hat and Neys reacted to news that Grand Admiral Karl Dönitz was now chancellor of Germany. They likely knew, however, that he was not in Berlin but in the north German town of Flensburg, near the Danish border. His main goal was to keep the Third Reich alive long enough to allow as many soldiers as possible to move west where they could surrender to American, British, and Canadian armies rather than be captured by the Red Army.

The Nazi leadership in the camps could see that the war was ending but, for the present, the Gestapo remained in control of the world within the wire. Canadian authorities refused a request for a memorial concert to commemorate Hitler. Nothing could be done to stop camp leader Wendt and his men from giving the Nazi salute with more than the customary feeling, or from staring down and threatening men who gave it with less enthusiasm, or who seemed to take the führer's death with equanimity.

The HARIKARI Club attacks never materialized. For POWs in North America, as for millions of soldiers around the world, May 1, 1945, was just another day, the 2,069th of the war. Allied troops were soon in every part of Germany, and war crimes investigators began combing files in Berlin and the newly liberated concentration camps in Buchenwald, Bergen-Belsen, Dachau, and elsewhere. Back in Ottawa, Colonel Streight wrote a letter to the war office in London telling the director of prisoners of war that a scheduled prosecution of two criminals in Medicine Hat would likely proceed.

For a moment, the odds on a prosecution looked good. A POW had told RCMP Lieutenant Thornton-Prehn in confidence that he was ready to spill what he knew of the murders of Plaszek and Lehmann. Before Thornton-Prehn, the Canadian policeman whose German language skills had proved so useful, could conduct an interview in the POW's native language he was killed in a car accident. A search of his files failed to turn up any record of the identity of the confidant. Only later did it come out that the two POWs Thornton-Prehn had hoped to prosecute were the doctors Nietzsche and Nolte.

This left Canadian authorities back at square one. Their witnesses either didn't know enough or weren't talking out of loyalty to the defunct Reich. Lance Corporal F. Dietz, for example, "would not admit that he knows Wittinger as taking any part in the murder." Dietz, in fact, was quoted as saying, "if Wittinger did do so, he certainly did a good job," words befitting a man known to be "an active Nazi."[45] The suspects were also uncooperative, and the evidence against them was insufficient. Corporal Bull interviewed Johannes Wittinger once more about Plaszek's murder in May and the POW "refused to make any statements or admission."

CHAPTER 6

From the German Surrender to the Plaszek Murder Trials

May 8, 1945 to March 6, 1946

ON THE MORNING OF May 8, 1945, the commandants of every POW camp in Canada ordered their prisoners to assemble on camp parade grounds. In Camp 132, they did so with what the author of the last issue of the Veterans Guard newspaper, *P.O.W. WOW*, described as "perfect timing and the utmost of military precision."[1] Some of the prisoners may have noticed an increase in the number of armed guards patrolling the perimeters, a precaution against a HARIKARI Club attack.

In Medicine Hat's Camp 132, the men stood under a cloudy sky in 1C° temperatures, unseasonably cold even for Alberta. The camp staff car arrived. Camp commandant R.O. Bull stepped out and climbed a dais where a loudspeaker had been set up. Camp Leader Wilhelm Wendt called out "*Achtung*" and some 12,000 men stood at attention. After Wendt saluted Bull, the commandant told him to stand his men "at ease."

With military ceremony out of the way, Bull read a proclamation in English, and then had it read in German. In the moments following this report of Nazi Germany's unconditional surrender, some of the prisoners stood stunned. Others, filled with emotion that the war was over and that their families' suffering had come to an end, broke down and sobbed. Still others cried for shattered dreams of German glory.

That same day, as thousands of their neighbours crowded into Medicine Hat churches for thanksgiving services, more than a thousand people gathered in Riverside Park, about five kilometres (three miles) from the POW camp, for a ceremony led by Alberta Senator Fredrich William Greshaw. "This is indeed a great day," he told the crowd. "As long as my memory lasts, I will look back on this occasion. It is the victorious end of a great struggle, and the end of one more ruthless enemy."[2]

After the Veterans Guard pipers finished playing, men, women, and children bowed their heads as Reverend T. Harris gave an invocation. Reverend R. B. Layton read from scripture. He was followed by Reverend L. T. H. Pearson, who gave a special prayer of thanksgiving. Before the crowd lent their voices to the hymns, "O God Our Help in Ages Past" and "From Ocean to Ocean," performed by the Salvation Army band and the high school choir, Reverend Paul R. Hedeger gave a benediction.

The men held in Camp 132 could not have missed the fireworks that the crowd on Second Street, not far from Joyce Reesor's home, enjoyed. In addition to the shooting stars, rockets and bombs (the celebratory kind) that "filled the air with loud explosions and sparkling patterns," as the *Medicine Hat News* reported on May 9, at 10:30 p.m. a "huge V-E sign made by bonfires appeared on the north hill overlooking the city. The fiery sign burned for over an hour." This was the same hill on which the water tower stood with its graffiti swastika. The POWs would not have been able to see the second bonfire, which floated on the South Saskatchewan River and which caused drivers to momentarily stop their cars and watch it float down the Bow River. Reesor may have been part of the fun, and surely would have known some of the teenagers who made up the snake dance that twisted its way through the city to the accompaniment of noise makers.

* * *

Days later, when officials in Ottawa compared reports from Canadian commandants with those filed in the United States, they could not have helped but notice the different reaction south of the border. Perhaps because most U.S. prisoners had been captured at Normandy and had seen the overwhelming might of the Allied armies, these men expected that Germany would lose the war; some were even "glad and relieved," and broke into cheers. In an act impossible to imagine of Wendt in Medicine Hat, one U.S. POW leader thanked the "Allies for freeing Germany from a government which was detested by the world."[3]

When the shock abated somewhat, more legally-minded POWs, like Lieutenant Schnorrenpfeil and former public prosecutor Herbert Schwab, must have realized that they now existed in a legal grey zone. Nothing in the Geneva Convention, or its predecessor legal instruments, such as "General Order Number 100" (the rules of war written by Francis Lieber and put in place by President Abraham Lincoln toward the end of the Civil War), foresaw the extinguishing of a POW's home government. Even after the Kaiser abdicated at the end of the First World War, the German state had persisted, with Friedrich Ebert becoming chancellor. Did the total dissolution of the German government on V-E Day dissolve the legal protections the Geneva Convention afforded POWs?

It was not a question anyone had asked in Europe. As the gates of Germany's POW camps swung open all over the continent, Allied POWs were immediately free men. For days, Canadian newspapers were full of stories of Canadian POWs embracing their liberators and being showered with chocolate bars and chewing gum before boarding planes to Britain.

There was no serious consideration in Canada, Britain, or the United States of treating the German prisoners differently than they had been under Geneva because of the unique situation created by the dissolution of the Reich. Public opinion would not have stood for it. Furthermore, no western government wanted to be in violation of Geneva with Nazi war crimes trials fast approaching. Nor, of course, was there any talk of simply opening the camp gates and letting the POWs walk free into the general population. None of the host governments had a clue as to what arrangements, besides berths on ships, would have to be made for their POWs to return to Germany. The men behind the wire could see that their ordeal would not be over any time soon.

* * *

The end of the war in Europe initially had little effect on RCMP Corporal Bull's methodical investigation of the murders in Camp 132. A report dated May 16, 1945, contains some new details picked up from a hard core Nazi. As a "Black," POW Erich Schracter was among the prisoners slated to be sent to Neys at the time Lehmann was killed. He told investigators that the last time he saw Lehmann was on the morning before the murder, September 10. Schracter and other students had presented their certificates for signing by their instructors, including Lehmann. If true, as RCMP corporal Bull noted, this threw into doubt the story that Lehmann had been called at 10 p.m. to sign the education certificates for the departing men.

On June 18, investigators drew up still another list of suspects in Lehmann's murder. Four of the six names on the list belonged to the U-boatwaffe. This suggests that the RCMP was working on the assumption that Lehmann's death and the arrival in Alberta of the seven medical officers from the POW camp in Bowmanville, Ontario, were linked. The POW camp in Bowmanville held most of the U-boat men sent to Canada, and it was those transferred medics who the RCMP linked with strengthening the Gestapo in the Medicine Hat and Lethbridge camps.

A more significant break came a month later when a second anonymous letter was found at Neys. A translation was sent to the Commissioner of the RCMP, Stuart T. Wood. Some of the letter's contents were garbled, and some of its assertions would later be disproved in court. Yet, if any single piece of evidence can be said to have broken open the POW murder cases, this was it.

The author of the letter wrote that in "the three years of my captivity, I have not experienced the slightest unpleasantness from the Canadian guards. But the types of persons, whom I will [illegible] for you, have made our life a real hell during this long period."[4]

Before setting forth what amounts to a legal complaint, the writer says that certain POWs deserved to be brought to justice: "They have made the life of their fellow prisoners behind the barbed wire, really hellish. They passed arbitrary judgement[s] in such a way that one would be inclined to believe they were doing it only to satisfy their perverse feelings."[5]

With the collapse of Germany, the letter continues, "it is now impossible for me to deliver the guilty parties to a regular court. I had always intended to do this.... May the enemy now be the judge."[6]

The body of the letter pointed a finger directly at POW Staff Sergeant Walter Wolf, the man who had led the Gestapo round-up of some fifty suspected dissidents in Camp 132, and who had been sweating and acting strangely and walking in the direction of Lehmann's barracks in the moments before the murder occurred:

> To satisfy his personal ego, [Walter Wolf] started the proceedings in most such cases. In that way he made himself important. Wolf and his staff were the instigators, in the cases of Plaszek, Koerber[7] and Lehmann.
>
> Plaszek was hanged on account of Wolf's provocation and not by the angry inmates in the camp as it was made known. The inmates' feelings had been created artificially by [Wolf] and his helpers.
>
> The case of [Sergeant] Koerber, who was beat in Medicine Hat, was also a victim of Wolf's. The whole affair was provoked entirely by Wolf himself.
>
> It is only ... Wolf himself, who is responsible for the case of Lehmann. Wolf acted with or without the concurrence of the acting camp leadership.
>
> Camp leader Elstermann who was in charge at that time, gave permission in the case of Plaszek.
>
> When the leadership hesitated, Wolf forced them to take action by pressure of his followers. To retain the camp leadership preferably, [Elstermann and his Nazified supporters] gave in in every case.[8]

On the strength of the implication of Wolf in Lehmann's death and the first link found between Wolf and Plaszek's killing, the RCMP withdrew its support for Wolf's early repatriation to Germany. (He had originally been approved at the end of April for repatriation because of unspecified health reasons.) Still, as a document dated the end of August shows, the RCMP treated the anonymous letter with skepticism, partly because investigators felt that Wolf, who had slashed his wrists the year before on May 26, 1944, was still "in a low mental state" the following September and not well enough to organize Lehmann's murder.[9]

Meanwhile, more information came in that was prejudicial to Dr. Nolte. The day before Lehmann's murder, a POW named Halbeisen who had been drinking the night before woke with more than a hangover. Realizing he had been badly beaten, Halbeisen went to see Nolte, who refused to treat him and told him to come back that afternoon. When Halbeisen returned, instead of treating him, Nolte told him he was being investigated and to return at 6 p.m. At this later meeting, Nolte read him the statements of three POWs, one of whom claimed that Halbeisen criticized how punishments were meted out in the camp. Another said that Halbeisen spoke openly of placing himself under Canadian protection. Halbeisen was further accused of having jumped to Lehmann's defence when it was mentioned in camp that he was a suspected homosexual. Though the evidence was piling up against Nolte, this information does not appear to have shaken the RCMP's benign opinion of the doctor.

Investigators now focused on the man with the swagger, Private Adolf Kratz and how he might be linked to Plaszek's murder. POW Paul Kazmierzak had previously implicated Kratz in Plaszek's killing. After being transferred to Neys, where he was badly beaten, Kazmierzak was moved again (to Lethbridge) where he gave investigators more detail on Kratz's involvement. His story now also involved Staff Sergeant Werner Schwalb, who had been seen returning to his barrack; like Wittinger, he, too, was seen with bloody hands, walking away from the hall where Plaszek died.[10]

With these added details, the RCMP believed it had enough to press charges in the Plaszek case. On October 11, 1945, RCMP Corporal Bull submitted an "information and complaint" to Medicine Hat police magistrate W.H. Ellis. The document named Adolf Kratz, Werner Schwalb, and Johannes Wittinger, all of whom had been accused by other POWs of participating in the hanging, and all of whom had arrived in North America on the same ship as Plaszek and Lehmann. The complaint said that they "did unlawfully murder August Plaszek, Contrary to Section 263 of the Criminal Code of Canada."[11]

* * *

Four days after Bull filed the complaint, the front page of the Monday edition of the *Medicine Hat News* screamed out what had been an open secret for more than two years: in late July 1943, a POW had been murdered within the city's limits. (The second murder remained an open secret for a few months longer.) Kratz, Schwalb, and Wittinger were arraigned in criminal court in Medicine Hat. According to the Canadian Press, none of the three men "smiled or showed any emotion" at the proceeding.[12] Schwalb's uniform was adorned with his Iron Cross and another decoration pinned over his left breast. Wittinger, too, wore a military decoration.

For weeks, news stories had been referencing the Geneva Convention in relation to the mistreatment of Canadian, British, and American POWs in Japanese camps, as well as the war crimes trials set to begin the next month in Nuremberg. A Canadian Press article, dated October 15, was the first to tell Canadians of their government's responsibilities under the Geneva Convention: specifically, that Canada was required to notify the German government of "the charge and details of the alleged offences against the men."[13] The story did not indicate that, in the absence of a German government, this information would be supplied to the protecting power, Switzerland.

Nor did the story explain why Canada departed from the wording of the Geneva Convention—and the practice in the United States, for example—of trying POWs in military court. According to an intelligence report that references a meeting in August 1945, the decision to assign the case to the regular criminal justice system appears to have flowed from the RCMP's lead role in the investigation. Under the title, "Special Information," the extract reads, "The RCMP are working with the camp staff in an endeavour to clear up the murders at Camp 132. Some information has been obtained and turned over to the police as the matter is one for the civil [criminal] courts* and is being taken care of [by] the civil authorities."[15]

The filing of the complaint did not end the investigation into Plaszek's death. Rather, with Kratz, Schwalb, and Wittinger arrested, more POWs felt secure enough to speak to army intelligence, including POW Gunter Pabst. Much of what Pabst reported underscored other prisoners' testimony but there was some new information, including that Schwalb had long expected to be formally accused of the killing. He had put together what amounted to a jailhouse legal team that understood the workings of the Canadian legal system. To help prove his innocence, he had lined up two prisoners willing to "commit perjury to get Schwalb acquitted." He was confident that prosecutors lacked the proverbial smoking gun. "If I always deny everything," he told Pabst, "they will not be able to hang me."[16]

Pabst said that he told Schwalb others had been condemned to death despite denying everything to the last, and pointed out the probative nature of circumstantial evidence in Canadian courts. After a few moment's pause, Schwalb said, "Well, we will get there alright!"[17]

---

* This decision will become a major issue in both the subsequent trials of the men accused of killing August Plaszek and Dr. Karl Lehmann and in the appeals of the death sentences.

In the latter part of his interview, Pabst told a story illustrating how the polarities of good and evil were anything but fixed in the artificial world of a POW camp. Schwalb, a man both the RCMP and many POWs considered a brutal killer, warned Pabst that fellow POW "Nietzsche is a bad one, be careful." His objection to Dr. Maximillian Nietzsche was not that he was suspected of murdering one or more POWs in North Africa. Rather, what concerned Schwalb was the doctor's fall from Nazi rectitude. During the Battle of the Bulge, at the end of 1944, Nietzsche had referred to Hitler as "a megalomaniac" and lamented that the bomb plot had failed. If it had succeeded, he said, "the German people would have taken a new course." Pabst shrugged off the advice to avoid Nietzsche and, after a heated argument, Schwalb warned, "Watch, that you don't find yourself one morning with an ax in your head!"[18]

Pabst also told army intelligence that he had once seen Schwalb sharpening a knife and asked him what he intended to do with it. Shwalb answered that he was going to kill an army intelligence officer, Lieutenant Paul F.O. Black, who had been working with RCMP Corporal Bull on the murder cases. Pabst claimed to have answered skeptically from behind a smile, "You will kill Mr. Black as much as you will others."[19]

* * *

With three suspects in custody, the Neys camp security officer, Major W. C. Pinkham, wrote a number of short reports in late October that provide both a time line of the murders and a psychological portrait of the relevant POW camps. Pinkham identified the cause of the murders as "barbed-wire psychosis," a condition first defined in 1919 as commonly associated with "a combination of despondency, touchiness, and worst of all self-absorption and self-pity," wrote sociologist Jean Cazeneuve in his book *Essai sur la psychologie du prisonnier de guerre* in 1945.[20]

Pinkham believed that barbed-wire psychosis was manifesting differently in some Canadian camps. In Ozada, Alberta, for instance, the Afrika Corps prisoners had gathered around the stalwart Nazi, Corporal Ernst Gurbat, to fight for what they believed was the "one valid legal institutive world's ideas, namely 'national socialism.'" To expunge their defeat in North Africa, the men felt the need to perform "a patriotic deed," which began as persecution of their insufficiently committed brethren, including French Legionnaires and suspected communists. The power of the stalwarts only increased in Lethbridge and, once these men reached Medicine Hat, they "hoped... to hunt down a job which would bring them recognition in Germany."[21]

Far from lessening tensions, the settled camp life in Medicine Hat, with its plentiful food and comfortable environment, exacerbated the tensions that naturally develop among thousands of men forced to live together. Trivial incidents that would seem molehills to those in the outside world were, within the camp, exaggerated into mountains. The Gestapo stirred the pot with "[s]landers, defamations and back-bitings" in order to further its own ends. Camp leader Wilhelm Wendt, according to Pinkham, had been a target of the hardliners for his failure to crack down on "communistic conspiracies" among POWs. The committed Nazis took Wendt's subsequent illness as a victory, one that was all the more important, wrote Pinkham, because the German soldiers were otherwise "condemned to stand idly in the struggle for their homeland."[22]

The camp's internal investigations of Schulz, who narrowly escaped his attackers by fleeing, white cloth in hand, to the camp perimeter, and of Plaszek began, Pinkham said, "according to law." They were carried out under the chairmanship of a professional, the pre-war lawyer Lieutenant

Hans Schnorrenpfeil. The camp Gestapo heightened tensions by yelping, "Those traitors should be hung." Schulz's dramatic run for the wire raised the level of excitement still higher and, for some prisoners, provided a justification for "lynch justice."[23]

Once Plaszek had been killed, Pinkham continued, the Gestapo dealt with "the-morning-after the-night-before-feeling" by "instigating tales and parlances to make [the prisoners] forget this 'hangover.'" Charges of communism and secret plans to overthrow the camp leadership "create[d] a frame of mind which belatedly... justifi[ed] the crime." By this circular logic, Schulz's attempt to save his life amounted to "desertion," and proved his guilt.[24]

Equally important was what Pinkham wrote about how the Germans viewed the Canadian investigation of Plaszek's death, and how it might have emboldened Lehmann's assailants later. Had a murder similar to Plaszek's occurred in Germany, justice would have been swift. The Gestapo took, and let it be known that it took, the Canadians' slow and methodical investigation as an indication that the detaining power "silently acknowledged this crime and... regarded it as justified." Only with the arrest and jailing of Kratz, Schwalb, and Wittinger did the POWs realize "that the Canadian System of Justice works certainly differently from that in Germany but that in the end it brings the culprits to deserved justice."[25] Pinkham couldn't resist patting himself and the investigators on the back by noting that several POWs told investigators they were impressed with the thoroughness of the investigation.

Pinkham believed that Wolf was responsible for Lehmann's death. Wolf and the men around him thought they were undermining the communist faction in the camp by committing the murder. They intended Lehmann's death to have two additional effects. Given that the hardcore Nazis were being moved to Neys, Ontario, it would serve as an example left behind in Alberta for the Camp 132 POWs of the Gestapo's power. Secondly, it would intimidate the recently-arrived POWs captured in Normandy, who as younger men were thought to be less convinced of the virtues of National Socialism. Wolf and the Gestapo wanted them to have "a concrete example" of what failure to be a good German could cost them.[26]

Like Corporal Bull, Pinkham saw Dr. Maximillian Nolte as a friendly presence in the camp. He does not mention that Nolte was suspected of murdering POWs in Africa while he, too, was a prisoner of the British. He describes the doctor as a "good co-operative spirit toward British authorities," and someone who worked "hard to maintain order and discipline" in Medicine Hat. It was true that Gurbat, Wolf, and others had tried to impose "Nazi ideologies" on Nolte, and that under these influences the doctor had "lost all conception of 'right' and 'wrong' of things—and in his irresolute attitude submitted himself to all and sundry innuendo."[27] But Pinkham still felt obliged to defend Nolte as simply lacking the mental and intellectual resolution to stand up to the Gestapo.

* * *

Beginning in November 1945, military tribunals struck by the Allies in Nuremberg, Germany, prosecuted prominent Nazi leaders for war crimes. Newspaper articles on the proceedings provided North Americans with a crash course in international law, the laws of war, the Geneva Convention, arguments about "victor's justice" (which were quickly dismissed by the recently-formed International Court of Justice) and the inner workings of Nazi Germany, including the still newly-named "Holocaust." On November 24, the *Winnipeg Tribune* shocked its readers with a front-page story relating that Hitler had told generals preparing for the invasion of Poland "to kill without mercy all the men, women and children of the Polish race or language," and that the rotund Hermann Göring, his highest ranking military official and minister responsible for the Gestapo, climbed on a table "and danced like a savage" in response.

On the same day, Lance Corporal Otto Krueger made a voluntary statement to Canadian investigators that would have made the military men standing trial at Nuremberg red with rage. Not only was Krueger a former French Legionnaire but before joining the Legion, he had helped organized the German Communist Party. Drafted into the Wehrmacht in early May 1941, he was captured in North Africa in July 1942. The picture he painted of how Dr. Nolte's circle lived "as parasites," depriving ideologically-suspect sick and injured POWs of the care and rest they needed, was a faint but distinct echo of the outrages perpetrated by those on trial in Nuremberg.[28]

After hearing this statement, RCMP Lieutenant Paul Black, conducting the interview, assumed Krueger was finished but, after a few moments, he continued and spoke of another prisoner, his friend Sergeant Heinz Wilhelm. The enigmatic story started off with Krueger saying that Wilhelm often came to visit him and that one day he "tickled me and patted me on the shoulder, a behaviour which formerly he had not shown," and which Krueger considered odd, especially in the presence of his roommates. Krueger asked Wilhelm "if he was homosexually inclined," and the blood drained from Wilhelm's face, although they soon sat down to play their usual game of chess. Krueger knew that homosexuality was illegal in both his and the Canadian army. Accordingly, he was walking a thin line when he told Black that Wilhelm had once remarked, "if one is to do a thing one should do it completely." Krueger was perplexed enough to ask Wilhelm the next day what he meant. Wilhelm did not want to discuss it, and Krueger had "never been able to fathom it."[29] Lieutenant Black's record leaves the impression that Krueger believed Wilhelm regretted not following through on his feelings for his friend and/or that Krueger had the same regrets.

Krueger went on to tell the RCMP officer that he was walking one night with Wilhelm, a week before Lehmann's murder, when his friend revealed foreknowledge of violence: "They are on the track of the ringleader," he said. Later, on the night before the two of them were sent to Neys, Wilhelm updated his friend, "They have the ringleader." Krueger, shielding his personal views, responded: "That's good. Then this matter will be cleared up the same as that of the deserters," a reference to the killing of Plaszek and the chase of Schulz.[30]

The same day Lieutenant Black interviewed Krueger, Pinkham sat down with Waffen SS Corporal Georg Herdel, whose view of the psychology leading to Plaszek's and Lehmann's killings matched those of his interviewer. More importantly, his views were based on what Wolf, still a chief suspect in Lehmann's death, had told Herdel. "To my opinion, the Plaszek murder was done by an incited crowd whereas the Lehmann murder was a secret affair deliberately premeditated and executed by a few," said Herdel.[31]

His pre-Waffen SS career is unknown, but Herdel was a careful listener. He noted that when describing how Lehmann had been beaten and killed, Wolf "always talked in the plural," using "*Wir*," (we). This left Herdel with the impression "that he certainly was connected with this affair," at minimum as an eye-witness. Herdel told Wolf that he and his accomplices had done something that "they couldn't get away with, not even in Germany." Wolf answered that their actions would be received differently at home because Communism "could not be brought in harmony with the honour of the Wehrmacht."[32]

In subsequent conversations, including one just five days before Herdel sat down with Pinkham, Wolf appeared to change his story, perhaps fearing, now that suspects in Plaszek's killing were headed for trial, that investigators were closing in on him. Wolf said he had not been directly involved in either of the Medicine Hat killings. There was still a suggestion that he knew something about what had transpired, or was somehow implicated: if called to give evidence, he added "he would not squeal on anybody." He also wanted Herdel to know that he was a tough guy, stating that he "could break the leg of a few if he so desired." Herdel ignored Wolf's chest thumping and told him, "he and he alone know how deep he is in these affairs."[33]

Two days later, Herdel met Wolf, who had seemed to be avoiding him, in the washroom. Wolf asked if fellow POW Krueger had been to see him, adding that Krueger had "softened up," meaning that he might squeal to the Canadians. Herdel played dumb, knowing that Krueger had already given evidence.

Herdel's read of Wolf's psychology, as related to Pinkham, was that he "feels guilty." The reasons for Herdel's assessment were four:

1) "Because no matter when and where we meet, he always brought up the talk to the murder affairs."

2) "Because he in his former talks appeared to be too well acquainted with these cases and details."

3) "Because he at present—after the Plaszek murder case started—tries to convince us of his innocence."

4) "Because he keeps away from me and he can hardly pass the time of day when I meet him, whereas [formerly] he visited me almost daily."[34]

For a man who expected to be charged with murder, Wolf was surprisingly loquacious, as Lieutenant Black heard that same day from another prisoner,

Private Helmut Porcher. When a group of POWs including Porcher stopped at Camp 132 for a meal on its way from Lethbridge to Neys, Wolf saw him and called out to his friend, "*Dicke Dinge sind passiert; Ich werde es Euch spaeter erzahlen!*" (Big things have happened; I will tell you about it later). When Wolf next saw Porcher, he told him about the decision to hang Lehmann, and included dramatic details from his last moments. Lehmann had been sitting at a desk, having just "unscrewed the cap of his fountain pen," as he'd done thousands of times in German classrooms, when he suddenly looked up and saw someone inside locking the hut door. It is unknown whether Lehmann responded to being locked in to the room.[35]

Porcher predicted to Wolf that "the Lehmann case will follow the Plaszek case," meaning that arrests were forthcoming. The braggadocio of Wolf's reply is less interesting than the mistake he makes about the Canadian criminal justice system's distinction between intent and act.[36] "They can give me only two or three years for my political actions," he said "otherwise I have no fear."[37]

A few days later, POW Otto Work gave RCMP Corporal Miller an earful about problems with the protective custody system. It relied upon a POW asking for protection, which only occurs when the man is already *in extremis*. Even then, the system "works much too slowly" to afford a person genuine security. A prisoner who asks for protective custody is "subjected to unnecessary publicity" which brands him "a traitor for life, with possible repercussions haunting one's existence for a lifetime." He is taken to safety but within the camp, forfeiting access to sports, moving pictures, and other activities. He also suffers the daily humiliation of knowing that he is ostracized by fellow prisoners who can be seen over the wire.[38]

Unless the POW is moved to a farm or some other facility, protective custody amounts to "another term for solitary confinement." Work advised the RCMP's Miller that if POWs were assured that they would be rapidly removed from camp after asking for protection, "in a manner simulating a normal transfer," and sent to camps where there was no Gestapo, more men would come forward to help Canadian authorities investigate the Plaszek and Lehmann killings.[39]

Around this time, Lieutenant Black received some useful information from another POW, Lance Corporal Hermann Schweizer, that must have made the Canadian officer think back to the concerns about the HARIKARI Clubs. Schweizer said that under the noses of camp commandant Bull, army intelligence officers, and the RCMP, the Gestapo—Schweizer called it the "security service"—had been manufacturing hand grenades (with the aid of matchheads) in a secret workshop in the boiler room of Hut D-4.[40] Presumably, the hut was quickly searched.

* * *

In some ways, December 1945 was more difficult than previous holiday seasons for the almost 36,000 POWs in Canada. The pain of being separated from their families was made more profound by the magnitude of destruction in their homeland, about which they would now know from both newspapers and letters from their families, and the fact that Russia, assumed (correctly, as it turned out) to be eager to revenge atrocities committed by the Germans, occupied half of their country. Film from Auschwitz, Birkenau, Bergen-Belsen, Buchenwald, and other concentration camps caused some Nazis in Allied POW camps to turn their backs on the cause, while others, die-hard past the end, sat stoically. A Luftwaffe officer named Brietenbach, who had been captured on D-Day while manning a radio-directional finding station near Cannes and imprisoned in Canada, initially doubted the veracity of the films "but eventually he did come to believe [them] and was heartsick," wrote David J. Carter, in his book about POW's in Canada.[41]

At Nuremberg, leading Nazis such as Joachim von Ribbentrop,[42] Hans Frank, Alfred Rosenberg, Albert Speer, and Göring had been convicted at trials that revealed to a horrified world the inner workings of the death camps.

The trial of SS Brigadeführer Kurt Meyer began on December 10 and, perhaps even more than the Nuremberg proceedings against top Nazi leadership, his must have hit home with the POWs. It was the first war crimes trial run by Canadians and, more importantly, it involved men like themselves who, having lifted their hands in surrender, expected to live.

Forty-eight Canadians who had been captured a few hours after they stormed ashore at Juno Beach had been massacred by Meyer's 12 SS Hitlerjugend Panzer Division. Among the six war crimes charges against Meyer was the following:

> COMMITTING A WAR CRIME in that he at his Headquarters at L'Ancienne Abbaye, Ardenne in the Province of Normandy and Republic of France on or about the 8th day of June, 1944, when Commander of 25 S.S. Panzer Grenadier Regiment, in violation of the laws and usages of war gave orders to troops under his command to kill seven Canadian prisoners of war, and as a result of such orders the said prisoners of war were thereupon shot and killed.[43]

On the first day of this trial in Aurich, a small north German town not far from the Dutch border, Alfred Helzel, who had been a POW in Hull, Quebec, told the court of Meyer's order "that prisoners will not be taken." Canadian prosecutor Lieutenant-Colonel Bruce MacDonald asked Helzel: "Did you understand by that order that you were not to take any prisoners?"[44] The answer was "yes."

Three days later, as the *Calgary Herald* reported that "lamp shades made from human skin" and shrunken heads had been submitted as evidence in Nuremberg, Canadians read also that evidence was given at Meyer's trial that prisoners were shot to save rations.[45] Meyer took the stand in his own defence and while admitting that prisoners were shot in his headquarters, denied he had given the order. On December 28, a board of Canadian officers found Meyer guilty on three of the five charges and sentenced him to be shot.[46]

December also brought POWs in Canada something they had not experienced since going behind barbed-wire: hunger. Days after Britain announced that food rationing would continue for another five years, the British government exercised its authority as the (legal) detaining power and instructed Ottawa to ignore the Geneva regulations that stipulated POWs were to be fed the same rations as nearby garrisoned troops. POW rations were cut to the level of German civilians, which was not high, given a food crisis in Germany brought on by economic collapse and a shattered transportation system. Since most of the POWs were younger, taller, and more physically fit than the average German civilian, the lowered calories per day was a hardship. While they carried out the order, the Veterans Guardsmen at Canadian camps resented it almost as much as the POWs. Both sides knew that Canada suffered no food shortages. Indeed, items were being stricken from Canada's list of rationed food almost weekly as Christmas approached.

* * *

Difficult as the holidays were, the new year brought hope of relief. The men who were formed into the first draft of POWs were told they were just weeks away from boarding a train to Halifax. From there, the men would sail to Britain, the first stop on their journey home, nine months after the war had ended.

The prospect of the POWs leaving Canada put pressure on RCMP investigators to make progress on the Lehmann killing. Constable George Krause, no longer under the alias Sapper King, was returned to the Medicine Hat POW camp where he revealed to the prisoners his German language skills. He interviewed a number of men in late January and early February, 1946.

The first prisoner on Krause's list was Flight Sergeant Willi Müeller, who had been shot down over Glasgow in May 1941. The RCMP hoped to pump Müeller for information about Walter Wolf and another POW allied with the Nazi leadership, Flight Sergeant Bruno Perzenowski. The investigators did not believe Müeller's claim that he did not know Perzenowski. Perzenowski and Müeller had lived in the same hut in both Medicine Hat and Neys. Nor did the RCMP believe Müeller when he denied having heard any details about Lehmann's death. POW Gunter Pabst, who had been helpful to investigators of the Plaszek murder, had dropped Müeller's name in connection with Lehmann.

Krause must have asked him outright if he'd been involved in the killing because he recorded Müeller's response: "I deny that I took part or was even present to the plan, committed the murder." The prisoner, who was also the camp boxing instructor, claimed to have spent his final night in Medicine Hat packing for the journey to Neys, and drinking beer at one of the farewell parties winked at by guards in Camp 132.[47]

A superior RCMP officer who had access to other Müeller interviews (now lost), was unconvinced by the prisoner's testimony and wrote at the bottom of Constable Krause's report:

> There appears to be indication that Müeller's self-assurance is decreasing, and I believe that if he were confronted with Wolf,

he might break down and provide the corroboration necessary to Wolf's statement. For this reason, I could request that arrangements be made to transfer Müeller from Lethbridge to Medicine Hat where further interrogation will be continued.[48]

By February 2, Constable Krause had concluded four more interviews. Three of these added significantly to the burgeoning file on Walter Wolf. Krause learned that Wolf spoke English and that before being drafted into the Afrika Corps, he had fought in France and had been awarded an Iron Cross Second Class. POW Private Bruno Krohl, a pre-war singer, told Krause he had been ordered out of his rehearsals in the education hut on the night Lehmann was later killed there. He reported that Wolf came into the room—the first time in the extant record that anyone placed Wolf close to the scene of the crime—and "was excited and sweating."[49] This is consistent with the testimony of POW Robert Schufart, who a year earlier said that Wolf had appeared strange and sweaty when he unexpectedly stopped Schufart to say goodbye and took off in the direction of Lehmann's barracks.

Schufart was interviewed again by Constable Krause and this time mentioned something he had neglected earlier. He had asked Wolf what was going on during their brief discussion. Wolf replied with "words to the effect that some communists had been caught." Both Krohl and Schufart reported that Wolf had been carrying "an iron ball."[50]

Camp leader Wilhelm Wendt had little new to say to Constable Krause. Rather, he came close to blaming the victim in Lehmann's death. After disingenuously stating that he may or may not have received a report about communists planning to overthrow the camp leadership, he admitted to assigning someone to investigate Lehmann, who was suspected of reading English newspapers to men in his hut. Wendt claimed

Lehmann had been fined and told not to repeat his behaviour. No other POW in the record told investigators about either the warning or the fine.

Wendt also told Krause that he had heard a rumour that Lehmann was the leader of the camp's communists, "but it was not investigated because there were never any grounds or proof for such complaints." No doubt guessing that the Canadians knew that several score men had been rounded up on charges of communism a few days before Lehmann's killing, Wendt added that he issued an order the day after that "inquiry" that said nothing had been proven against the arrested men, that some were "possibly partly to blame through foolish comments," but none were to be molested in the future and all was in order again. Questions of translation aside, the order must have struck investigators as an equivocation: "possibly partly to blame" is rather different than "nothing was proven" against these men and, of course, very different from "innocent."[51] And the notion that everything was "in order again" was far-fetched for a camp roiled by the impending move to Neys and the murder of one of its ranks.

Wendt's testimony left Krause shaking his head. From "the knowledge which we have of the conditions then existing in the camp, it is most improbable that subordinates would take upon themselves the responsibility of the killing of Lehmann without the implied consent of the camp leadership." Wendt, he observed, "is a very smooth person and although the investigation to date has not implicated him in the plot, it is possible that he did have prior knowledge."[52]

* * *

POWs boarding the three special trains out of Medicine Hat on the night of February 10, 1946, saw their last heavy Canadian snowstorm. In the days prior, they had packed the kit bags supplied for them by the Canadian government, each costing $1.28, the *Calgary Herald* told its readers. Each man was allowed fifty pounds of kit, with another fifteen pounds eligible to be shipped to Germany through the Red Cross. What they couldn't pack or ship, including musical instruments, sports equipment and, no doubt, some of the ship models they had spent endless hours building, were sold at fire-sale prices.

The thousands of men, divided into groups of fifty, one of whom understood English and, thus, could transmit orders to the rest, were lined up on the railroad siding near Camp 132. They would have found the large white tags hanging from their chests only slightly less demeaning than the red targets on the back of their warm winter coats. The tags bore each man's name, POW number, and a number assigned to him for the journey to Halifax. To ensure that the fifty men in each car had been assigned to it, the white tag had to be matched with a red tag before boarding. To handle any discrepancies, Canadian officials had on hand each POW's dental records, although it is not recorded if any guard needed to turn on his flashlight and peer into a POW's mouth.

Once the men were on board, some of the guards who had been standing at the perimeter also climbed on the train. Despite the war being over (or, perhaps, because it was over and the Canadians still feared HARIKARI Club attacks), these guards were better armed than the rifle-bearing soldiers who had brought the POWs west years earlier. Now, the guards carried Sten submachine guns and, more savvy about escapes, they took up positions on the right-of-way on each side of the train as it approached a siding. After dark, still other guards, using trigger-equipped searchlights, swept the sides of the coaches looking for unusual movement.[53]

While most of prisoners held in Canada were seasoned soldiers, and many of them might have been, at the very least, complicit in war crimes, the fact remains that they showed strong emotions on leaving Medicine

Hat. "They may have been tough fighting men but they are sentimental as hell," one senior Canadian officer said.[54] They were sentimental for their homeland and the families they hoped to see soon, but also for the place that had been their home for several years. Many packed diaries they had kept in camp. Some memorialized their time behind Canadian barbed wire in scrapbooks filled with pictures of Hollywood starlets. One prisoner used his fifteen-pound package to send back an entire collection of the famed Varga Girl pinups from *Esquire* magazine. A surprising number of others used precious packing space to bring home copies of *Webster's English Dictionary* and several might be seen as suggesting their political leanings by stowing *The Life and Writings of Abraham Lincoln*. To while away the long hours on the train and aboard ship, some read a then-popular book less complimentary to Lincoln, *Gone with the Wind*.

The train cars easily accommodated their fifty men, three abreast, though the berth formed by folding down the seats was a tight squeeze for each group of three. Lest Canadians worry that the POWs were being treated too well, officials told the press that their first dinner consisted of hamburger, potatoes, carrots, bread pudding, and coffee, while the guards had a chicken dinner. In Halifax, the trains stopped at Pier 21, the same pier that beginning in 1928 welcomed thousands of immigrants to Canada, and from which Canadian troops sailed to war. The pier was surrounded by barbed wire. Searchlights turned night into day as the POWs walked up the gangway to one of the world's great ocean liners, Cunard's *RMS Mauretania*, still doing war work.

It took just under two weeks to get the prisoners to the United Kingdom, by which time W.R. Howson, chief justice of the Supreme Court of Alberta, had impanelled a jury in *Rex vs. Werner Schwalb*. The first of three defendants charged with the murder of Private August Plaszek was about to go on trial.

CHAPTER 7

Rex v. Werner Schwalb

February 25 to March 5, 1946

THE INITIAL STATEMENT FROM the bench in Canada's first-ever murder trial of prisoners of war was not to the accused, nor to the defence attorney or the Crown prosecutor. Rather, Alberta Chief Justice William R. Howson reprimanded a potential juror who arrived late. A second juror also failed to arrive on time, although the judge was more understanding in his case. The man was delayed because of a nosebleed.

The three POWs charged with Private August Plaszek's death were slated to be tried together. No sooner had the charge sheet been read, in English and in German, however, than Louis S. Turcotte, selected by then Canadian justice minister Louis St. Laurent to act for the defendants, and paid for by the federal government, moved to sever the trials. Hearing the case, Justice Howson took one look at the pile of books Turcotte brought to support his petition, told the accused to sit down, sent the jury out of the courtroom, and settled in for a long morning.[1]

Turcotte, born in Quebec, had been eight years old when his family moved to Lethbridge in 1912. He had graduated from high school at age fifteen, from the University of Alberta at seventeen, and from law school at twenty. He liked to joke that he had been chosen as defence counsel for this trial simply because he was one of the few breathing Liberals in Alberta, and Louis St. Laurent was a Liberal. But partisan allegiances aside, Turcotte was a talented and well-respected lawyer. He also represented Japanese internees forcibly removed to Alberta from their homes on the Pacific coast in 1942. He later served as mayor of Lethbridge, the first chancellor of the University of Lethbridge, and an unsuccessful candidate for the federal Liberals.[2]

Turcotte urged Justice Howson to sever the trials because it would be "absolutely impossible" for members of a jury to keep in their minds what evidence was against each defendant individually in the course of a long trial. In addition to a number of witnesses who would testify against all three of the accused, five witnesses were scheduled to give evidence against Werner Schwalb, seven against Adolf Kratz, and four against Johannes Wittinger, respectively. Turcotte told Justice Howson that in all the testimony only one witness in "any way implicated two of the accused and none of them implicated the three." Were the jury to conclude that one man was guilty, he feared it might say, "Oh, heck, the whole works is guilty, let it go at that." To support the application to sever, Turcotte cited precedents from Britain, British Columbia, Alberta, and the Canadian Supreme Court (this last ruling from 1921) stating that the crown "would not be embarrassed or prejudiced by the accused being tried separately."[3]

The Plaszek case was sufficiently important for the deputy attorney general of Alberta, H. J. Wilson, KC, to assign himself as lead prosecutor. A native Albertan and a veteran of the Great War, reputed for a keen legal mind and being quick on his feet, Wilson disagreed strenuously with Turcotte's motion. Justice Howson did not have to sever the trials at all, he said, and certainly not at this juncture. The accused were charged with a joint offence, and, as such, "should be jointly tried even though there may be some prejudice against the accused."[4]

Wilson's argument was rooted in the riotous circumstances of Plaszek's death. The defendants were not charged for rioting *per se*, which, then as now, could see individual rioters tried jointly. Nevertheless, Wilson intended to proceed as if the charges were under the Riot Act. The crown's "whole case against these men is being part and parcel of a riotous mob, and that their actions were those of jointly participating in murder." The Crown, accordingly, was not "say[ing] that any one of these men committed murder;" rather, it was saying "they are joint participants and thereby under the provisions of the Code they are guilty of murder."[5] As for Turcotte's concern that a suspicion toward one defendant would carry over to the others, Wilson told the judge it would be simple for him to instruct the jury not to apply evidence from one man to another. No appeal had ever been successful on the grounds that the trial judge had not severed cases, Wilson added, before citing his own list of precedents from various jurisdictions.

The court broke for lunch, leaving Justice Howson with a decision to make. A former banker, bill collector, real estate agent, lawyer, and leader of the Alberta Liberal party, Howson would turn sixty-three in the course of the trial. As with Turcotte, connections to the federal Liberal party had been important to his career: justice minister Ernest Lapointe had appointed him to sit on the Alberta Supreme Court Trial Division in 1936, from which he advanced to the appellate division and in 1944 to chief justice of the trial division. When the court reconvened after lunch, he severed the trials, using the phrase "fair trial" almost as a mantra, as he would in days following.

Wilson elected to try Schwalb first, and a jury of six men was duly impanelled. Another six men would hear *Rex. v. Adolf Kratz* later in March. Johannes Wittinger's trial would follow but come to an abrupt halt after just three days when it became known one of the jurors was not yet twenty-six, the age of eligibility to participate in the proceedings. Wittinger's new trial would take place in June.

Perhaps in an effort to counter the argument that these trials were another example of victor's justice, a criticism dogging Nuremberg and other war crimes tribunals, the crown was magnanimous in its opening statement. Schwalb was introduced to the jury as a pre-war baker and cook who had been born in June 1915 in a part of the Rhineland that was occupied by France after the First World War. Wilson told the jury that despite the fact that Schwalb was a prisoner of war and, as such, an enemy, he was "entitled to the same safeguards of British justice as any other citizen of our country."[6]

The prosecutor next began laying the foundation of his case by calling three technical witnesses. Two were engineers who vouched for the scale models of Camp 132 that would be used to trace the movements of POWs on the day of the crime. Another was the police photographer who swore to the veracity of the pictures available to both the crown and the defence. These witnesses were followed to the stand by RCMP Corporal Bull, who attested to what he had seen in the camp's west recreation hall, including a long trail of blood, a frayed rope, and the large overhead beams from which Plaszek had been hanged.

Corporal Bull told the court that after surveying the crime scene, he had proceeded to the funeral home, where he met RCMP Lieutenant Thornton-Prehn, who had information on the corpse. This led to clinical descriptions of the rope wound twice around Plaszek's neck, his tongue protruding, his contusion-marked face and blood-matted hair. Bull calmly painted a picture of a painful and harrowing death, the pathos of which, Wilson hoped, would be strong enough to overcome any notion that Plaszek was just "one more dead Heine," as RCMP Constable George Krause had written in his report after spending time in the enclosure in 1943. Wilson's point was that no matter how Plaszek died, he did not deserve his fate. Turcotte did not have much in the way of cross-examination. He pushed Bull on his details, including which door he had used to enter the recreation hall. It was small beer compared to descriptions of a man who had died "with foamy matter exuding from the mouth."[7]

Most of the people in the court room would have seen POWs in uniform on supervised walks through town, and by now they would have been accustomed to seeing Schwalb at the defendant's table in his infantryman's uniform.[8] Still, watching Regimental Sergeant Major Richard Elstermann walk to the front of the courtroom, swear on the Bible and sit in the witness box in the impressive uniform of an NCO in Hitler's Wehrmacht must have caused more than one person in the courtroom to take a deeper breath.

Acting camp leader Elstermann's testimony that day confirmed what some newspapers had already reported: in the distant reaches of Canada, German POWs had set themselves up as so many Heinrich Himmlers, arrogating to themselves as camp leaders the powers to police, investigate, and interrogate their fellow prisoners for perceived offences against the Nazi leadership. Elstermann took the court through the workings of the court of honour, his decision that Private Christian Schulz had contradicted himself and would be held under arrest, and Schulz's run to the wire. He recounted how he had been called out of his hearings when Lieutenant William A. Dawe's party was detained by the POW crowd around his office, and how he walked the Canadians to safety, returning to find Plaszek's body in the west recreation hall. Elstermann initially described the crowd of prisoners, numbering hundreds of men, as "a little excited." Pushed by Wilson, he called it a "mob devoid of discipline."[9]

None of the reporters covering the trials discussed what surely struck the people in the courtroom as strange and new: German officers claiming the authority to hold courts of honour under German military law within the city limits of Medicine Hat.

As he sat in the witness box on the second day of the trial, the former state legal advisor First Lieutenant Hans Schnorrenpfeil must have felt that the Canadian criminal justice system was woefully inefficient. He told how Elstermann had deputized him to do a preliminary investigation into whether several men were seeking to overthrow the camp leadership, something he'd already explained to a preliminary inquiry a few weeks earlier. Again, he went over how the POW court of honour operated on July 21, 1943, including the production of a transcript, and the fact that several men sat behind a wooden divider listening to ensure that proper military procedures were followed. He reviewed the interrogation of Schulz, and his order to detain Schulz. Since he had been interrogating Burkhardt during Schulz's run from the mob, Schnorrenpfeil was not asked about it. He was, however, asked about the warning shot. "I never troubled myself when I heard a shot," he replied with Olympian disdain. He had continued his questioning of Burkhardt until he heard the cry, "That's a traitor," and the crowd had stormed into his room. Mistaken for Burkhardt, Schnorrenpfeil was punched in the jaw before Dr. Nolte arrived to prevent further violence.[10]

Even through the translation of Schnorrenpfeil's answers, it is apparent that Turcotte's cross-examination, which began after lunch, offended the proud German lawyer's *amour propre*. The defence attorney zeroed in on Schnorrenpfeil's statement that two POWs were listening to the interrogations from behind a divider. Had Schnorrenpfeil actually seen them in the hut? "I take it that I did see them," he said, adding later, "I take it as the natural course of things since it had been decided the evening before." These answers did not satisfy Turcotte: "But you never saw them at all during the day," his rising tone turning the declarative statement into a question. "Nien," said Schnorrenpfeil.[11]

Turcotte's options were limited in defence of his clients. He lacked character witnesses or others who might bring testimony that mitigated the circumstances of the crime or his clients' actions. Nor did he think it wise to put each defendant on the stand. Accordingly, in this and each subsequent trial, he concentrated on challenging the crown's witnesses and trying to shake their credibility. Schnorrenpfeil described hearing the disturbance caused by the crowd looking for the traitor, Burkhardt. Turcotte seized on Elstermann's previous use of the phrase "a mob devoid of discipline" to describe the scene, and with a relentless, almost mocking cross-examination, forced the witness to backtrack and admit that, indeed, he had heard the riotous mob outside his door. Turcotte hoped this about-face might give at least one member of the jury pause.

* * *

The next three witnesses were Sergeant Major Wilhelm Weidemann, Sergeant Major Ludwig Kammermeier, and Private Schulz. Neither the transcript nor the newspaper accounts record the shock of the men and women in the courtroom when Weidemann refused to kiss the Bible after swearing "To tell the truth, the whole truth and nothing but the truth. So, help you God."[12] We know of it only because it is part of the transcript of a subsequent trial. We do not know Weidemann's reason, although, given his fidelity to the Nazi cause, it is reasonable to assume that his objections were ideological. Hardcore Nazis rejected the authority of the Bible in favour of Hitler's *Mein Kampf*. Until after the end of the war, Nazi leadership in the POW camps actively discouraged Catholic and Protestant observances and veneration of the Bible. At all events, Justice Howson was satisfied with Weidemann's raising his right hand and repeating the oath.

Both Weidemann and Kammermeier testified that they were supposed to ensure that their collecting of men for Schnorrenpfeil to interrogate remained secret. Weidemann traced Schulz's run, describing how he "turned around like lightening" as he exited the hut."[13] He had tried to cut off Schulz, but once the former Legionnaire crossed the wire, Weidemann decided to give up the chase and hold the crowd back (no witness substantiated this latter claim). While other witnesses would give different estimates for the size of the crowd following Schulz, Weidemann said it approached 2,000.

Turcotte's questioning of Weidemann managed to produce more confusion on the partitions shielding the several listeners from view, and which doors to the hut (which was the same size as the men's barracks and subdivided into a number of rooms) were opened and which were closed. The jury heard for the first time how the mob had got its hands on Plaszek. Weidemann had taken him to another room in the hut to await questioning. He was discovered there and grabbed by a small group of men, one of whom struck him in the head, before he was thrown outside into the arms of a crowd baying for blood.

Kammermeier, too, described how he had rounded up first Schulz and then Plaszek for their interrogations. Under cross-examination, he told Turcotte that he had left the two men and gone to the mess hall, 150 metres away, when Plaszek was thrown to the mob. Kammermeier said he had not noticed anything out of the ordinary at the time this happened, claiming that 600 men clamouring to finish their meals in the allotted fifteen minutes produced noise that would have drowned out the mob that had grabbed Plaszek. Turcotte managed to get Kammermeier to admit that he was not certain if he ate at the first or second seating that day because seating schedules "changed every week."[14]

Private Schulz told of his fear of being held in custody, his run, and the terrifying moments when he was being stoned by his fellow prisoners after having crossed the wire. Attempting to explain the ferociousness of the mob, he spoke of "one small black man who stood there in front of the crowd, and he behaved as a beast."[15] He was speaking metaphorically, perhaps assuming some level of racism in the court or among the jury. While Schulz would have served with African soldiers while in the French Foreign Legion, Nazi racial theories classified Africans, as they did Jews and Slavic peoples, as *Untermenschen* (inferior people), and they were not part of the Wehrmacht.

The former commandant of Camp 132, R. O. Bull, now retired, told Schwalb's trial what he had seen in the enclosure and at the crime scene, but his major contribution was to explain his standing order of April 1, 1943, which outlined the duties of the German camp leader of POWs. "The Camp Leader, under the Commandant," it read, "is in Command of all P.O.W. interned in the camp." All fourteen articles of the standing order, which made the camp leader responsible for translating and transmitting orders, keeping the camp clean, and appointing various deputies in the camp, were read into the record. One of these, restating Article X of the Geneva Convention, made clear that the POWs remained under German military law.[16]

Bull told the court that he had no knowledge of the camp leader holding a court of honour, and his belief that the camp leader had no authority to do so. But Bull may have been aware that something resembling a Gestapo was either operating in camp, or had the potential to do so.

The last article of his standing order suggests as much: "Prisoners are forbidden to take any collective physical action against any other P.O.W. Bullying is despicable, and will not be tolerated. Disciplinary action against any P.O.W. lies in the hands of the Commandant or through him, in the hands of the camp leader."[17]

* * *

The next seven witnesses in Schwalb's trial were Veterans Guardsmen who, together, corroborated Schulz's testimony, adding a few details.

Guardsman Reginald H. Back told the jury that he had been in Tower No. 7 and had fired a warning shot with a .303 rifle. Had the crowd (he estimated it at 1,000 men) rushed the wire, he had another 999 rounds, as well as a Sten gun with a 200-round clip. The same armaments were available to the guards in each tower. Turcotte took aim at Back's contention that "there were four men dragging [Plaszek], two on either side."[18] He asked the guard for the distance between his tower and the main door of the west recreation hall, and then doubted that Back had been able to see clearly from what he estimated to be five hundred feet. Gilbert Hummel testified that he had given his boots to Schulz so he could climb the barbed wire fence and escape to the detention yard without stepping from the perimeter back into camp where the mob would have had something approaching a legal right to seize him. It was left unsaid that the men in the guard towers likely would have opened fire on the crowd to defend Schulz who had already been granted Canadian protection.

No doubt primed by this challenge to Back, Turcotte later seized upon a statement by Guardsman Frederick C. Byers that from Tower No. 8 he had seen "about eighteen men dragging [and kicking] something" toward the west recreation hall. "Now, you say there were about eighteen men. Did you count them by any chance?" The guard retreated: "No, I just made an approximate guess at them." A few questions later, the bench intervened when Byers said that after the door to the recreation hall had closed, with Plaszek inside, one man came out and told the mob to disperse, and they did. "Just a second," Justice Howson said. "Was this order to disperse given in English?" Byers said it wasn't. "Well do you speak German?" asked the judge. Byers again retreated: "A man just came out and waved his hand and shouted something and they all dispersed."[19]

Byers said that sometime later a group of men had gathered at the recreation hall and seemed to be "going in and out" and "viewing something." Again, Justice Howson did not wait for Turcotte to object. Byers had already told the court he had not been in the hall, and, therefore, could not say that the men "seemed to be viewing something." The most Howson would allow was the statement, "they were coming in and going out," which didn't add much to the court's understanding.[20]

Canadian Guardsman Knut Nielsen's testimony was especially helpful to the crown's strategy of connecting the murder to a riotous environment. In response to a question from Wilson about his presence in the camp's scout centre, Nielson responded, "I stayed there until the riot started." When Turcotte didn't object to use of the term, Wilson picked it up and asked what Nielson did "after the riot started." Several questions later, seeking to get on record a legal definition of a riot, Wilson asked, "And you spoke of a riot. What do you mean by a riot?"[21] The witness obligingly described a scene with a thousand prisoners of war milling about the main gate of the camp.

Guardsman Nielsen also told of following acting camp leader Elstermann into the west recreation hall, which was filled with prisoners. About ten or twelve feet into the hall, he saw a pool of blood on the cement floor. Four or five feet further, he saw a large blood stain. Pointing to a support stud on the model before him, Nielsen said, "the feet was right up against this stud here and the body lying up against the cement wall." Wilson inquired as to the condition of the body. "It had a rope around its neck, sir. It was pulled very tight around its neck and there was about six inches of loose rope."[22] The rope was so tight around Plaszek's neck that Neilson had been unable to get his finger between rope and skin. There was so much blood on the floor and on the body that Nielsen turned the body expecting to see a stab wound. There was none. The blood had come from an inch-long cut on the back of the victim's head.

* * *

There was more gory testimony from the witness who followed Neilson to the stand: Captain Dr. William M. Hall, Royal Canadian Army Medical Corps. He had examined Plaszek's body in the morgue and confirmed to the court that there was "a considerable amount of blood about the face" and lacerations on the scalp.[23] He described how the victim's tongue slightly protruded from the cold body.

Some of the jurors and others in the courtroom must have wondered why Turcotte let stand a number of Hall's answers containing the phrase "I believe." For some speakers, this expression is a mere verbal tick or a placeholder. It can even be an intensifier when used by someone in authority, such as Justice Howson. In Hall's case, however, it came across as what linguists call a "hedge," undermining the veracity of the rest of his words. His "I believe" rendered otherwise declarative statements into sentences admitting slight uncertainty. Even when the crown asked simple questions such as the date of the autopsy, Dr. Hall answered, "I believe it was the next day." He answered another query: "I saw the same body the night of the 23rd, I believe."[24]

If Turcotte had not noticed this locution when Hall was questioned by Wilson, he could not have missed it during his cross-examination.

"Now, was the neck swollen?" asked Turcotte.

"I believe we reported swelling," said Hall.

"What about the cut on the head, do you remember about that?"

"Well, there were two cuts, one, I believe, somewhat deeper than the other...."[25]

In almost every other instance of witnesses waffling in this matter, Turcotte had cut in to ask something to the effect of, "Did you or did you not make this remark?" Often, he would next produce a document demonstrating the facts of the matter. Hall was excused his hedges, likely because Turcotte thought that by repetition, Hall's "I believe" was weakening his testimony. The defence attorney had further opportunity to attack Hall's credibility later in the cross-examination on another aspect of his testimony.

"Well now, are you quite sure that what you saw on the lungs was congestion and not hypostasis," asked Turcotte.[26] Congestion is an abnormal accumulation of fluid; hypostasis is the accumulation of blood or other bodily fluids in the parts of the body lowest to the ground because of the effect of gravity after death.

Hall came close to stuttering in his response: "Well, in my report, I believe I made the remark that the congestion was—there was generalized congestion—of the lungs. Well, in hypostasis, congestion is not generalized. It [hypostatic congestion] is a settling of the blood to the dependent portions of the lungs and it is usually demonstrably different."[27]

"So, you think that it is quite easy," jabbed Turcotte, "that you can see the difference between those two ideas, the blood settling and the blood being congested as a result of injuries?"

"Well, I wouldn't say it is easy," answered Hall. "In some case it may be so, at other times there may be some confusion about it."[28]

Turcotte did not ask Hall to explain what would make one case easy and another difficult. He wasn't really interested in determining whether Hall saw congestion or hypostasis. Plaszek was dead, and no one doubted that he had been strangled. The defence attorney's aim was simply to shake the jury's faith in the crown's most expert medical witness, planting the seed of a reasonable doubt. He got what he wanted when Hall used the word "confusion."

* * *

The final group of witnesses called to testify was the POWs. One of these was Private Georg Jaeschke, who took the jury back into Camp 132's west recreation hall on that hot July afternoon where, in one corner, he had been using his seaman's skills to weave rope he would use to repair soccer nets. Drawn to the hall's main door by the sound of the crowd, he arrived in time to see Schulz bolt and go over the wire. A short while later, when Jaeschke was seven or eight paces inside the hall, he saw through the open sliding doors five or six men hauling another man toward the hall.

Jaeschke's testimony highlighted the problems of producing a precise trial transcript from translated testimony. The witness said that he saw the five or six men pulling toward the hall another man who "was bleeding from the head and that his clothes were blood." After some discussion amongst the judge, the court interpreter, Captain Gerald James Ryan, and the prosecutor Wilson, Howson ordered the transcript to read: "I took it for granted that he had been hit since he was bleeding from the head."[29]

Not long after, another translation crux emerged. After hearing Ryan interpret one of Jaeschke's answers as, "I saw how a man ran to him with a large piece of earth," Sergeant Paul Papsdorf, who was responsible for confirming the translation, signalled Howson and said that "Boden" could also be rendered as "clay." The court then heard an explanation of how normally, a piece of clay would be called "Lehmstrueck" with "Bodenstrueck" meaning a piece of earth. Lacking knowledge of German himself, Howson ordered that the word "Boden" be entered into the transcript. He then added that "the jury understand[s] that in English 'clay' is earth and earth is 'clay" and then turned to Jaeschke and said, "I think it is quite clear to everybody. Now do you understand all we have been saying?" Jaeschke answered affirmatively.[30]

Wilson had barely restarted, asking about "the man who struck the man on the ground with the piece of clay or earth," when Howson interrupted. "I don't think the witness said that he struck him with it, he said he threw it at him.... And he could see that the piece of earth or clay was broken into fragments."[31] Admonished, Wilson asked the witness what happened next.

"A number of people came into the hall and the man was then dragged to the other side of the hall," replied the witness. Not wanting to be "mixed up in the business," Jaeschke said he left the hall—but not before hearing Plaszek cry out, "I am not guilty and I have a wife and child."[32]

In his testimony, Jaeschke had mentioned repairing the nets with a private named Eric Hielscher, who also testified. Hielscher placed the defendant, Schwalb, closer to the crime scene, telling the court he saw that "Sergeant Schwalb had him the front by the leg." A rope was placed around Plaszek's neck and tightened before he was dragged across the hall "to where he was hanged." Wilson, using a photograph, tried to get Hielscher to pinpoint where Plaszek had been hanged. Turcotte objected to what he considered a leading question, which prompted a debate between Howson and Wilson over the nature of a leading question. Howson ended it with another admonition: "I don't want the slightest suggestion made to this witness."[33]

Turcotte's cross-examination of Hielscher elicited from the POW that he had "continued working while they were hanging the man."

The defence lawyer, sounding incredulous, asked, "Is that an ordinary occurrence in your life?"

"I said to myself immediately, 'I haven't lost anything thereby,'" replied Hielscher.

"Did you still continue to think about your work while they were hanging the man?"

"Yes."

"A very faithful worker," smirked Turcotte, knowing that his words left a faint echo of "I was only following orders."[34]

Given the questions about Dr. Maximillian Nolte's enigmatic influence in the POW camp and suspicions about his involvement with the murder of POWs in Africa, putting him on the stand was a gamble for the prosecution. But he was a medical doctor and as the camp's only German officer, the highest-ranking German to see Plaszek hanging. Under Wilson's questioning, Nolte's testimony was uneventful. He told how a POW had come into the hospital yelling that he was needed in the west recreation hall. Although he had entered through the canteen door, Nolte noticed that the main door to the hall was open and about 100 men were milling around the body hanging from a crossbeam. Nolte said that he ordered the body cut down. He checked for a pulse but did not find one. He had the body moved to a part of the hall with better light. The rope had so deeply cut into the man's neck that he couldn't get it off.

Turcotte asked why the doctor had not tried artificial respiration on Plaszek. Nolte answered that he already determined that the man was dead and that artificial respiration would require removing the rope, which he could not do because removing it would violate the rule against "touch[ing] a dead body before the police arrived and investigated." This cut little ice with the defence attorney: "I see. So you weren't worrying a great deal whether he was dead or not, at least, you weren't trying very hard to save his life."[35]

POW Rudolf Faber's testimony of how he helped cut down Plaszek's body might have seemed extraneous, especially because he did not mention seeing the murder or hearing who had done it. The line of questioning did serve a purpose for the prosecution, however. Faber had entered the hall a few steps behind Nolte. When the doctor asked for a knife, Faber took out a razor blade he used to carve wood. He gave two answers as to how he got to the cross beam to cut the rope. First, he said, "I climbed—I must have got hold of the wall somehow," and a few moments later claimed, "several people pushed me up, held me and I cut the rope."[36]

Turcotte took the bit in his mouth and ran with it:

"And when you cut the rope, what happened to the body or what happened to the man that was hanging?"

"It fell down."

"Nobody attempted to hold it up at all?"

"I don't know."

"Well, you were there, you saw it?"

"Yes, I cut it down and he fell down."[37]

This testimony not only added to the pathos of the scene but elucidated what appeared to be "an indignity to a dead human body," another offence under Canada's criminal code.

The next group of POWs called to testify shifted the focus from the dead man to the men accused of killing him. Sergeant Walter Koerber told of how after Weidemann entered the hut where Plaszek was waiting his interrogation, he (Koerber) heard the "noise of a fairly considerable scuffle and then a man was thrown out" of the door. As soon as the man, whom Koerber recognized as Plaszek, was outside the door, a corporal "hit him on the head with a large bolt," plausibly the sort of blunt object that would have caused the scalp wound identified by Dr. Hall. More importantly, Koerber testified that Schwalb, emerged from the hut carrying a coiled rope. In an attempt to muddy the waters, Turcotte zeroed in on Weidemann, who had not been charged, and got Koerber to say he was the one who told his fellow POWs, "People be quiet, otherwise the Canadians will come and take this man [Plaszek] away."[38]

POW Paul Kazmirzak confirmed Koerber's account of Plaszek being thrown out of the hut and dragged to the recreation hall. He followed the crowd and a few minutes later saw Plaszek hanging and Schwalb standing in the middle of the hall "with blood on his hands."[39] Newspaper accounts withheld Kazmirzak's name, referring to him as "a young barber," a courtesy extended to all of the POW witnesses to protect their families in Germany from retribution.[40]

Turcotte did his best to pick apart Kazmirzak's story. The witness's statement to the court that he had entered the hall through the main door differed from his account at the preliminary hearing that he had entered through a smaller door. "It is possible that I was confused then because I myself went through the small door," Kazmirzak admitted.

Having established that Kazmirzak and Koerber were standing near each other, the defence attorney opened some daylight between the two men's stories when Kazmirzak said he had no memory of Weidemann telling the crowd to quiet down lest the Canadians arrive. Turcotte also asked for an explanation of the difference between Kazmirzak's statement at the preliminary hearing—"I saw Schwalb with his hands dripping with blood"—and what the court had heard minutes earlier, "with blood on his hands."[41] Kazmirzak blamed the difference on the translators.

Turcotte also aimed to undermine the witness's character. Had Kazmirzak been brought before the camp leader in 1944, he asked. The witness admitted he had.

"And that was under Section 175 of the German [Military] Code, is that not correct?"

"Yes"

"And that has to do with the committing of what is known as buggery?"

"Yes."[42]

Having given the six jurymen permission to consider Kazmirzak a moral reprobate—homosexual acts were illegal in Canada, the United States, the United Kingdom, and Germany at the time—Turcotte next attempted to paint him as psychologically unstable. Had the witness ever said he was "going to commit suicide?" Justice Howson was visibly annoyed by the question, which was not based on evidence but on a rumour of a letter on one in the court had seen. Still, he did not instruct the jury to disregard Turcotte's impugning of Kazmirzak's mental health. Turcotte, having accomplished all he wanted, told Howson, "Well, we will let it go, my Lord."[43]

Another POW, Josef Kauer, also testified to seeing Schwalb outside the recreation hall with "blood on his fingers." Other prisoners asked him what was happening. "Go into the hall there," said Schwalb. "There is somebody hanging there." Kauer, who had known Schwalb since they were in the Lethbridge POW camp, pushed his way towards him and asked, "Sergeant, what have you done?"[44] Along the same lines, POW Max Winkler testified that Schwalb came into their barracks with blood splattered trousers and bloody hands.

Winkler's testimony became controversial when he reported Schwalb saying, "*Ich habe noch nach den strick vertlangte*," which could be rendered into English as "I was still looking for the rope." The court translator first rendered it as "I asked for the rope." Turcotte, seeking something less damaging to his client, questioned the meaning of "*noch*" and "*nach*," which led to a discussion with Wilson and Howson about German verbs. Turcotte's insistence on pushing the witness to explain the meaning of the words infuriated Wilson. He jumped up to "very forcibly register my objection to this kind of cross-examination and I would like it noted on the record because it seems to me that this is absolutely inadmissible from any standpoint."[45]

Turcotte continued to pursue the translation question, which brought more objections from Wilson, who accused the court's interpreter, whom he had chosen, of not giving translations but interpretations. The judge was irked by Wilson's style: he was acting more like the deputy attorney general of the Province of Alberta than a prosecutor in Howson's court. "Now, when you address me, stand up," he demanded. Wilson obliged as Howson asked, "Now what is it you have to say?" Wilson's attempt to explain that because they were hearing the witness' words through an interpreter, they were getting an interpretation generated more heat than light, as can be seen from Howson's tart response: "Well, I don't see your point at all."[46]

After what everyone in the courtroom must have found to be a close-to-mind-numbing excursus into German grammar and the pitfalls of translation, "*Ich habe noch nach den strick vertlangte,*" went into the transcript as, "I demanded the rope."[47] This rendering cast his client in a worse light, but Turcotte could at least hope that the linguistic wrestling match had shaken the jurymen's faith in Winkler's words.

The prosecution's penultimate witness, POW Kurt Wendorf, testified that in the Neys camp, Schwalb had said "he was nervous and slept badly because he was present at the incident at Medicine Hat."[48]

The final witness, POW Gunter Pabst, described seeing a man hanging and, as the body still swung from the makeshift gibbet, prisoners throwing sand on the pool of blood saying, "There's traitors' blood."[49]

The more important part of Pabst's testimony concerned his interactions with Schwalb at Neys, where they had become friendly. Having lived in German East Africa (Tanzania) until he was six-years-old, Pabst was teaching Swahili to Schwalb and other prisoners. He said Schwalb told him that the police had come, interviewed him, and accused him of being involved in "the incident." Schwalb said he had told the police he wasn't involved, and added to Pabst that the investigators "did not know very much about the matter" because they had been "very friendly" to him. Pabst further told the court that Schwalb had arranged with a fellow prisoner to "say that he had not been in the head barracks that day to wash his fingers." This confession prompted Pabst to ask Schwalb directly about his involvement. Before answering, Schwalb looked around and said, "Yes, I was actually there.... To you I can say I was actually there."[50]

Despite having lined up a man to perjure himself as protection, Schwalb worried about who had seen him walk with bloody hands and clothes from the recreation hall to his barracks. "This walk can lead to a hanging for me," he told Pabst. After another translation debate, this went into the record as, "This walk has led to suspicion falling on me."[51]

"Did he say anything further to you at all," Wilson asked the witness.

Pabst testified that Schwalb had said, "Should they hang me, I will die as a German soldier.[52]

After this statement, Turcotte's cross-examination, Wilson's re-examination and the defence's second cross-examination, Wilson stood and said, "That is the case for the crown, my Lord."

Howson looked at Turcotte and said, "Defence, Mr. Turcotte?"

"No defence," he replied.[53]

Howson then told the court that given the complexity of the case, including the difficulties of translation, the attorneys needed some time to prepare their final addresses. He adjourned the court until ten the following morning.

* * *

The next day, March 5, ten more trains carrying several thousand German POWs who had spent years in Camp 132 chugged eastward across the prairies, the first leg of their journey home. That same day, Joyce Reesor would sit in court, seeing the face of Werner Schwalb for the first time, and, shortly after ten o'clock, hearing prosecutor Wilson begin his summation to the six-man jury in *Rex v. Schwalb*.

It had been established that August Plaszek was killed by hanging in the late afternoon of July 21, 1943: his corpse had been seen by POWs, including Nolte and the acting camp leader, Richard Elstermann, camp staff, the RCMP, and a Canadian army medical corps doctor.

A number of witnesses had described Schulz's run to the wire and that in the minutes after, hundreds or thousands of men in the enclosure were in a riotous frame of mind. The crown had the murder weapon, a bloody noose.

To connect that weapon to Schwalb, the crown relied upon the defendant's own words as reported by other POWs. The *Calgary Herald* on March 5 reported on its front page that Wilson quoted a POW as saying Schwalb had "realized the damning evidence of his own acts." Trial fatigue is likely why the *Medicine Hat News* relegated the story to page three, but the local reporter played up a witness testifying that Schwalb had told him he was "nervous and slept badly because he was present at the incident at Medicine Hat."[54] If believable, these statements proved that Schwalb was a joint participant.

Turcotte's address to the jury noted that some of the witnesses were confused about times and places. Others were "too positive" to be believed, given the two or three years that had passed since many of the events.[55] The men responsible for Plaszek's death, the "true murderers," Turcotte said, were the camp leadership: Elstermann, Schnorrenpfeil, and Weidemann.[56] Despite their oaths as witnesses, these men had "lied throughout" their time on the stand.[57]

Judge Howson's charge to the jury ran for fifty pages and took four hours to read. He reminded the jury to "erase from your minds any preconceived notions" and to "consider such evidence as was presented in this Court during this trial."[58]

As her "punishment essay" would show, high school student Joyce Reesor listened carefully to the explanation of "reasonable doubt," and how in Canadian courts the accused is under no burden to prove his or her own innocence.

Jurors were bound, Howson told them, to accept his word on the applicable law, and were not to concern themselves with penalty, which, they almost certainly knew, was death. Having explained the distinction between direct and indirect evidence (something a witness testifies that he has seen or heard vs. circumstantial evidence), and that the jury could convict on indirect evidence, Howson moved on to the legal definition of murder. The crucial part was that "everyone is a party to and guilty of an offence who (a) actually commits it; (b) does or omits an act for the purpose of aiding any person to commit the offence; and (c) abets any person in commission of the offence."[59]

After the jury had been sent to consider its verdict, Turcotte objected to Howson's explanation of the difference between murder and manslaughter. After much discussion amongst Howson, Wilson, and Turcotte, the jury was brought back for further explanation, and was returned to the jury room at 5:23 p.m.

Thirty-seven minutes later, the jury returned to a breathless courtroom where, as Reesor wrote, "[e]ven the ticking of the clock seemed exaggerated."

The clerk of the court asked, "Gentlemen of the Jury, have you arrived at a verdict. If so, say so by your foreman."

More moments passed than in most trials, as the interpreter's low monotone voice translated these words.

The foreman stood up, faced Howson, and said, "We find the accused guilty of murder."

At least one person, young Joyce Reesor, wondered what the condemned man thought. To ensure that the guilty verdict was, indeed, unanimous, the clerk polled the jurymen, and with the sixth "yes," the verdict became official.[60]

Said Justice Howson:

> The sentence of the court is that you be taken from here to the Provincial Gaol at Lethbridge, and there be kept in custody until the 26th day of June 1946. On that day you will be taken from the gaol to the place of execution, and there you will be hanged by the neck until you are dead, and may the Lord have mercy on your soul.[61]

As Werner Schwalb stood up and stepped out of the prisoner's box, Reesor saw in his face a "mask of arrogance." Before his guards led him away, the condemned man turned to the court's interpreter and gave him "a forced smile."[62]

Reesor watched as he "walked haughtily from the court-room," with guards by his side.[63]

CHAPTER 8

Rex v. Adolf Kratz
March 7 to March 16, 1946

BEGINNING ON MARCH 7, 1946, Adolf Kratz, his swaggering stilled, was the next POW on trial for his life. For the press and officers of the court, large parts of his trial for the murder of August Plaszek were a twice-told tale. Of the twenty-nine witnesses called, twenty-one had appeared in Werner Schwalb's trial, including all but one of those called to establish the foundation of the prosecution's case. Judge Howson and the other officers of the court listened patiently as these men pointed to new models and plans and photographs; Louis Turcotte, concerned that the writing on the exhibits used in the previous trial would taint this one, had successfully petitioned the court for replacements. There was also a new prosecutor, Walter Donald Gow, K.C., a well-respected local lawyer with an impressive record of public service behind him. Gow followed H. J. Wilson's script from the first trial when questioning witnesses. Turcotte, by contrast, had studied the transcripts and spotted weaknesses he now set out to exploit in an attempt to save the life of a soldier who had fought on three fronts: France, the Russian front, and in North Africa, where he was captured on May 29, 1942, at Tobruk.

Turcotte bore down harder on RCMP Corporal Bull than he had before. For instance, he asked what had happened to Plaszek's bloody shirt, which Bull testified he had seen at the funeral home. Bull answered that when his men had tried to retrieve it, they learned that it had been destroyed along with other items of clothing, casting a shadow on the RCMP's handling of evidence.

When Turcotte asked Bull whether the windows of the west recreation hall were frosted or whitewashed, the juror's might have wondered where he was headed. Bull's answer, however, was helpful to the defence attorney. "My memory is not clear to be specific on this point," said Bull. "I recall that as I entered the hall from the outside sunlight, you had the impression of going into a subdued light, and it is possible that the west windows may have been frosted to some extent, but I would not be positive on that point."[1] Turcotte had lured the only police officer testifying at Kratz's trial into saying that his memory was "not clear" while also putting on record that the lighting in the recreation hall was poor. These were small but significant gains.

Having seen in Schwalb's trial how important the functioning of the camp Gestapo was to the crown's case, Turcotte adjusted his strategy, aiming to show that his client had acted under a reasonable understanding of military orders. His opening came when former acting camp leader Richard Elstermann stated baldly what had only been implied at Schwalb's trial, that he had "the right and the duty" to investigate rumours that Plaszek and other veterans of the French Foreign Legion were planning to move against the camp leadership.

Turcotte linked efforts to put down the rumoured rebellion with the activities of camp education director Corporal Ernst Gurbat, whose role was described as "seeing that the people of the camp thought in the right manner."[2] A picture emerged of a camp leadership organized and determined to enforce ideological solidarity and military discipline.

And just after 2 p.m. on the first day of the trial, Turcotte renewed his duel with Hans Justus Schnorrenpfeil. The first lieutenant and former state legal advisor filled some gaps in his previous testimony. Retelling how he had been mistaken for Burkhardt, the man he was interrogating, and needed to be rescued by Dr. Maximillian Nolte from a mob of prisoners, Schnorrenpfeil testified that instead of going to eat after the incident he had gone back to his hut to nurse his sore jaw. It was only then, he said, that he heard about Schulz's run, that Plaszek had been seized by the mob, and about the killing.

Turcotte wasn't buying it. He asked if the witness by chance had had cotton in his ears while conducting his interrogation, or if he "perhaps suffered from temporary amnesia as a result of being hit in the face by that crowd." When the German lawyer answer "*Nien*" to these facetious questions. Turcotte pulled out all stops:

> Well can you give us any reasonable explanation why, if there was a crowd which dragged another person from the building you were in to the hall just north of there, and this man [was] being kicked and hit with stones and with bolts, and before that was thrown out of the hallway next to you after a scuffle and after someone said, 'Be quiet for the Canadians will come and get him.' Can you tell us any reason you didn't hear any or all of that?[3]

Schnorrenpfeil's answer was unconvincing:

> I have an explanation for that. First of all, I had a definite task before me. I busied myself with completing that task through questions and answers. The answers were given to me I then worked out and dictated. For this reason alone, I was concentrating.[4]

On the prosecution side, crown attorney Gow knew that Christian Schulz's testimony about his run to save his life had been effective in establishing the existence of a riotous mob at Schwalb's trial. Shultz's personal details were fleshed out to further humanize him. The jury learned that he was a former manager of an electro-plating factory and that he had come to Canada as a prisoner of war on May 28, 1942, aboard the *Queen Elizabeth*. He had been in the German army for only a year, having been called up after failing to win a deferment as a worker. Schulz's testimony also served to humanize the victim, Plaszek, whom he described as a friend from the French Foreign Legion and a "quiet man" who "joked with everybody."[5]

Captain Dr. Maximillian Nolte testified again in the Kratz trial but in a different light. Turcotte was interested in the doctor's role in camp discipline. On paper, he should have had no role at all. He was a medical officer, full stop. It came out under questioning, however, that Nolte had attended a meeting called by Elstermann to plan the inquiry into rumours that the Legionnaires were conspiring to oust camp leadership. Nolte was the highest-ranking German in the camp and was part of the leadership cabal. He was a target of the rumoured insurrection, Turcotte insisted, and therefore an interested party.

Turcotte asked Nolte why, if he had nothing to do with camp discipline, he had accompanied Elstermann back to the recreation hall after

Plaszek had been killed and his death had been reported to the authorities. The doctor said Elstermann had asked that he join him. "I see," said Turcotte doubtfully. "But you didn't have anything to do with the maintenance of discipline at all in the camp?" Nolte again replied, "No."[6]

Nolte added somewhat to his account of finding Plaszek hanging from a crossbeam. The man had no heartbeat, no eye motions, and his "eyes were broken, that is to say, the cornea was dry and cloudy," said Nolte, because dead men don't blink. A quick test showed the man's skin did not redden when scratched, indicating he was dead. Asked if he'd formed an opinion as to the cause of death, Nolte said he couldn't be definite without a post mortem, but he "personally believe[d] that the cause of death was strangulation."[7]

Turcotte returned to his dispute with Nolte over the doctor's treatment of the corpse. On the one hand, Nolte claimed that he did not cut away the rope from around Plaszek's neck "in order to take no proof from the hands of the police." Turcotte found Nolte's posing as a law-abiding prisoner concerned for the integrity of a police investigation difficult to swallow, especially given the doctor's other actions. The attorney asked Nolte why he had not ordered some men to hold Plaszek's body as it was being cut down, and came close to accusing Nolte of contributing to Plaszek's death: "But you didn't think about taking some precautions to see that he did not fall or drop to the ground as he was being cut down?" Nolte answered, "*Nien.*"[8]

As for the role of the swaggering Kratz, whose boxing instructor's physique gave mute testimony to his penchant for violence, the court heard from POW Paul Kazmirzak that "Plaszek was thrown out of the hut. As he got to the doorway and stood there, Kratz had a stone in his hand and hit him on the head." (For those who had been at Schwalb's trial, this presumably filled in the blank left by Private George Jaeschke's testimony that a man had run up to Plaszek and hit him with a "boden.") Kazmirzak also said that Plaszek was "pulled down by the people" who kicked him and yelled "Strike him dead" before he was dragged to the west recreation hall. Turcotte tried to shake Kazmirzak's testimony about where exactly Kratz was standing during these events. He also noticed that the witness, in his preliminary hearing, had said Plaszek was dragged through the small doors of the recreation hall; now he was saying that the victim had been dragged through the hall's large sliding doors. Kazmirzak did not do much to clarify his testimony: "It was not absolutely clear to me at the time because I myself had gone through the small door and I must have mixed it [up]."[9]

As he had in Schwalb's trial, Turcotte also attempted to use Kazmirzak's homosexuality to discredit him as a witness, suggesting that his "conviction" under Section 175 of the German Military Code, which dealt with homosexual activity, had ostracized Kazmirzak within the camp and given him ample reason to want revenge on the camp leaders and their acolytes, including Kratz. Secondly, Turcotte knew that branding Kazmirzak as homosexual would tend to undermine his credibility with the six-man jury.

* * *

POW Hugo Stolte was the first witness to report Kratz's words. Stolte had returned to his hut shortly after Schulz went over the wire. He testified that Kratz came in not long after and said: "there was somebody there [at the recreation hall] that he [Stolte] knew and he [Kratz] was going to take part in hanging him." Kratz immediately left the hut. Stolte followed to the hall and "found that somebody had been hanged."[10] For a few moments, he was not sure if the man was Corporal Kafka or Plaszek, for both were bald, but he soon realized it was his friend Plaszek from Cologne, where they were inducted into the 361st Regiment together.

Stolte further reported that Kratz had said, "now we have hanged one of these swine." Knowing that this did now quite implicate Kratz in the crime, the crown pushed further, asking Stolte about a conversation the following day. "He told me in detail what had taken place," said Stolte. "The way they hanged the man. The way they had put the rope around his neck and hanged him." The witness said he didn't ask Kratz anything further, fearing that he might also "be hanged at any moment."[11]

Turcotte's approach to Stolte was similar to his questioning of Kazmirzak, pointing out small but significant differences between the witness's testimony at trial and during the preliminary inquiry. In the inquiry, Stolte used the word "somebody," not "swine." Stolte couldn't explain the discrepancy but was "prepared to guarantee" Kratz had said "swine."[12]

Before the witness left the stand, Howson allowed a juror to ask the witness if he could explain why Kratz would have alerted Stolte to the hanging of his friend. The answer went a fair distance toward explaining how effectively Corporal Ernst Gurbat and his circle had been in enforcing commitment to Nazi ideology. "Kratz had become a perfect little Nazi," said Stolte, "and as such he had lost all his brains, and I take it that was the reason—he wanted to be the good Nazi."[13]

Noting that Stolte was much older than Kratz, the same juror asked if he had made "any attempt to convert Kratz from the Nazi thought to rational thought?" Although likely amazed at the juror's naïveté, Stolte answered politely, "I would never have attempted such a thing. It would have cost me my life."

Before he left the stand, another juror asked Stolte, "Were you, then, a very good Nazi at the time?"

"I have never been a good Nazi," answered Stolte.[14]

Private Adam Jansen later corroborated Stolte's account of what Kratz said after he came into their hut: "I have assisted to hang a swine."[15]

Yet another witness, Lorenz Kasmirzak, would also testify about Kratz but prosecutor Gow first asked him a question not asked of any other POW: where had he been taken prisoner. His answer, Tobruk, likely explains the reason. Being captured at this storied battle gave Kasmirzak more status than had he simply been captured in the sands of the western desert. Kasmirzak went on to testify that he had heard a conversation in which a POW said to Kratz, "you have taken a good part" in these events. Kratz's reply was, "It is my duty. One must hang all these swine."[17]

More startling was POW Fritz Dorrenseiff's testimony that Kratz came into the hut they shared on the evening after Plaszek's killing and, while lying on his bed eating an egg, said: "The egg tastes that much better because I have helped hang a traitor." Dorrenseiff was, like Plaszek, also a member of the Legionnaire-heavy 361st Regiment, which meant that his blood ran cold two evenings later when Kratz said, "There is no room, there is no place in this hut for Legionnaires and more of you will be hanged."[18]

Turcotte challenged all of this testimony regarding statements by Kratz, and managed to muddy the waters by demonstrating inconsistencies in the language attributed to the accused. Had he said "hang" or "kill"? Had he meant that he had killed a traitor or that a traitor had been killed? Was Plaszek killed? Was he "done away with?" Was his death "brought about?"[19] Among other terms, the three German words for murder—*umbringen*, *toten* and *amorder* [which probably should have been *mord*] were carefully parsed. It all had the effect of undercutting the precision of the prosecution's case.

Although he spoke English, Sergeant Walter Koerber requested a translator, which gave him a few more seconds to compose his answers. As he had at Schwalb's trial, Koerber described for the jury how Wilhelm Weidemann, who had been conducting the interrogation of the suspected mutineers, threw Plaszek out of the hut and into the arms of angry Nazified POWs. Plaszek was hit on the head with a bolt and dragged by his arms and legs away from the hut. Asked to identify one of the men who had done the dragging, Koerber answered "Kratz," and pointed to him in the courtroom.

Under cross-examination, Turcotte sought to deflect blame onto Weidemann, who was not on trial, but who in response to the angry group's call for blood said, "I will have this man [Plaszek] thrown out." It was not Turcotte's best moment. He inadvertently clarified the scene for the prosecution. Turcotte asked what part of the victim's body Kratz was holding, and Koerber answered without hesitation that "he had him by the foot" and his "face was up."[20]

A short time later, Turcotte asked some seemingly innocuous questions about how long Koerber had known Kratz by name. The witness claimed he had known the accused as "Addie," short for Adolph, and had only learned his surname "when I came for interrogation by Inspector Bull." Turcotte found this unlikely. "Yes," he said, "Addie, a man that you slept with, talked with, worked with for two years and you didn't know his last name." Gow, alert for any imputation that his witness was an active homosexual, jumped out of his seat: "He didn't say he slept with him."[21]

"Slept next to him, all right," growled Turcotte.

"I wasn't with the man for two years," Koerber sputtered.[22]

Having complicated Koerber's profile in the jury's mind, Turcotte went on to question the witness about other elements of Camp 132's operations. Koerber had mentioned that camp education director Gurbat provided "religious instruction" to prisoners. Turcotte wanted to know what other kinds of instruction were provided, and asked specifically about politics. Koerber allowed that politics were part of the instruction.

"Well," asked Turcotte, "are you mixing politics and religion now? Is that the same subject in the camp?"

Koerber said that Gurbat "continually told of Nazi affairs."

"Gurbat was what you might call the Minister of Propaganda in the camp?" asked Turcotte.

"The Dr. Goebbels," agreed the witness, putting the first mention of a Nazi Government official on the trial record.[23]

All the news given out by Gurbat and his associations, Koerber said, was from a distinctly Nazi point of view. This confirmed to Turcotte's satisfaction the power of the Nazi element in the camp, and demonstrated that it had the tools and inclination to promote Nazi ideology and enforce discipline among the prisoners. Koerber's testimony fit neatly with what Stolte had said earlier of how "Kratz had become a perfect little Nazi and as such he had lost all his brains."

"That is all, thank you," said Turcotte, obviously hoping the jury would appreciate the pressures Kratz was under in the camp.[24]

As at Schwalb's trial, Turcotte declined to call witnesses for Kratz's defence.

* * *

On March 15, 1946, the crown prosecutor Gow stood before Justice Howson to deliver his summation in the case of *Rex v. Kratz*. The first part was similar to his performance in *Rex v. Schwalb*: a precis of Schulz's run, the finding of Plaszek's body, the riotous tenor of the camp. When he turned to Kratz's actions, the crown chose loaded words to describe what had happened to the victim: "I have never read about any other lynching in Canada, nor have I ever heard of one except in the murder of Plaszek. I hope we never have to deal with another."[25]

No matter what the law of Germany might say about suspected traitors, concluded Gow, the law of Canada had to prevail. Plaszek, he reminded the jurors, was a "quiet chap," who, unlike Schulz, did not even have the chance of running for his life. He was the victim of a "cold-blooded murder."[26]

As he had two weeks earlier, Turcotte argued that the evidence against his client was weak. Indeed, no witness could confirm that Kratz was in the recreation hall when Plaszek was killed. The camp leaders, Turcotte charged, were responsible for what befell the victim, and had covered their actions with "a pack of lies from start to finish."[27] From our distance seven decades later, it seems Turcotte erred in not telling the jury in this agricultural town that Kratz, the pre-war carpenter, had worked in the sugar beet fields while at the Lethbridge POW camp.

Beginning at 10 a.m. on March 16, Justice Howson delivered his charge to the jury, the bulk of which was identical to the one that had impressed Joyce Reesor. The case went to the jury at 1:20 p.m. Forty-five minutes later, following Turcotte's objection that Howson had not fully explained culpable and non-culpable homicide, the jury was recalled so that the judge could clarify his explanation. The jury returned to its room at 2:35 p.m.

At 6:05 p.m., the foreman of the jury told the clerk of the court that the jury was deadlocked. Howson ordered that dinner be provided and that the jury return to its work. Before returning to the jury room, the foreman asked an unexpected question: "Your Lordship, before retiring, there has been a question that has come up in the jury room. Is the jury permitted to bring in a recommendation with the verdict?"

"Yes," said Howson, before adding, "if you arrive at a unanimous verdict, you can bring in whatever recommendation you wish."[28]

Within the hour, at 6:50 p.m., the jury returned to the courtroom with its verdict. "The jury," announced the foreman, "finds the accused guilty as charged, with a strong recommendation for mercy."[29]

Chief Justice Howson passed a sentence of death but made the following statement to Kratz:

> The jury has found you guilty of the offence for which you have been charged, and have brought in a strong recommendation for mercy. Under the circumstances I have no option but to sentence you, but I wish to assure you that I shall forward to the secretary of state for Canada, who in turn will forward to the minister of justice, who in turn will deliver to the governor general the jury's recommendation. Now in saying that, I am not in a position to assure you of anything, but the recommendation made by the jury will go forward with all the papers and I know will receive conscientious consideration of those who are at the head of the department of justice and the administration of justice in Canada.[30]

Unlike their American counterparts, Canadian jurors are bound by an oath of secrecy about what occurs in the jury room. We cannot know for sure what prompted the recommendation for mercy. Kratz's age, twenty-four, which meant he had been a soldier since he was eighteen and had come of age in Hitler's Germany, almost certainly had something to do with it. Equally likely was Turcotte's strategy of emphasizing at trial that Kratz had, in his friend's words, "lost all his brains." Especially for younger soldiers, the effects of defeat and lengthy incarceration were psychologically and intellectually disorienting, and Kratz appeared to have fallen under the influence of the Camp 132 Gestapo, with its insistence on properly worn uniforms, the stiff-armed salute, the celebration of Hitler's birthday, and a hard line against any dissent in the ranks. Turcotte's emphasis on the camp's propaganda machine seems to have paid off with the jury. When Howson sent the report of Kratz's trial to Ottawa, the covering letter reported that the six men who had heard the evidence and convicted Kratz did in fact recommend that the governor general in council use the royal prerogative and grant the POW mercy.

CHAPTER 9

The Appeals in the Plaszek Murder Trials, *Rex v. Johannas Wittinger,* and the Execution of Adolf Kratz

April to June 1946

THE FINAL EDITION OF *P.O.W. WOW*, the Camp 132 newspaper produced by the Veterans Guard, prophesied that the enormous prison of war facility, hurriedly built mid-war on the outskirts of Medicine Hat and doubling the local population almost overnight, would soon be abandoned "to gophers, cactus, and rattlesnakes."[1] Through the spring of 1946 that transformation of the camp neared completion. Its only inhabitants were a skeleton staff of guards and those prisoners slated to be witnesses in either the Lehmann trial, or Johannas Wittinger's for the murder of August Plaszek.

Appeals for the two men already convicted of killing Plaszek moved forward. In April 1946, defence attorney Louis Turcotte challenged both the conviction and sentence of Werner Schwalb at the Alberta Court of Appeals. He cited seventeen instances in which he believed "the learned trial judge" had erred. He began by questioning Chief Justice Howson's decision to ignore Schwalb's election to be tried by judge alone and proceed with a jury trial. Another point argued that Howson had tilted the table against Schwalb when he told the jury "the accused in a criminal court is not bound to say anything and he is not bound to do anything." Turcotte believed this unfairly reminded the jurors that Schwalb had not testified in his own defence. The defence further maintained that Howson should have instructed the jury that murder requires "malice aforethought," which, perforce, a rampaging mob cannot have.[2]

In his report to the secretary of state for Canada on *Rex v. Werner Schwalb*, Howson appears to have been most concerned about three points he assumed would be central in Turcotte's appeal, including the judge's presentation—or lack thereof—of the law relating to the lesser charge of manslaughter in his original charge to the jury. It was only when the jurors had retired that Turcotte raised the matter and Howson called the six men back into court and explained the law around manslaughter. "I had no intention of explaining to the jury the law relating to manslaughter," Howson told the secretary. He had seen "nothing in the evidence upon which" a manslaughter finding could be established. In his opinion, the evidence presented at trial left the jury with two options: "the verdict must be murder or nothing." He believed that by belatedly dealing with the question of manslaughter, he had given the accused "a protection to which he was probably not even entitled."[3]

As Turcotte filed a similar appeal for Adolf Kratz, questions arose about the convicted prisoners' rights. Schwalb's prosecutor, Henry Wilson, in his capacity as Alberta's deputy attorney general, was seeking guidance from Ottawa. Wilson noted that when a death sentence is meted out to a POW, the Geneva Convention dictates that the circumstances of the offence must be delivered as soon as possible to a neutral intermediary, or protecting power, for "transmission to the power in whose armed forces the prisoner served." Further, the "sentence shall not be carried out before the expiration of a period of at least three months from the date of the receipt of the communication."[4] Since both Schwalb and Kratz were sentenced to be executed on June 26 and it was already 4 April, Wilson believed Alberta was already in contravention of the Geneva Convention.

A week later, Frederick Varcoe, the Canadian deputy minister of justice, telegrammed back to Wilson saying that the Swiss government had been removed from its role as Germany's protecting power by the Big Four (USSR, US, UK, and France). Since the Swiss "(have) ceased to be the protecting power," he continued, "there is no protecting power." The transmission of the suggested communication to Geneva for delivery to Germany "must therefore be dispensed with." Varcoe added that "no ground for reprieve on this account appears to exist."[5]

That might have been the end of the matter but another memo written to Varcoe the day his telegram was sent advised him that while a three-month long reprieve was not necessary, "it would be proper for the detaining power (Canada) to endeavour to give to these prisoners of war the protection which [the Geneva Convention]... intended to provide." In the absence of a protecting power, the government's lawyers suggested the case be outlined for the benefit of a Mr. Maag at the International Committee of the Red Cross in Montreal. Maag, they believed, should be able "to make representations in support of a commutation of the death sentence, or any other action he may consider appropriate."[6] In fact, Maag himself had suggested just such an arrangement to Canada's department of external affairs seven months earlier, when the complications of the extinguishment of the Nazi German State and the continued holding of POWs first became manifest. According to David J. Carter, who wrote a book on POWs in Canada, Prime Minister Mackenzie King "protested in writing to the British Foreign Office in London that the Canadian government did not approve of the removal of the Swiss as the Protecting Power," but his objections were swatted aside by the British.[7]

On May 21, 1946, the Alberta Appeals Court unanimously dismissed the appeal of Schwalb's and Kratz's convictions. There was no reporter present at the release of the court's decision, and no reasons for it were made public. A few days earlier, however, Alberta's deputy attorney general wrote a memorandum that indicated the appeal court's logic in the case of *Rex v. Werner Schwalb*. After reviewing the trial transcripts, the three-judge panel found that "there was no prejudice to the accused" in Howson's remarks. The court did not believe that Howson had overstepped the line by reminding the jury that the accused had declined to give evidence. The judges agreed with Howson that "there was no evidence in this case to justify a verdict of manslaughter" and, therefore, no need for him to explain manslaughter to the jury. Indeed, the appeals court was of the opinion that "if the jury had brought in a verdict of manslaughter, and the crown had appealed, the court would necessarily have ordered a new trial." Furthermore, the court believed "that there was no unlawful act or insult [by Plaszek] which would justify the actions of the crowd." Rather, the "evidence clearly showed that [Schwalb] intended to murder Plaszek"[8]

The deputy attorney general's other memorandum, in the case against Kratz, suggests that the decision of the appeals court was identical to that in Schwalb's case, save for one additional point. The judges dismissed Turcotte's argument that the trial judge had "failed to adequately point out to the jury certain discrepancies in the evidence of the witnesses."

Such discrepancies, said the court, were "matters for the jury to decide, because juries are the judge of facts."[9]

After the Appeals Court ruled against his clients, Turcotte played the last card available to him, writing to Canada's governor general, Viscount Harold Alexander, to request the "royal prerogative of mercy." Although Turcotte noted that Justice Howson had already forwarded the recommendation for mercy made by Kratz's jury, the attorney did not build his case on this. Rather, he wrote that the evidence at trial failed to demonstrate that either Schwalb or Kratz had hanged Plaszek. The camp leaders who had testified at the trials committed perjury, argued the defence attorney, as did at least one of Sergeant Koerber and Regimental Sergeant Major Weidemann; the former said the latter was present when Plaszek was thrown out of the hut, while the latter denied being there.

Turcotte also raised the matter of the status of German military law within the enclosure. "If a Canadian in a German prison camp had had an honest belief that one of their group was a traitor and, in a melee, this Canadian was killed, surely the Government of Canada would not execute Canadian soldiers who had taken part in the melee."[10]

Perhaps clutching at straws, Turcotte further submitted that a killing under the circumstances of mob hysteria was "not as culpable as killing in cold blood." He admitted that "Canadian courts have held that mob hysteria is not, in law, a reason for reducing a charge from murder to manslaughter,"[11] and, therefore, based his argument on a four-page quotation from the second edition of George F. Arnold's *Psychology Applied to Legal Evidence*. Arnold argues that an accused's crime is mitigated by the psychological effect of being part of a certain type of emotionally driven crowd. Turcotte quoted Arnold quoting the psychologist Hugo Munsterburg: "To be a member of [such] a crowd is always sufficient to weaken" the countervailing force of an individual's reason. Turcotte also referenced Gustave Le Bon's famous work, *The Crowd: A Study of the Popular Mind* (1895), maintaining that Schwalb and Kratz were essentially hypnotized by the rioters around them: "The active part of the brain is paralyzed." The ability to judge right from wrong and exercise will are lost. The man of the crowd "becomes a barbarian, a creature acting by instinct" alone.[12]

Through Munsterburg, Turcotte also enlisted the theories of the pre-Freudian American psychologist William James to explain how the Nazi party used the psychology of "political and religious associations" to control its adherents. The mental processes of an individual man, wrote James, "are profoundly modified by virtue of the fact that he thought, felt, and acted as one of a group and in reciprocal action with other members of the group as a whole."[13] Turcotte took this as confirmation that Kratz, as POW Hugo Stolte put it, had "lost all his brains" to Nazism.

* * *

The last of the trio accused of murdering August Plaszek did not finally stand trial until June. The transcript of Johannes Wittinger's second trial (his first was quickly aborted because one of the jurors was found to be too young to serve) is missing. But a report filed by Justice Howson with the deputy minister of justice contains a summary of the prosecution's evidence against the accused. It suggests that the case against Wittinger, a former truck driver who fought in France, Russia, and North Africa, was very similar to those against Schwalb and Kratz.

POW Franz Schmidbauer, who knew Wittinger from their hometown in Austria, recognized him as one of four men who dragged Plaszek into the recreation hall. After the murder, Schmidbauer and three other men, including POW Ferdinand Fandel, "saw Wittinger with his hands covered in blood." Fandel testified that Wittinger remarked, "Now I have beaten one to death with a stone and afterwards took him… and hung him." The other witnesses, according to Howson, used different words, but the "substance of their testimony is… that [Wittinger] admitted to being implicated in the murder."[14] Yet another POW, Franz Crepaz, testified to hearing Wittinger boast of smashing Plaszek's head with a stone.

Schmidbaeur also told the court that the day after the killing he confronted Wittinger: "You have killed a family man."

"Hold your tongue," Wittinger shot back. He claimed to have had instructions from camp leadership to commit his acts.[15]

Unlike the previous two murder trials, Turcotte called witnesses for the defence: Schwalb and the accused himself, Wittinger. Arranging for Schwalb to testify required negotiation with Justice Howson, who was reluctant to have the convicted murderer moved from Lethbridge to Medicine Hat and back to Lethbridge just days before he was to be executed on June 26. Satisfied that his testimony was necessary, the judge issued the necessary orders. On June 21, Schwalb appeared in the same courtroom where he had been tried and sentenced to death.

Turcotte faced a difficult task in establishing why the jury should trust Schwalb. He opened with some personal questions and the court learned that the convict had been born 50 kilometres west of the Rhine, and that he had been captured as a soldier in the Haifa Pass in north west Egypt. It was also revealed that Schwalb's primary occupation in Camp 132 had been head referee of the soccer games, perhaps an attempt by Turcotte to paint his witness as a man concerned with rules and fair play.

Knowing that if he didn't, the Crown would, Turcotte also asked Schwalb about the reputation of the 361st Regiment in which Plaszek served. "The average soldier did not want to have anything to do with this regiment," said Schwalb, who had earlier noted that it was composed mainly of former French Foreign Legionnaires, "but the reputation of the regiment in battle was high."[16]

In Schwalb's version of events the villain of the piece was Regimental Sergeant Major Wilhelm Weidemann, who had been assisting with the interrogations of suspected dissidents. Schwalb said that after entering the hut in which Plaszek was held, he heard a POW ask, "is he [Plaszek] guilty?" Weidemann answered "yes" and said that he would be "handed over to the crowd." Schwalb testified he was outside the hut a short while later when Plaszek "flew out of the building just like a torpedo" and fell on the ground with "three or four heavy thuds."[17]

In Schwalb's own trial, the jury had almost certainly believed that when he told a fellow prisoner that he couldn't sleep because of what he had seen at Medicine Hat, Schwalb really meant that he couldn't sleep because of what he had *done* in Medicine Hat. Now, in Wittinger's trial, Schwalb for the first time gave a jury an account of his actions. Once Plaszek had been pulled into the recreation hall, he said, he was dropped onto a sports mat. Concerned that Plaszek's blood would soak into the mat, Schwalb "picked [Plaszek] up by the shoulders and pulled him off the mat and onto the floor." From the way Plaszek's head fell backwards, Schwalb concluded that "the man was either dead or most certainly unconscious," which, a moment later, he qualified as "heavily unconscious."[18]

The rope that played such an important part in his trial was not, Schwalb said, brought to the scene of the attack by either himself or Wittinger, nor had either of them used it. Rather, at "the moment I was about to pick up the sports mat [to move it to storage], two men were occupied by tying a rope around the neck of [Plaszek] and one man said, 'Go away, I can do it better than you.'"[19]

Turcotte then addressed what had been the most damning evidence against Schwalb, the fact that his hands were covered with blood. "They were bloody," said the witness, "because I had lifted the blood-soaked sports mat."[20] Leaving aside the question of whether this testimony would have helped Schwalb if it had been produced at his own trial, Turcotte clearly believed this version of events would help Wittinger, who in Schwalb's telling was absent from the scene.

The crown began its attack on Schwalb's testimony by having him remind the jury that he was condemned to die. This fact underscored that he had been convicted of a capital crime; at the same time, it risked giving his words something of the status of a death-bed confession. Schwalb was asked if he waited until now to implicate Weidemann in Plaszek's death to buy himself time: if Weidemann were charged, Schwalb would be a material witness, and his execution would in all probability be postponed.[21] Schwalb acknowledged that this eventuality had crossed his mind but said it did not affect his testimony.

The crown also directed the jury's attention to a short note Schwalb had written to RCMP Corporal Bull some weeks before Wittinger's trial. No doubt knowing the chances of his sentence being commuted were not good, Schwalb wrote, "I wish to see you because I have to say [to] you some important point in the case of Lehmann." Bull met with Schwalb two days later. The convict offered to reveal certain things he knew about the Lehmann case if Corporal Bull "could do something for me." When Bull said he couldn't do anything for him, Schwalb told the RCMP officer, "it was therefore unnecessary that we should speak about these matters to each other."[22] The crown believed the attempted deal was fatal to Schwalb's credibility.

After leaving the witness stand, Schwalb was returned to confinement and greeted with bad news. A telegram had arrived from Ottawa stating that his excellency the governor general in council "is unable to order any interference with the sentence of the Court in the Capital Case of Werner Schwalb sentenced to death by the Honourable Judge Howson STOP."[23]

Schwalb's fellow convict received far better news: "I am commanded to inform you that his Excellency the Governor General in Council is pleased to commute to a term of life imprisonment… in the case of Adolf Kratz."[24]

The third man to be tried, Adolphus Wittinger, now took the stand. He was a pathetic sight. An active member of a Nazi paramilitary organization in Austria before the war,[25] he had contracted tuberculosis in Lethbridge's prison while awaiting trial and lost so much weight that sitting caused him unbearable pain. Justice Howson allowed him to sit on a pillow while testifying on his own behalf.

Wittinger told the court that after he saw Schulz go "over the wire," he returned to his hut. A short time later he heard someone yell, "a man has been hanged." Wittinger not only denied making the comments attributed to him about his role in Plaszek's death, he said he "had no knowledge of ever having spoken to at least two of the witnesses."[26]

After the summations of the crown and Turcotte, the former leaning on POW testimony that the accused had admitted the crime, the latter relying on testimony that Wittinger was nowhere near the scene, Howson delivered a two-hour charge to the jury.

Howard Millin, the same man who had been delivering a load of soda pop to the camp on the last day of August Plaszek's life, says that he and his fellow jurors "studied the testimony and looked at the documents. We gave it a thorough going over. We felt that there was no way they could prove that Wittinger was at the scene and that was critical to us. After three hours, it was decided to take our first vote. It was a secret ballot."[27]

Decades later, Millen's memory of the last moments of the trial remain sharp:

[The jurors] came out and I could see the POW standing at attention looking over at us. He was very pale. When the verdict was read and interpreted, it didn't sink in. His face was sort of blank. It seemed like an eternity. Man, the light on that man's face, I'll never forget. Undoubtedly, he thought that everyone else had been condemned to die, he was the last one, automatically he figured he would die. He just couldn't believe it, the tears and smiles of joy! Unforgettable! I was very happy to be on the jury that we could bring in 'not guilty' as the verdict.[28]

Not everyone in Medicine Hat was as pleased as Millen at the outcome. Residents had accepted with equanimity the presence of 12,000 POWs within their city limits, but Nuremberg and the revelation of Nazi killings of Canadian prisoners after D-Day had darkened the mood. When Millen and the other jurors left the court house and for some time afterward, they were jeered as "Nazi lovers."[29]

* * *

In the early hours of June 27, 1946, Sheriff Toombs of the Lethbridge judicial district, Herbert Holt, warden of the provincial jail in Lethbridge, and J.S. Wray, the jail's surgeon, put their names to documents that testified to the execution of Werner Schwalb. When, in the waning minutes of June 26 and the first moments of June 27, it became clear that no telegram would arrive commuting his death sentence, the executioner placed the black hood over the head of the thirty-one-year-old former member of Rommel's Afrika Korps, and positioned him over the steel trapdoor.

Schwalb, the only person to die for the killing of August Plaszek, called out in English, "My Führer, I follow thee."[30]

CHAPTER 10

The Lehmann Murder Trials

June 24 to July 2, 1946

"I am of the opinion that the land comprised in the Prisoner of War Camp, No. 132, at Medicine Hat, is part of the Dominion of Canada,"

—Judge Howsen

FOUR MEN STOOD ACCUSED of murdering Corporal Dr. Karl Lehmann, each in his early thirties, and each with an impressive military record.

Bruno Perzenowski, a tall well-built man with a long face, had been a policeman in Elbing, then a city in Germany, before joining the Luftwaffe in 1935. He served with distinction, earning an Iron Cross, First Class before his Heinkel bomber was shot down over Wales in April 1941. After spending fifteen days in a hospital for head and spinal injuries, he was transferred to a British POW camp and later to Canada.

Sergeant Major Heinrich Busch, a dark-haired man with features that Leni Riefenstahl, Hitler's favourite film director, would have lingered over with her camera, had worked as a clerk in a clothing store prior to joining the Luftwaffe in 1934. He earned an Iron Cross First Class and an Iron Cross Second Class before his twenty-sixth flight, when his bomber got tangled in the wires of a barrage balloon (one of the common defences against aircraft attack) and crashed over England on February 18, 1941.

Flight Sergeant Wilhelm "Willy" Müeller's plane didn't survive the first day of the Greenock Blitz over Scotland in early May 1941, and because his parachute did not fully deploy, he almost didn't survive his fall to earth. He spent six months in two different English hospitals recovering from broken arms and several vertebrae before being sent to a POW camp in Bury, a camp near Manchester, England and, later to Canada. A talented artist and well liked, Müeller had completed eighty-six flights before being shot down and had earned both an Iron Cross Second Class and an Iron Cross First Class.

Staff Sergeant Walter Wolf enlisted in the Wehrmacht in 1937. Part of the invasion force that conquered France in 1940 and later transferred to the Afrika Korps, he earned an Iron Cross Second Class and was captured at the Haifa Pass on January 17, 1942. Arriving in Canada later that year, he worked for several months in a Manitoba lumber camp before he was moved to Medicine Hat. He was fluent in English and married with no children.

While planning for the trial of the four men accused of murdering Karl Lehmann, the crown considered filing joint charges against them. Perhaps because this had been tried—and failed after defence objections—in the Plaszek case, crown prosecutor Walter Gow decided to bring separate charges against Perzenowski, Busch, Müeller and Wolf. Ironically, when Gow noted during his first outline of the case that most of the facts he would cite as evidence against Perzenowski would be presented in three subsequent trials, George E.A. Rice, the defence lawyer chosen by the federal government to represent the accused, averred that they should have been charged together. The trial began on June 24, 1946, before a jury of six men.[1]

Unbeknownst to Rice, he almost ended up on trial himself. Seven weeks earlier, the crown considered charging him with obstruction of justice for allegedly tampering with a crown witness. In reporting to his superiors on the background of this matter, RCMP Corporal Bull said that on May 2, the second day of the preliminary hearing for Bruno Perzenowski, Rice had asked to speak with the four defendants prior to the opening of court. "I permitted Mr. Rice to interview these men privately as I believed I was entitled to do," wrote the RCMP corporal. (Rice was, after all, their lawyer.) Later that day when Wolf was called as a crown witness, "he refused to give testimony" against his fellow defendant. The next day, Müeller and Busch also refused to give evidence against Perzenowski. This clearly surprised the prosecutor, Gow, who immediately ordered that the POWs "be kept apart and not permitted to communicate with anyone."[2]

Gow believed Rice had given the defendants instructions not to testify for the crown, which would have violated Section 180 of the Criminal Code. Gow wrote the RCMP that he considered the matter "an emergency and urgent," and that he had also written to the deputy attorney general of Alberta to consider charging Rice for "having obstructed the aims of justice."[3]

In addition to writing his letters, Gow instructed Corporal Bull to interview Walter Wolf, Willy Müeller, and Heinrich Busch, "not as clients of Mr. Rice but as probable witnesses in any action that might be taken against Mr. Rice."[4] The RCMP investigator obliged. The three prisoners each told him essentially the same story. Rice had met with the four POWs twice before the proceedings against Perzenowski, the first to stand trial, began. At each meeting, when the issue of their giving evidence came up, Rice declined to give them advice. He impressed on them, said Wolf, "that we were all in the same position" and encouraged them "to make a decision on the evidence we should give." An intelligent young man who, before joining the army in 1937 had been a financial inspector, Wolf pointed out that since he was one of Rice's clients, he "did not feel it was fair that [Rice] should defend one of his clients against the evidence of the others."[5] Wolf told Rice that he had decided not to give evidence against the others and that he had reached that decision on his own. Müeller's and Busch's statements said the same for themselves. The RCMP found no evidence of corruption of witnesses and no charges were laid against Rice.

* * *

The prosecutor headed into this first of the Lehmann trials with an advantage the crown had lacked in the Plaszek case. Gow had signed confessions from all four of the accused. The first jury wouldn't learn this until the trial was well along however. The prosecution still had to build its case and it would need more than confessions to win convictions. The question the defence would ask again and again in all four trials was whether the accused POWs were within their rights—as German soldiers following orders—to kill a man in their midst who was considered a traitor. It was a killing to be sure. But was it unlawful?

Moments after the tall, long-faced Perzenowski pleaded "not guilty" to the charge that he "did unlawfully murder Karl Lehmann," and before his plea was entered into the court records, Rice jumped to his feet to object. He was questioning the very foundation of the trial: the competency of Justice Howson's court to hear the case. "The accused is a prisoner of war and this offence, if any was committed in a prisoner of war camp, should be tried by a military court martial," Rice told the judge. "You have no jurisdiction to try him."[6]

Howson asked if Rice intended to make an argument. "Not at the present time, my Lord," he replied. He simply wanted the objection noted, and it was—before Howson overruled it. Citing the Alberta Appeals Court's rejection of a similar argument in the Plaszek murder case, Howson held that "this Court has jurisdiction to try this or any other offence against the Criminal Code of Canada."[7]

Howson then turned to Perzenowski, and asked in the stilted language of the law, "How say you to this charge?"

His answer to Judge Howson's question was "not guilty." After the clerk of the court repeated the question, Perzenowski again answered "not guilty."[8] To confirm he had heard the plea correctly, the clerk asked, "Hearken to your plea as the court records it, you plead not guilty as within charged." The seldom used word "hearken" was just close enough to its German root "*Horchen*" for Perzenowski to understand.

Gow opened his case by flattering the jury. After telling its members they should wipe from their minds anything they had heard about the case in the streets or in newspapers and that they must be governed solely by the evidence presented to them at trial, he said, "You will, of course, bring to bear upon that evidence your knowledge of worldly affairs as reasonable men of the world, and it is as reasonable men of the world, and experienced, that you are chosen as the jury to determine the fact in this particular case."[9]

Wanting to avoid giving grounds for a mistrial, Howson stepped in before the first witness was called to ask if Perzenowski required an interpreter. Assured by Rice that he did not, the judge allowed Gow to question RCMP officer Jonathan McConnel Campbell. The witness testified as to the veracity of the model of hut DZ, where Lehmann's body was found, and pictures of the body, its position (kneeling), the piece of rope wound around Lehmann's neck, another piece tied to the gas pipe above, a bloody rag found nearby, numerous blood stains, and the condition of Lehmann's body.

RCMP detective sergeant Jack W. Stanton followed and added grisly details to the scene. The court heard of "blood oozing from the nostrils and mouth" of the victim, of his badly swollen eyes, face, and his protruding tongue. Blood had dripped "down the front of his clothing forming a pool on the floor."[10]

Rice's cross-examination seemed almost cavalier but he could not risk letting this gruesome image become fixed in the jurors' minds. "Did you make any test as to whether this was human blood you referred to?" he asked.

"Well, I was satisfied it was human blood," said Stanton, confident in his common-sense judgment.

"It is not what you are satisfied with, it is your sworn testimony, witness, we are after," said Rice, pointing a rhetorical finger at Stanton and emphasizing the word "witness." He then upped the ante.

"You are swearing to God it was blood. You made no test to see what kind of blood it was."[11]

Rice's aim, of course, was not to suggest Stanton had perjured himself or somehow had missed that a pig's blood had ended up beneath Lehmann's body. His aim was to lead at least one juror to think that there might be an important technical lapse in the RCMP's investigation, and thereby, plant the seed of reasonable doubt.

Changing direction, Rice asked about the politics inside the wire with a seemingly innocuous question: "I suppose as a police officer you hear lots of reports as to what has been going on in these camps?"

THE LEHMANN MURDER TRIALS

"A certain amount," Stanton answered.

"I believe that there was a General Smidt [Schmidt] held in a prisoner of war camp here about that time?" pursued Rice.

"Well, I [can] answer that only from hearsay information," said Stanton.

"Well, that's good enough," said the lawyer.[12]

Rice, Gow, and Howson then exchanged views on whether or not hearsay information was "good enough," with Howson determining: "The witness can say whether or not he knows it or whether it is pure hearsay. He is an experienced witness."[13]

Witness Stanton continued and confirmed for Rice that Canadian authorities were fully aware of how the camp Gestapo worked: "There was a rumour in circulation that [Schmidt] had issued certain orders to the German prisoners."

The nature of the orders, according to Stanton, was that "any traitor they might find they should dispose of them."

"They should be disposed of?" asked Rice.

"And make it appear as if it was a suicide."[14]

This fit neatly into the defence attorney's contention that the killing had been ordered. Rice hoped that the jury would make allowance for the military concept of following orders, especially when the man ordered killed was a traitor.

Testimony from the next three witnesses, POW Wilhelm Dittrich; coroner, Sydney Francis McEwen; and undertaker, John Jessop Nott, laid the foundation for most of Gow's case. Dittrich identified the body in RCMP photos as Lehmann. McEwen concluded that Lehmann died of asphyxiation. Nott testified as to the condition of the body and its disposal.

* * *

What the crown wanted from POW Albert Schurr in the witness box was straight forward. He was the first to see Lehmann's body hanging in the hut, where he had gone to study for future university exams. He alerted camp leader Wendt to the death and was sent by him to find Captain Dr. Maximillian Nolte. Before the court heard any of this, however, Schurr surprised everyone by saying, "I do not wish to swear on the Bible."[15]

Justice Howson, who had dealt calmly with a similar refusal by Sergeant Major Wilhelm Weidemann in the Plaszek trials, asked why Schurr didn't "wish to swear on the Bible?"

"That is my conviction," said Schurr, hardly charting a path forward.

"Well, how do you take an oath then, or how do you pledge yourself in Court, by affirming?" asked Howson.

After some back and forth, Schurr made his oath *sans* Bible. It was rendered into English by translator Captain Anthony Robert Lendi as, "I swear before Almighty God that before this Court I shall speak the truth, the pure truth, and nothing but the truth."[16]

Gow took what he expected from Schurr and handed the witness over to Rice, who steered Schurr in a new direction: "And while you were [in Camp 132] were there any such things as sexual crimes, I think you call it?"

"Oh yes. There were some but I didn't pay much attention to it," said Schurr.

"And they were dealt with by your camp spokesman and his assistants?"[17]

Although Schurr again said he didn't pay much attention to such crimes because he did not participate in them, he did confirm that the camp leader and his assistants were responsible for enforcing laws against homosexual activity. He also confirmed that men whom Rice termed as "homosexual perverts or men that were guilty of that crime" were brought before courts of honour and stripped of their decorations, if not worse.[18]

The next witness, POW Victor Freelandt, told Rice that after one degradation ceremony, some men beat the POW convicted of homosexuality (Sergeant Hermann Koerber, no relation to the POW Walter Koerber who testified during the Plaszck trials) because they were "angry over the fact that they had been living with such a swine."[19]

"And by homosexual crimes, just what do you mean by that?" asked Rice.[20]

"I believe it is the same as it is in English."

"Buggery, do you know what that means?"

"There is no translation to the word 'buggery,' sir. It is homosexual practice. That is the translation."

"Sodomy, do you know what that is?"

"No. I don't know."

"I am referring to Tremeear's Criminal Code, 'Buggery.' This offence, called sodomy, is defined as carnal copulation against nature by human being with each other or with a beast."

"I understand that."[21]

The point of the learned discussion of Tremeear's definition of "Buggery" was that a Nazi court of honour operated in the Medicine Hat POW camp or, as Rice put it to the witness, "your own court, consisting of German prisoners of war, dealt with [sexual crime] and punished the culprit."[22]

Both Freelandt and Schurr testified that it was the responsibility of camp leader Wendt or men operating under his instructions to carry out justice in these matters. With the thoroughness that earned him the admiration of his legal colleagues, Rice continued to explore the functioning of this extra-Canadian legal system, and soon had Freelandt saying, "Yes, it went according to German criminal law, military law."[23]

With that settled, Rice turned his attention to Lehmann, not his sexual habits but his loyalty to the Reich. Posing for a moment as the proverbial "old country lawyer," Rice asked, "I believe you told me when you were examined before that Lehmann was regarded by members of the camp as a traitor?" Freelandt agreed, and Rice continued.[24]

"And I think you also said that Lehmann had been accused of bringing false information into the camp and disseminating it?"

Freelandt told the Court "that while in England Lehmann had spread false news" and that "he had met with strong resistance in the camp in consequence." He had "almost been hanged"[25] in the Oldham POW camp [in Britain] for it.[26]

Not content to let Rice's view of the camp leadership take root, prosecutor Gow asked to re-examine the witness. Soon he had Freelandt admitting that his contention that Sergeant Hermann Koerber was humiliated and stripped of his rank for homosexual activity was based on hearsay. Gow asked how Freelandt knew Lehmann was a traitor. The witness's claim that this was "practically a general topic in the camp" cut little ice. His claim that fellow defendant Walter Wolf had confirmed Lehmann's guilt cut even less. Asked whether anyone else had told him the same, Freelandt said, "I believe but I cannot say exactly. It is quite a long time ago since. That was in 1943, 1944,"[27] His testimony left what Rice had constructed a smoking ruin.

Instead of dismissing the witness, Howson used his prerogative to ask: "All that you have told us is that there was gossip in the camp that Lehmann was a traitor?"

Freelandt's answered affirmatively, adding that he could not remember any names of other POWs who had told him about Lehmann's traitorous actions. Howson wanted to know how long before Lehmann's killing the witness had heard these rumours? "I cannot say exactly," said Freelandt." Quite some time. Quite some time."[28] All of which served to underline Gow's demolition of the defence on this point.

* * *

Alerted by Schurr's refusal to take an oath on the Bible, Justice Howson watched carefully as other POWs were sworn in, and found POW Werner Neumann's attempt to kiss the Bible wanting.

"Did you kiss the Bible or did you kiss your thumb?"

"Thumb."

"Well. Just take the Bible in your hands and we will have no more thumb kissing here."

The transcript here breaks from its usual structure to indicate, as if a stage direction: "The witnessed kissed the Bible."[29]

Scarcely mollified, Howson asked, "Why did you kiss your thumb?"

After some attempts to excuse the thumb kiss as a result of the positioning of the Bible in his hand, Neumann cut to what he thought was the heart of the matter: "I understood it was just a symbol and I thought it would be just the same."

Howson was having none of it. Did Neumann believe in God? Neumann said he did. Then, thundered the judge, "why did you kiss your thumb in this court?" Neumann fell back on the positioning of his thumb vis-à-vis the Bible. Howson could barely contain his anger: "You had better learn that when you come into this court and you are asked to take an oath that the Bible means something in Canada, if it doesn't mean anything anywhere else to you."[30]

(The religious sensitivities of the court were strained almost to the breaking point a week later when POW Hermann Schweizer explained to Howson that rather than swear an oath on the Bible he preferred to take his "on the sword."

"I beg your pardon?" asked Howson.

"On the sword."

"Is the sword of more importance to you than the Bible?"

"Yes."

"You believe in the sword rather than the Bible, do you?"

"Yes."

"Do you believe in God?"

"No."

"What religion have you?"

"None."

"You have no religion?"

"No."[31]

Likely in deference to the sensitivities of its Christian readers, the *Medicine Hat News* made no mention of this exchange. By doing so, the paper passed up the chance to show how old Prussian militaristic norms had persisted in the Wehrmacht even though Nazi ideology and rites differed significantly from those associated with Prussia.)

Once Neumann had affirmed that he would tell the truth, Gow had him identify himself as a teacher of history and sports before turning to events on the night of September 10–11, 1944. The witness remembered the evening well, as a group of men was preparing to leave in the morning for the POW camp at Neys. Perzenowski had come to him and asked "that I should go to Corporal Lehmann and tell him that after the evening meal, after supper, he should come to the school room."[32] (The pretext, the court heard from different POWs in different trials, was always that Lehmann needed to sign certificates of study for the transferred POWs.)

Rice ignored Neumann's bit part in the Lehmann drama and focused instead on getting the POW to talk about camp discipline. "And what happened regarding persons that committed any homosexual offence in the camp?" he asked. They were punished and stripped of rank, said Neumann. Pushed further, he admitted that they were also beaten.[33]

Having established again that the camp leadership punished homosexuals and condoned violence against them, Rice asked the witness: "Do you know anything about Lehmann?" Neumann said he knew him, and that "he was regarded as a traitor" as well as a leader of the camp communists.[34]

POW Heinz Riehme's testimony brought the courtroom into the hut where Perzenowski, Wolf, Busch, and Müeller awaited Lehmann. Once Lehmann arrived and sat down on a bench, Perzenowski began speaking with him. Riehme couldn't remember Perzenowski's exact words, but he asked Lehmann "what he knew of riotous organizations in the camp." Before Riehme could answer, Justice Howson interjected: "What he knew of what?" Riehme responded with the same words. Driving this home for the jury, Gow repeated: "A riotous organization in the camp." Riehme wasn't sure exactly how Lehmann responded but, after Howson confirmed he could convey the substance of Lehmann's words, Riehme said, "He replied in the negative."[35]

"Well, then, what happened following that?"[36] asked Gow, coyly underplaying the moment. He knew what was coming next from the preliminary hearings.

Riehme said the "following incidents happened so fast and in such quick succession that I cannot remember all the details." What he did remember was that the bench on which Perzenowski and Lehmann sat fell over. "There was general turmoil. I first saw Sergeant Major Busch and then someone shouted, 'The rope.'"[37] The witness saw Busch fasten a rope to a pipe on the ceiling. (At Busch's trial two weeks later, Riehme would repeat this story, adding the gruesome detail that after the accused tied the rope to the gas pipe and Lehmann's body was allowed to drop, the rope broke, and Lehmann's bloody and unconscious body crashed to the floor.)

As for the actions of the accused, Perzenowski, Riehme recalled him having a cloth in his hand and bending down near Lehmann's body. He did not say what Perzenowski did with the cloth, likely because several RCMP officers had already testified that when they found Lehmann's body, a bloody cloth had been shoved in his mouth.

The defence lawyer's cross-examination concentrated on camp discipline. Rice asked Riehme what he knew of homosexual crimes in the camp and how they were punished. In the course of this questioning, for the first time the court heard that every evening the POWs received news from Germany from one of the camp's hidden radios. Even more importantly, the Hatters learned that the thousands of POWs who had lived just down the street, were issued orders over these radios. "And were you bound by those orders that came in over the radio from Germany?" Rice asked. The witness answered that the orders, from military sources, had to be obeyed.[38]

Rice asked Riehme if an order had come into the camp over the radio shortly after the failed attempt to assassinate Hitler. Before the witness could answer, Gow jumped to his feet: "I must object to this question, my Lord. The witness has already stated that he did not hear the radio, therefore he is not in a position to answer that question." The judge disagreed, noting that it was up to the jury to decide how much weight to put on the testimony. But Howson went on to raise what amounted to an epistemological point that threatened Rice's defence. "The natural thing is that if he did not know where the radio was, if he never heard the radio, he does not know if the message came from Germany or Medicine Hat." Rice sought to undercut Howson's philosophical point—how does Riehme know what he knows?—by referencing something few in the dominion of Canada, least of all Justice Howson, would deny. "My Lord, we might not know personally there is a King of England. We believe in it and act on it. In a prisoner of war camp, they are not advertising to everyone in there where a hidden radio is."[39]

After the clerk of the court re-read the question about orders in the wake of the 1944 Hitler bomb plot, Rice asked the witness: "An order was published, and the effect of that order was that traitors were to be summarily disposed of?... That if [even] a private found an officer to be a traitor, it was his right and duty to immediately shoot him?"[40] Riehme agreed.

* * *

Had the Jewish German cultural critic Walter Benjamin not perished, (on the Spanish border in 1940 while attempting to flee Vichy France), he would have recognized the legal context in which the POWs lived. Hitler was more than just the holder of executive power, as Benjamin would have put it. As supreme warlord, Hitler embodied and enacted a kind of sovereignty that took shape in the Baroque period (1600–1750), when the antecedents of the German military code were formulated by Frederick the Great's military lawyers. "The ruler," Benjamin writes with reference to a series of *Trauerspielen* (mourning plays, not unlike *Hamlet*), "is designated from the outset as the holder of dictatorial power if war, revolt, or other catastrophes should lead to a state of emergency." The legal "state of emergency" is meant to achieve "a complete stabilization, an ecclesiastical and political restoration... [in which a prince's] constitutional position guarantees the continuity of the community, flourishing of feats of arms and in the sciences, in the arts and in its Church."[41]

It follows that once Hitler declared a state of emergency, Perzenowski, who believed Lehmann to be a traitor, had no choice but to arrange for him to be destroyed: that many of the 900 men about to be shipped to Neys were either members or supporters of the Gestapo and particularly loyal to the führer added an urgency to the move against Lehmann.

Knowing that this extraordinary legal notion, that a soldier of lower rank could judge one of higher rank, ran counter to what the jury and everyone else in the court knew about Canadian military law, Rice put the Wehrmacht's military disciplinary manual into evidence. It was marked Exhibit Twenty-Four. The court translator read a section of the manual that would end up occupying nine legal-sized pages in the transcript.

While Hitler's government had augmented the manual, the bulk of it dated to before the First World War. However odious the Nazi regime, it was the legal government of Germany, having been installed by President Paul von Hindenburg in January 1933, and it had passed the usual tests of legitimacy by being recognized by Britain, Canada,[42] France, the United States, and, after the Molotov-Ribbentrop pact of 1939, the Soviet Union.

The following were among the most important sections of the disciplinary manual read into the record:

- "It is applicable to all persons who are under military discipline, that is not only for soldiers and employees of the army... That is for those on non-active service but also for persons who are with

the army in the field of operations and prisoners of war, also it extends to foreigners and Germans in the field of operations."
- "The laws regarding disciplinary action in the field extend over prisoners of war who have been ordered by the highest-ranking officer at their domicile [i.e., country in which they are held or POW camp] that the laws of war exist for them."
- "An order is an expression of will. It is a demand for a certain behaviour on the basis of personal legal relation of power."
- "There is a death penalty in the armed forces for the following… this fact is especially directed against all pacifist attempts to weaken the morale of the people or undermine discipline [in the army]."
- "Mere doubt about the purpose [of an order] by his superior does not entitle or oblige the lesser rank to disobey the given order."
- "Whoever commits in the field treason to his country… will be punishable by death for treason. Offenders can be soldiers and employees of the army, prisoners of war, foreigners or Germans in the war theatre. He who in Germany or as a German in a foreign country during the war assists an enemy power during the war… can be punished by death or life imprisonment."
- "He who in the inland or as a German in foreign countries incites or acts against the German Reich and assists the power with which the German Reich is in a state of war will be punished by death or life imprisonment."
- "Prisoners of war are subject to all regulations and law for all offences committed during their captivity."

Another section of the manual must have suggested to Prosecutor Gow and Judge Howson that, at least from the German military standpoint (which still governed the POWs, according to the Geneva Convention, as did Canadian law) the legitimacy of the entire trial was at stake: "A surrender of prisoners of war from the military courts to the civilian courts is not tolerable."[43]

These clauses bore directly on the question of *mens rea*, or criminal intent, although neither lawyer used the term at trial. The common law maxim, *actus reus non facit reum nisi mens sit rea*, holds that an individual is not culpable for an illegal act unless he or she has a guilty mind (or, after the development of the defence of insanity, is capable of forming criminal intent). If Perzenowski owed fealty to the Reich, he could not be guilty of murder, for the killing was indistinguishable from an execution that a military tribunal might order, or the shooting of a deserter on a battle field by a second lieutenant. German military code forbade disobeying an order even if its veracity was doubted. Asked if any of the men involved in the killing were "just carrying out an order," Riehme said, "Yes, I am certain of it."[44]

As an answer to Rice's military disciplinary manual, Prosecutor Gow placed on the record the Geneva Convention of 1929, the cover of which was embossed with the words, "Ottawa, Edmond Cloutier, Printer to the King's Most Excellent Majesty, 1942." It had been proclaimed by the president of the German Reich (of the defunct Weimar Republic), the president of the United States, and the king of Great Britain, Ireland. Howson allowed the convention to become Exhibit Twenty-Five.

Gow was interested in only two articles of the Geneva Convention. The first, Article 45, stated that "prisoners of war shall be subject to the laws, regulations, and orders in force in the armed forces of the detaining power."[45]

"Of what power?" asked Howson.

"The detaining power," said Gow, no doubt silently thanking the judge for underscoring his point. He continued to read: "Any act of insubordination shall render [POWs] liable to the measures prescribed by such orders, regulations, and orders" of the detaining power.[46]

Gow also read Article 2 of the convention into the record: "Prisoners of war are in the power of the hostile government, but not the individuals or formations which captured them."[47] This was meant to protect soldiers taken on the battlefield from abuse, reprisals, and theft of personal items by the capturing soldiers. Effectively, it distinguished POWs from regular criminals, treating them more as a sort of political prisoner; their offence, if that be the correct word, was being on the wrong side on the battlefield. With that, Gow delivered his "checkmate" to Rice's introduction of the German military disciplinary manual.

* * *

Up to now, the jury was still unaware that the man on trial (and the three other accused POWs) had confessed to killing Lehmann. Knowing that each confession would be challenged by the defence, Gow went about his business to this point as if the admissions did not exist. He established who had been killed, the method by which he had been brought to his death, as well as the motive and opportunity of the accused murderers. With his next witness, POW Max Voigt, Gow would show the court how the murder occurred. Before hearing this, Howson had to navigate yet again the tricky question of oath taking. Voight refused to take an oath kissing the Bible. He would only hold the Bible. Howson grudgingly allowed this improvisation, after which Voight told the court why Lehmann had fallen off the bench while sitting beside Perzenowski in the hut: "Willy Müeller hit Lehmann with his fist in the face."[48]

During the tumult that followed, said the witness, Wolf jumped on Lehmann to hold him down so that his hands could be tied behind his back. Ordered away from the scene by Müeller, Voigt had taken one last look and saw Lehmann "hanging near the wall from a rope."[49]

Predictably, by this point, Rice ignored Voigt's evidence about the killing and instead focused on the requirements of German POWs to follow orders from superior officers and Germany itself. Voigt told the court, "For prisoners of war in foreign country prisoner of war camps, the regulations are even strengthened in relation to this German military law." When asked how much time should elapse between someone being found to be a traitor and his punishment, Voigt answered, "He should be shot immediately."[50]

"And, if you didn't have a shooting iron [firearm] what were you to do, hang him?" asked Rice.

"According to the opportunity offered at the moment," agreed the witness.[51]

Rice seamlessly moved from the regulatory requirement to execute traitors to the question of punishing homosexuals in the camp. Voigt confirmed what the court had already heard about Hermann Koerber's degradation ceremony. He also testified, and this was new to the court, that the degradation ceremony involved three other POWs. Voigt's reticence to specify the sexual offence Koerber and the others had committed led to another reading of Tremeear's definition of "buggery." The witness further testified that Koerber had been so badly beaten that Voigt had to take him to the hospital.

In almost every examination or cross-examination at the Plaszek and Lehmann trials, the lawyers began their questioning of POW witnesses by asking about their backgrounds: where they were born, where they had served, where they were captured, how they came to Canada, and when they arrived in Medicine Hat. But Rice waited to run over this ground with Voigt. The POW was a member of the U-boatwaffe, perhaps the most respected, and feared branch of the Nazi forces, and the only one to attack Canada (in 1942 and 1944 during the Battle of the St. Lawrence). Though irrelevant to the trial, Rice had Voigt boast of helping to "sink 70,000 tons of shipping." It was a means of bolstering the prestige of the witness, a lowly machine technician, when he testified that Müeller said the command to deal with Lehmann "was an order from higher up."[52]

In his redirect examination, Gow had Voigt cover Perzenowski's first words to the victim on entering the hut: "Corporal Lehmann, sit down on that bench," as well as Müeller's punch. Voigt said that he also watched as Wolf jumped on the stunned victim and, moments later, saw Lehmann hanging from a rope. But it was what Voigt said about Koerber or, to be more precise, the men who beat him up for homosexuality, that would have discomfited the defence. "Four of these men were put before a Canadian court—I don't know what kind of a court it was—and they were sentenced to one year's imprisonment."[53] Gow had the witness repeat that a Canadian court had exercised jurisdiction over POWs in Camp 132, even though the assault in question, which went by the bland name of "comradely admonition," was part of a degradation ceremony under the aegis of camp leadership.

The punishment for homosexuality would continue to be important to the trial, albeit for different reasons for the prosecution and the defence. Gow believed degradation ceremonies and beatings were evidence of the Gestapo's terror in Camp 132. Rice presented them as the legitimate (if regrettable) machinery of army discipline. As a member of the Gestapo in another camp justified the beatings: "I give a comrade such an admonition, it is proof that I have not given him up altogether, but I have still some hope for him, and by beating him up I am bringing him to his senses."[54] Rice was able to show that the

Canadian camp officials sometimes turned a blind eye to the Gestapo's "admonitions."

* * *

The narration of the crime in Perzenowski's trial, as well as in the other three, was straight forward, largely because of Willy Müeller. The first of the accused men to testify, Müeller was also the first to publicly confess his role in killing Karl Lehmann. He told the court that Perzenowski informed him that a "court" of three or four men had determined that Lehmann was "the head" of a communist group seeking to overthrow camp leadership. Perzenowski also told Müeller "he had received an order from the highest authority to remove" Lehmann, and that Müeller had to "assist" him. The good-natured Müeller asked, "Why me?" Perzenowski said Müeller was "a decent fellow, a good soldier, and a strong man."[55] It was clear that while Müeller had not read the order that Perzenowski purported to have in hand, he felt bound by German military law to follow what he had been told was an order. Failure to do so, he knew, could result in charges against him.[56]

Müeller recruited a few other men to help entice Lehmann to the hut the evening of September 10. Perzenowski and Wolf were waiting in the hut, and joined after a time by Busch and POWs Voigt and Riehme. According to Müeller, Wolf said, "I hope [Lehmann] will come soon and if he doesn't come, I will get him." A short time later, someone said, "He is coming," and Perzenowski went to greet the man who had been teaching him languages.[57]

Müeller further testified that Perzenowski led Lehmann to a bench and began asking him what he knew about communistic activities in the camp. Lehmann's expected answer, "*Nein*," was the signal for Müeller to drive his right fist into Lehmann's face. The upper cut, which Müeller, the camp's boxing instructor, told the court was used to knock a man out, dropped Lehmann to the floor. Wolf, Busch and Müeller grabbed the prone man and Müeller took a rope with a slip knot out of his pocket. He and Busch slipped the noose around Lehmann's neck while Perzenowski stuffed a rag in the victim's bloody mouth. "Then we lifted Corporal Lehmann and I believe it was Sergeant Major Busch, but I cannot say exactly, who then fastened the rope or tied the rope" to a gas pipe.[58]

Gow ended his examination of Müeller by asking him why Perzenowski, the man on trial, had met with him earlier in the day. Müeller answered that there was only one possibility: "To kill Lehmann."[59]

Rice's examination of Müeller added little of substance to the court record. He again asked questions about homosexuality in the camp, radio messages, orders to kill traitors, and Müeller's understanding of his requirement to follow what Perzenowski said was an order. It may have seemed small beer given that Perzenowski faced hanging, but Rice made sure to get Müeller on record that Perzenowski "always spoke rather well of [Lehmann]" and said he was a good teacher.[60] This, combined with Müeller's knowledge of rumours of a communist revolt in camp were intended as further evidence that Perzenowski (and, by extension, the other assailants) were, as Hitler's paladins were "working towards the Führer," or seeking to fulfill Hitler's will, when they eliminated Lehmann.[61]

* * *

Once Müeller vacated the witness stand, the prosecution called former camp leader Wilhelm Wendt who gave some valuable testimony on the inner-workings of POW leadership. He explained that he was responsible for discipline in Camp 132 and answered a question that had been lingering since 1943 when RCMP Corporal Bull noted in a file the "enigmatic" nature of Captain Dr. Maximillian Nolte's power: "As far as the disciplinary powers are concerned," said Wendt, "there was only one man above me and that was Dr. Nolte who, as an officer, was in charge of disciplinary powers in the camp." Only an officer, he continued, "could be responsible for discipline among German soldiers."[62]

After Wendt explained that as camp leader/spokesman, he was responsible for transmitting Commandant Bull's orders to his fellow POWs, prosecutor Gow introduced a document he wanted admitted as evidence. Rice was quick to object. "I don't know what is in it," he told Judge Howson, adding that the defence was entitled to know what evidence would be adduced. Howson agreed and said Rice could look at it. That wasn't enough for Rice, however, who wanted the document translated. Gow offered to make everything clear in the course of questioning Wendt: "If my learned friend will just give me the time." But Rice was in no mood to compromise: "You are asking to have it marked as an exhibit. I object to it. I think the time to have it marked is when we know what it is."[63] Howson ordered the document translated and adjourned the court until the next morning.

At 10 a.m. the next day, June 27, the court re-convened and Rice immediately withdrew his objection to Gow's document, which was now introduced into evidence. The translation showed it had neither bark nor bite, which the somewhat embarrassed prosecutor admitted to the court: "Until such time as I had seen the translation, I thought it was an order but it appears to be more in the nature of a communication to the prisoners of war at Medicine Hat, and signed by Colonel Bull, the commandant at the time, May 10, 1943."[64]

Howson was unamused: "If it is only taking out time we might as well not be bothered with it. I had no idea it was a goodwill letter or anything like that. I had a notion it was a regulation affecting the prisoners of war." Howson asked the jury if they wanted to hear it. Gow must have inwardly cringed when he heard a juror say, "I don't think it is of any interest to the jury, my Lord."[65]

Gow tried to get his case back on track by asking Wendt a number of questions about camp discipline and investigations, all designed to show that Wendt issued orders and investigations were carried out. The most salient point concerned an investigation of Lehmann for "conducting certain meetings in a hut" during which he read news from Canadian papers to other POWs, likely after D-Day. Wendt considered this to be a minor infraction and, instead of punishing him, warned him "that in the future he should leave such things alone."[66]

For a prosecution witness, Wendt gave the jury little to chew on. Rice, on the other hand, dined out on the former camp spokesman. He had Wendt tell the court: "we punished refusals to obey orders in the camp and offences against Canadian orders, for instance, the non-saluting of officers, the hanging of blankets in the huts, the taking of lumber from empty huts or the entry into empty huts."[67] The significance of this testimony was that Canadian authorities recognized and, in fact, relied upon the Gestapo to maintain discipline in Camp 132.

"Let us step a little deeper into the mire," said Rice. "What about homosexual crimes, they came under you?" After referencing "some light cases of this nature," Wendt said Koerber's case bordered on the criminal "as he had tried to debauch some of the younger soldiers in the camp." Rice wanted the issue crystal clear: "That is to commit buggery with them, is it?" No one in the courtroom had to wait for the translation when Wendt answered "*Ja.*"[68]

What of the Canadian authorities, Rice asked? Did they expect "you to deal with those cases?" Again, Wendt answered "yes," adding a rhetorical question that indicated his power. "Where would things have ended if I had not stepped in?"[69]

Sensing he was on a roll, Rice quickly followed up: "But it was the Canadian authorities that knew about it and wanted you to handle it?" Wendt didn't quite say that Commandant Bull turned a blind eye to comradely admonitions and degradation ceremonies, but he went far enough: "Of these cases, the Canadian authorities knew very little and we took very little or hardly anything at all as we intended to deal with these matters ourselves, taking the slogan that the dirty linen should be washed in your own house."[70]

(During Busch's trial, Rice again cross-examined Wendt, and asked whether some of the "perverts" were "let out of the camp after they had been arrested" by the Gestapo, as was the case with Koerber who had "defected." Wendt said yes. Howson stepped in to ask, "Did you sign an order for the execution of Lehmann?" Wendt denied doing so and said that he had "not been able to determine" who had ordered the execution. Seizing the moment, Rice interjected, "It is a military secret," establishing what he wanted to portray, that POWs remained military actors responsible to the chain of command.[70]

In Müeller's trial, the same issues caused tempers to flare. In an intervention that today would almost certainly be grounds for a mistrial, the bench asked Wendt, "Witness, why do you assume that in Canada the authorities recognize homosexual offences as a proper thing [i.e., there being no punishment for homosexual activity]?" No doubt thinking of the protection extended to Koerber, Wendt answered, "Because offenders of homosexual crimes are not or have not been punished." Howson harrumphed: "Before you leave this country, I want to tell you that I do not propose that you will stand up here in a Canadian Court and insult the Canadian people or the Canadian authorities, and if that is your German mind, you had better change it. Now that is my advice to you."[72]

Wendt's response, an attempt to pour oil on troubled waters, failed miserably. "I did not intend to cast any slur on the Canadian people, but it is a fact that these men had not been punished by the Canadian courts, and, therefore, I have come to the conclusion of that kind, and I do beg the court that it not be interpreted as an insult on the Canadian people." The courtroom, however, was Howson's. "I have heard all I want from you. You can go."[73])

Since Rice was arguing that Perzenowski was following orders, it might have seemed strange that the defence would let Wendt testify that he had not ordered a second investigation of Lehmann, still less his execution: "And there was no officer in the camp who had any power or authority to order the death of Lehmann?"

"In my opinion, No."

"So that those who did kill Lehmann just took it upon themselves to kill him?"

Wendt's answer, which Rice would have known was coming, explained his tactics: "Yes, I assume that these men who committed the deed used the radio broadcast from Germany as their source of authority."[74]

The court had already heard that the German military disciplinary manuals demanded that soldiers not wait for orders from their superior officers to kill traitors, a point reiterated by the orders issued after the Hitler bomb plot. Wendt couldn't remember the wording of the broadcast order, but he said that "immediately upon having taken it down from the radio, [it] was spread through the camp in order to warn every man of the seriousness of the situation."[75]

Wendt went on to say that "according to the wording of the order, every soldier was not only justified but it was his duty to destroy traitors."

Speaking for many in the courtroom whose sense of legal fair play was offended by the order, Howson intervened: "You would kill them first and investigate after, according to your theory?" Wendt's answered "no," which cleared up very little.[76]

"Aren't you saying that every person who thinks that another one is a traitor has a right to destroy them?" asked Rice of Wendt.

"If according to the order issued, yes."[77]

Wendt added that his personal position was less clear cut, suggesting there was a role for due process, but Rice had got what he wanted of the witness. The fact was that under Nazi law, it likely would have made no difference if Wendt had authorized an investigation of Lehmann: simply being investigated for a crime against the state was tantamount to a finding of guilt. As legal scholar Rudolf Lehmann (no relation to the victim) wrote: "it was not the mandate of military courts to find truth as such—which did not exist—but rather to guarantee the existence of the community that had given power to the court." The court was not an independent entity, as it was in a common law jurisdiction such as Canada. Rather, it "was the most distinguished form of the Führer's orders."[78]

* * *

The next morning, the jurors had barely sat down before the crown asked that they be excluded from court for the first hearing of coming evidence. This *voir dire*, or trial within a trial, concerned not so much the veracity of the signed confessions Gow wanted to place into evidence but, rather, how they were obtained. That is, were they either coerced or given with the expectation of a favour.

The first person examined was RCMP Detective Corporal George Henry Miller, who testified that when he first interviewed Perzenowski six months earlier at the POW camp in Neys, Ontario, he gave him the standard warning: "You need not say anything. You have nothing to hope from any promise or favour and you have nothing to fear from any threat, whether or not you say anything, but that anything you do so may be used as evidence."[79]

At first, Perzenowski denied being involved in Lehmann's killing. Indeed, he stressed that he respected him. Expecting that answer, Miller led the discussion toward the question of whether "there were German regulations which would authorize the death penalty in the manner the death penalty was carried out."[80] Although his answer was not presented in court, Perzenowski appears to have again denied any involvement. Miller ended the cat-and-mouse game by slyly appealing to their shared profession:

> I finally stated… that I was rather surprised at the stand he was taking in this regard… that as a former German police officer—he had told me in the meantime that he had been in the German police force for five years—he would realize the weight of the evidence against him.[81]

Miller also appealed to the POW's pride, telling him: "I fully expected that his defence would be quite different to the flat denials that he was advancing." He told Perzenowski: "I expected that you would probably adopt the line of defence that you did the killing on the strength of orders from your superiors and were obliged to carry out those duties in the capacity of a German soldier."[82]

Miller again skipped over some of the intervening conversation, but something he said changed Perzenowski's attitude. Not long after, "the accused admitted that he gave the orders to dispose of Lehmann and that he himself was present when the crime was committed."[83]

When Miller asked if he was prepared to make a formal statement to this effect, the POW said, "I have told you I took part in the murder and you can hang me if you want to."[84]

Wanting to avoid the appearance of pressuring the witness, Miller told Perzenowski to sleep on it and that he would be provided with paper and pencil in the morning. At 8:30 a.m. the next day, Perzenowski told Miller, "I am prepared to give you a statement. You write it down and I will sign it."[85]

With this on the record, Gow asked Miller what seemed like housekeeping questions: did Perzenowski fully understood the gravity of making and signing the statement, and was the statement in Miller's handwriting the exact one signed by Perzenowski. Gow then casually asked Justice Howson to enter the signed statement as an exhibit.

The judge said, "No."

Gow argued that it was necessary for identification—to establish the veracity of the confession Perzenowski gave and signed. Howson again refused and reminded the prosecutor that the purpose of the *voir dire* was simply "to give me the opportunity of ascertaining whether or not this statement that you propose putting in is a free and voluntary one on the part of the accused, but it doesn't go in for identification."[86]

Gow proceeded with Miller and the court learned that Perzenowski did not, in fact, sign the confession on that second morning. Miller pushed him gently, suggesting that the POW think it over during the coming night, and offered "there may be something further that you wish to add to your statement."[87] The next morning, a short paragraph stating the confession was his was added to the statement and Perzenowski signed it.

Miller had a tougher time during Rice's cross-examination. "The only further evidence you wanted—be straight on this constable—all you went there for was to get a confession, isn't that right."

"Well, yes," said Miller.

"Sure," snorted Rice.

Stung, Miller backtracked, "I wouldn't say my sole purpose was to get a confession."

"It wouldn't hurt you to speak up?" said Rice.

Gow stepped in to defend the witness: "Let the man answer the question."

Ignoring Gow, Rice continued: "You went there, you had the information that he had issued the order, but what you wanted was to get an admission that he had issued the order?"

"That wasn't my absolute objective," said Miller. "I also wanted to get further information on possibly others that were implicated in the crime."

"You wanted to get that. Did you tell him that?"

"I told him in the first place that my purpose, the purpose for me being there was to make further enquiries into the murder of Dr. Lehmann."

"Yes, and your real purpose of further inquiries was to get a confession from the accused that he was the one that issued the order that helped kill Lehmann, that is right?"

"He stated that he was the one that issued the orders and that he was present when Lehmann was being killed."

"But before he denied it?"

"But before he denied it, yes."[88]

Rice suggested that Miller had leaned on the fact that Perzenowski had been a German police officer in order to push him to make a statement. "Why didn't you walk away when he told you he had nothing to do with it [Lehmann's killing]?"

"I would be a poor policeman if I did that," said Miller.[89]

Although the detective had done nothing illegal, Rice had managed to make his dealings with the POW at least look morally questionable.

The court heard much the same story from the next witness, RCMP Corporal Bull, with one exception. Rice asked why Bull had to interview Perzenowski to get another written confession a day after receiving one in the POW's own handwriting. "You went there to get a proper confession to patch up one that was no good," suggested Rice.[90]

"Yes," answered Bull.

"And then something misfired on that one, I take it."

The first confession, Bull told the court, "did not set forth quite explicitly... that it had been thoroughly explained to him the fact that he may have been acting under orders would not constitute a valid defence."[91]

"And to shorten that up, corporal, you were sent back to Medicine Hat to get a proper confession or one that the authorities figured would hold water."

"Yes."[92]

Rice also pushed Corporal Bull on other subtle pressures applied to Perzenowski and his fellow POWs. He found it significant that the suspects were kept isolated in a dark cell block, and interviewed on a Sunday, the least appropriate day of the week. To the defence, these measures amounted to psych-ops.

(Rice expressed this theory most cogently at the same stage in Wolf's trial:

> I am submitting that the circumstances surrounding the manner in which this statement was obtained were not voluntary. The accused was taken from [a POW camp] and practically put in jail. He was first questioned, and after the police could get no information from him, he was practically put into jail and kept there over-night. Then, the next day the police apparently decided that he had started to wilt a bit, although the accused

made no statement, and he was put back in jail again and kept overnight.[93])

Rice, in fact, missed an opportunity to invoke the Geneva Convention. Article 9 bars POWs from being confined or imprisoned "except as a measure indispensable for safety or health, and only so long as circumstances exist which necessitate such a measure."[94] Neither Wolf nor the other three accused POWs represented a threat to the "safety or health" of the public and there was no threat to their "safety or health" in the POW camps.

After the clerk of the court read Perzenowski's two confessions into the record, Howson said he was satisfied that they were given "freely and voluntarily" and could be presented to the jury.[95] He called for the jury to be returned to the courtroom. Bull was again put on the stand to swear to the veracity of the confession, which was then read in open court.

(The judge did more than overrule Rice's objections to entering the confessions into evidence. Howson actually quoted them in his charge to the jury in Perzenowksi's trial, as well as in the Wolf and Busch trials. Rice fought harder in Müeller's trial and managed to demonstrate that the RCMP had tried to break Müeller down: first by showing him pictures of Lehmann's broken body and the murder scene and then by telling him that his fingerprints were found on the pipe at the scene of the crime, which turned out to be, in Rice's words, "an infernal lie." The result, however, was the same. Howson allowed the crown to enter Müeller's confession into evidence.)

* * *

Although Rice cross-examined both Wolf and Müeller, he declined to put them or the other two defendants forward as witnesses for the defence.

There seemed nothing left but for the counsels to begin their summations when Rice rose and returned to the objection he had introduced at the beginning of the trial. Howson once again ordered the jury out of the courtroom.

Rice then discussed Canada's status as a detaining power and argued that Howson's court did not have jurisdiction to try Perzenowski (he would do the same at the three subsequent trials). Perzenowski, captured by the British Army, was properly a British prisoner. His presence in Canada was incidental to his status as a POW. What's more, said Rice, even if one were to grant his status in Canada was more than incidental, Canada's War Measures Act stated that if a district military officer was unable to administer a summary sentence or otherwise dispose of a case, "he shall take steps to bring the accused to trial before a military court." It was true that the statute gave the district military officer scope to communicate with civil powers "in order that the accused may be dealt with by a civil court or criminal jurisdiction." But, Rice insisted, "there is no evidence before you that the district officer commanding this district requested this court to deal with the charge against the accused." Therefore, this "court has no jurisdiction."[96]

Rice further noted that under military law, death sentences could only be passed "by the concurrence of all members" of a panel or jury "who must be five in number."[97] At a time when the general populace was more familiar with military affairs than is the case today, Rice did not have to underscore that such a court would be made up of serving military officers, not civilians, which was closer to the common law requirement that trials be held before a "jury of one's peers."

Trying a POW in a civilian court, Rice continued, was like asking a commanding officer who shot a battlefield deserter to be shipped back to Canada to stand trial for murder. "That is why the commanding officer

THE LEHMANN MURDER TRIALS

is given a discretionary power to deal with the situation, and in the field of war you cannot apply the same principles as you do in the field of peace," said Rice. "The accused here was enclosed behind barbed wire with soldiers in front of him with machine guns. They were in the field of war for all it had been transplanted to Canada."[98]

Rice finally asked the court to consider the definition of murder. He reached back two centuries to the most important synthesis of common law, Sir William Blackstone's *Commentaries on the Laws of England*: "Further, the person killed must be a reasonable creature in being and under the King's peace at the time of the killing. Therefore, to kill an alien, a Jew, or an outlaw, who are under the King's peace and protection, is as much murder as to kill the most regular-born Englishman: except he be an alien enemy in time of war."[99] Indeed, Rice added with regard to wartime foes, the "King should laugh with glee if the whole of them were killed, they are all his enemies."[100]

Rice's focused on the phrase "under the King's peace." Perzenowski (like his fellow defendants) owed no allegiance to the British crown. He was "an avowed enemy of the King, kept here during the war."[101] Could it fairly be said that he was "in the King's peace?" Prisoners of war, insisted Rice, were a special case of persons not covered under the King's peace. The rights of POWs did not spring from the common law and the King but from international covenants and the role of the protecting power.

Among the case law cited by Rice was *Queen v. Sattler* (1848), in which Lord Campbell of the criminal appeal court in England wrote, "If a prisoner-of-war, who had not given his parole [promise not to do violence], killed a sentinel in trying to escape, it would not be murder." Rather, it would be an act of war.[102] Rice moved from there to noting that no one would think of putting Perzenowski on trial for the men, women, and children killed during his other acts of war including more than sixty bombing runs over England.

Rice also brought the court back to the question of the duty owed by the POWs to Germany. By his lights, the question was settled in 1907 in *De Jager v. The Attorney General of Natal* (South Africa), in which the appeals court ruled that "British law demands of a British subject continuous allegiance to the crown even if in enemy-occupied territory." It only makes sense, Rice told the court, that "if we hold this rule of law as regarding ourselves, then we must concede that an enemy alien held in an internment camp during hostilities must be bound by continuous allegiance to the government of his country." [103]

Rice told the court that Perzenowski's deed had to be "regarded as political" rather than personal. Judge Howson asked if Perzenowski's was indeed a "political offence," and if Rice was arguing that the case should be withdrawn from the jury, or that the bench should direct the jury to deliberate on a "reduced charge." Rice answered that "the accused would be in the same position who committed a political offence in Germany and had escaped to this country. We would grant him asylum." After some back and forth, Howson asked, "What you are saying is this: that the internment camp out here is, in essence, a part of Germany?... And the law of Canada does not apply, that is what you are saying?"[104]

"That is what I am saying, my Lord."[105]

Rice then drew a distinction between a crime to rob Lehmann of gold or to have killed him to further one's own position in the camp, as opposed to Perzenowski's "patriotic motive." The defendant had "a right to do what he did, that he was carrying out an order of the German army." Rice continued:

The fact that he was in a prisoner of war camp in Medicine Hat thousands of miles away from the scene of the conflict is beside the matter. He is just the same as though he was immediately back of the lines or in the front lines… He is in the position of any other German soldier carrying out an order or carrying out the direction of the German military law…. An order came to destroy a traitor…. The fact that this camp was in a peaceful community is beside the matter. This camp was a seething hotbed of people who were the avowed enemies of our King.[106]

The defence attorney did not use the term "double bind," meaning a choice between two irreconcilable demands or courses of action. Yet, that was what Rice was describing. (He sharpened the point in Wolf's trial, stating that had the defendant not complied with the order to eliminate the traitor in Camp 132, he was liable to be shot on returning to Germany. If he did comply with the order, and Howson's court had jurisdiction, Wolf faced the prospect of being hanged for murder in Canada.) Rice suggested to Howson that given the competing legal regimes under which the accused found themselves, the judge should reduce the charge and declare that "under our civil law… all he [Perzenowski] should be found guilty of is manslaughter."[107]

The crown's rebuttal took issue with Rice's claim that the military authorities did not communicate with civil authorities, as evidenced by the camp leaders' calls to Medicine Hat's coroner and the RCMP. He dismissed Rice's claim that Canadian law did not cover the entire country, and interpreted the part of the Geneva Convention that said "prisoners of war are in the power of the hostile government, but not the individuals or formations which captured them" as allowing the transfer of authority for them to Canada from Britain (as, in practice, had occurred).[108]

As if in a game of poker, Gow saw Rice's use of the almost century-old *Statler* case and raised him with a reference to the more recent decision in *Rex v. Kaehler* (1945). In that case, Justice Stephens took issue with *Statler* and argued that obedience to the law is not administered "for the common benefit of a community of which the alleged offender is for the time being a member, but for the benefit of a community of which he is an avowed and open enemy." According to Gow, Rice erred by claiming that Lord Campbell's statement about killing a sentry being an act of war covered Perzenowski. His case much more resembled the one anatomized by Stephens: "If, however, a prisoner of war committed a crime unconnected with an attempt to recover his liberty (for instance, rape or arson), he would be liable for the same punishments as other persons."[109]

Justice Howson was curt in his rejection of Rice's application, noting at the beginning that he was "of the opinion that the land comprised in the Prisoner of War Camp, No. 132, at Medicine Hat, is part of the Dominion of Canada," and that the camp was "merely an area of land fenced in for the safe-keeping of German prisoners of war." It followed that the "law of Canada relating to criminal offences within that area is the same as applies to all other parts of Canada." Further, this "court has jurisdiction to try criminal offences committed in Alberta by those persons residing within that enclosure in the same manner as by those persons residing outside of its boundaries."[110]

* * *

The outcome of Perzenowski's trial was placed on page three of the *Medicine Hat News*, and deeper in other Canadian newspapers. The summation of Rice's defence in the *Medicine Hat News* didn't mention its most interesting part, perhaps in deference to the religious sentiments of its readers:

> You have here a man [Perzenowski] who had been going to school with a person and had no grudge against that person whatever,

THE LEHMANN MURDER TRIALS

he did not want his property, he did not want his position, he was not hurting him in the slightest until one Saturday night he wakes up to the fact, along with others, that they have a traitor in their midst, like Christ when he found Judas. If a man's patriotism when he is fighting with his back to the wall, and having flown sixty trips or more over England, over enemy territory, if that won't stir his passions then nothing will, he is just dead. That is the picture you have on this fateful ... evening.[111]

Before sending the jury to consider its verdict, as he had in the Plaszek murder trials, Howson reviewed what he found to be the key pieces of evidence pertaining to Perzenowski, explained the roll of the jury in determining the veracity of the evidence, and the law relating to murder. Sixty minutes after retiring to the jury room, the foreman reported it had reached a verdict.

"Perzenowski to Hang Oct. 16," was the headline on the city page of the July 2, 1946, *Medicine Hat News*, right up against an advertisement for Gust's Food Store, "Medicine Hat's Popular Food Market," listing hot house tomatoes at 29 cents per pound.

Karl Lehmann's four attackers in their separate trials all left court with the same dreaded words from the bench ringing in their ears. "I sentence you to hang from the neck until dead," said Chief Justice Howson. "May God have mercy on your soul."[112]

CHAPTER 11

Lehmann Appeals and Pleas for Clemency

September 6 to December 17, 1946

WITHIN DAYS OF DEFENCE attorney George Rice filing a notice of appeal of the guilty verdicts and death sentences handed down, letters pleading for clemency for Bruno Perzenowski, Heinrich Busch, Walter Wolf, and Willy Müeller started landing on then Justice Minister Louis St. Laurent's desk.

The first to arrive was written on September 6, 1946, by Hermann Boeschenstein, who worked for the YMCA's War Prisoner's Aid division headquartered in Toronto. Boeschenstein knew Perzenowski from his visits to the POW camp at Neys, where Perzenowski had been camp leader. Boeschenstein had found him to be a quiet and "very co-operative man." As would other petitioners, Boeschenstein attributed Perzenowski's illegal action to "having grown up under... dictatorial conditions." Though the YMCA was no longer a strongly religious organization, Boeschenstein nevertheless resorted to religious language in telling St. Laurent that, while he had met the other three defendants only once, he had reason to believe "that they too now regret and hate the soul-destroying indoctrination which turned them into murderers."[1] Boeschenstein closed his letter by telling the justice minister that he would contact Sir Ernest MacMillan, the chair of the YMCA Committee for Canada and that the minister should expect to hear from him and other members of the Red Cross Committee.

Six days later, a package of letters from Heinrich Busch's mother, sister, and pastor reached Ottawa. A version of the sister's letter had arrived at Chief Justice Howson's chambers a month earlier after she read about Busch's trial and death sentence in a German newspaper. Howson responded, telling her that he had forwarded copies of her letter to both defence attorney Rice and the under-secretary of state for Canada. The judge explained that "in this democratic country" executions were not automatic, that the final authority lay with the governor general, who would review the sentence if the appeal that had already been filed was unsuccessful.[2]

Busch's sister claimed her brother Heinrich was "uncapable (sic) of murder." Her definition of murder, "to kill anybody willfully," ignored the fact that Busch was a bomber pilot while indicating that the German newspaper had said nothing of his signed confession. She assured Canadian officials that neither Busch nor her family "mingled with politics." She blamed both his plane crash and "depression" caused "by the time he spent behind the barbed wires" for whatever erratic behaviour he exhibited. The paragraph that praises his patriotism and love of his "native country" displayed something of a tin ear. The same could be said of her attempt to blame the victim. Relying on the article that (wrongly) stated "Lehmann was killed after a very heated political dispute," she wrote that "most probably Karl Lehmann also had his share of fault therein." Executing Busch "would break my poor mother's heart."[3]

Busch's mother's letter begs for both her son's life and "reliable news." She, too, said he "suffered from a nervous disorder" caused by his long years as a POW. Whatever Busch did, she was sure, was the product of an "overexcited passion." Her letter, containing the words "if... he is the perpetrator," shows that, like her daughter, she was unaware of Busch's confession. The widowed Mrs. Busch ended her entry by telling the Canadian government that both Busch and his family have "been an opponent of Nationalsocialism (sic) at all times."[4]

Busch's pastor, Karl Wessendorft, of the Greater Hesse Confessional Church (*Bekennende Kirche*), wrote Ottawa to say that Busch's entire family "enjoys the best reputation and is honoured in the community." They "never were party members of the NSDAP [Nazi party], but on the contrary were always outspoken against the party." Given the risk they would have run by publicly opposing the regime, these last words were almost certainly an overstatement. Still, the fact that they did not join the Nazified *Deutsche Evangelische Kirche* but remained in the communion of the Confessional Church (its most famous member being the murdered anti-Nazi minister Dietrich Bonhoeffer) does indicate that the Busch family kept a certain distance from Hitler's party. As in the correspondence of Busch's mother and sister, pastor Wessendorft lays the blame for whatever the POW did on the fact that he "has not been master of his sense since considerable time."[5]

* * *

Each of the appeals made similar arguments to those presented in the trial.[6] First, Rice contended that Justice Howson did not have jurisdiction to try the men because:

a. There was no evidence that the military authorities had waved jurisdiction;
b. There was no evidence that the military authorities had asked the court to assume jurisdiction;
c. Since the men were captured by the British, they were accountable to the British;
d. The men were not "in the King's peace";
e. The killing of a German POW by fellow POWs is not a crime but "an act of war";
f. Under Article 45 of the Geneva Convention, German POWs who commit crimes "should be returned to Germany to be dealt with according to the law of Germany."[7]

Rice also argued that Howson failed to instruct the jury that a finding that the men had "committed a political offence" would have been a mitigating factor. Nor did Howson explain to the jury what the law would have been had it determined that the accused were simply "carrying out an order of his military superiors." Howson also failed to explain "the effect of finding that the accused did something which he thought was right, but was wrong under our civil law."[8]

As Turcotte had before him in the Plaszek trials, Rice argued that Howson should have instructed the jury that it could have substituted a verdict of manslaughter. "The learned trial judge erred in admitting as evidence a confession signed by the appellant" and by discussing the confessions in his charges to the jury.[9]

Howson, Rice asserted, voided the trial in his charge to the jury when he said, "as a matter of law—and you must accept your law from me—that there was no law in force in that camp which authorized any one to give an order, or any other authority to kill Lehmann. There was no court, or other tribunal, or committee of any kind whatsoever in that camp that had the power to sentence Lehmann to death. If, as a fact, there ever were such an order in existence, no matter from how high up it came, it was an unlawful order, and was an unlawful act, and those who carried out that unlawful act were themselves guilty of an unlawful act."[10]

The six-page appeal ended with Rice asking the honourable court for an order "(a) quashing the conviction or in the alternative, (b) an order reducing the conviction to manslaughter, or in the alternative, (c) an order for a new trial."[11]

Since oral arguments were scheduled for the last week of October and Howson had set October 16 as the date for the POWs' execution, the judge postponed their execution to November 13.

There was a case precedent that would have bolstered the defence's appeals, although Rice (and perhaps the crown) were not aware of it. The Canadian government, however, *did* know that two POWs convicted of murdering another in South Africa had been sentenced—not to death—but to five years at hard labour. Ottawa knew because on October 8, 1946, the office of the high commission for Canada in Pretoria wrote the secretary of state for external affairs about the case. The two POWs had killed a POW named Haensel, accused of being a traitor and a spy. Ottawa had a special interest in the two killers, Paul Wallet and Walter Warner, because they had ended up in a Canadian POW camp. (As noted earlier, tens of thousands of prisoners were transferred via South Africa to Canada, which had the space, supplies, and camps to house them.) According to a note written by Lieutenant Colonel A.C. Wygard of Canada's MI7, Wallet and Warner had been transferred back from Canada to South Africa to stand trial for the murder. From Wygard's note, it appears that the investigation took place in Canada and, when completed, the "cases were handed over to External Affairs [presumably in Ottawa] and the South African High Commission in Ottawa." Subsequently, the "witnesses and suspects were transferred to South Africa via the U.K."[12]

Wygard's note refers to a report number 266 that informed the Canadian government that the South African courts recognized the dilemma that at least Müeller faced after Perzenowski recruited him.[13] According to the high commissioner, Wallet and Werner, in obeying the order to execute Haensel, committed an offence against South African law. On the other hand, had they disobeyed the order, the judge averred, there was "a grave risk that Wallet and Warner themselves would be regarded by their fellow prisoners as being guilty of conduct prejudicial to military discipline." The judge further recognized that the accused feared retribution could be taken against them and their families after the end of the war. "The circumstances surrounding the death of Haensel," the judge found, "were thus such as to exterminate the offence committed by Wallet and Warner and it was for this reason that the case did not call for the infliction of the death penalty" but, rather, five years at hard labour.[14]

* * *

While the accused waited for Rice to present oral arguments to the appeals court in Calgary, another batch of desperate letters arrived in Ottawa pleading this time for Sergeant Major Walter Wolf's life. A letter written on October 2, 1946, from a man named Emile, who worked at a hospital with Wolf's father, praised the convicted POW as being an honest and well-educated son. One of Wolf's former teachers, a man named Reinhard, wrote that the German NCO "always behaved himself in a blameless way, while attending elementary school" and that he was known for his "sincere and upright character."[15]

The Wolf family belonged to an Evangelical church (again, not the Nazified *Deutsche Evangelische Kirche*) in the parish of Crumstadt, fifty kilometres south of Frankfurt. The church warden Peter Michel praised the family. With forgivable hyperbole and, obviously, without knowing of Wolf's signed confession, a parson named Walter, added, "nobody in the whole parish can believe that he [Wolf] was capable of the bad action imputed to him."[16]

The longest letter was written by Hans v. D. Au, PhD, pastor and professor. No doubt hoping that he would be read by an equally religious mind, Wolf's former religion professor said that "in his very soul [Wolf] sympathized with the matter" taught in church classes. The pastor still remembered "how the young man strove in great earnest [sic] after the solution of the problem of truth." He obviously was not aware that Wolf had confessed: "When he burdens his Canadian comrades and affirms he is not guilty of a crime, I expect from him that he would be courageous enough to speak the full truth, the more so as now his situation has a poor chance, and I cannot believe that Walter Wolf could have committed the crime imputed to him."[17]

* * *

On October 16, the day his clients had originally been scheduled to hang, Rice stood before the three judges of the appeals court in Calgary. In addition to resuming the arguments made in his written submission, he reached back to his trial summation and pleaded for the four men's lives by presenting a hypothetical case. Would we be asking for the death of Canadian POWs who killed William Joyce (the British traitor, dubbed "Lord Haw-Haw," who broadcast from Berlin)? Two interventions by the judges reported by the press suggest that Rice's arguments were meeting with some favour. First, Chief Justice Horace Harvey quoted him, "These people killed one of their own. It was an act of war."[18] Secondly, in an exchange with Rice, Mr. Justice Frank Ford appeared to agree with Rice when he reminded the defence counsel "that the trial had been held after the cessation of hostilities" and that Rice himself had expressed doubt that "the sentences passed on the men could be carried out because of the absence of a protecting power," which formerly had been Switzerland."[19] When a reporter for the *Saskatoon Star Phoenix* asked Rice how far he would go in making his appeals, the defence attorney replied with brutal honesty: "I'm willing to grasp at every straw."[20]

The following day, although the editors of the *Calgary Herald* buried the story on page 19, they still fairly gloated: "Calgary Huns To Be Hanged."[21] Despite his intervention during the hearing, Harvey joined the other justices: "We are unanimous in the opinion that the appeals fail and must be dismissed."[22] The *Saskatoon Star Phoenix*'s story (on page five) ended by quoting Rice that "it is unlikely the four Germans will be hanged November 13 as the public hangman is 'engaged' in Ontario on that date." On October 30, Justice Howson signed the order delaying the executions to December 18.[23]

* * *

Three days after the appeals court rejected Rice's submission, a letter written by Prime Minister Mackenzie King showed that even before the formal request for clemency had made its way through the bureaucracy, the highest levels of the government were considering the condemned men's plight. King's letter was triggered by a missive from Francis P. Carroll, bishop of Calgary. Carroll had heard about the four men headed to the gallows from the Catholic jail chaplain in Lethbridge and from a cable sent by the president of the Lutheran Church in Greater Hesse, Germany.

To avoid the charge of special pleading for his co-religionists, Carroll tells the prime minister that none of the four condemned men are Roman Catholics. His claim that "he was not familiar with the details of the case" was designed to cast him as being a disinterested observer. "Yet judging from its intricacies as published in the newspapers," he wrote, likely referring the issue of following orders, "leniency may be possible."[25]

Carroll avoids making a religious argument for mercy. Instead, knowing that King had been in power for more than two decades and had negotiated war-time alliances with Britain and the United States, he appears to have expected that the political leader would respond to realpolitik. Accordingly, he wrote: "I feel that leniency would create a good impression of Canadian justice in Germany."[26] To the untrained ear, King's response appears to hold out some hope. Those familiar with government boilerplate would recognize it for what it is: "I shall be pleased to bring the representations of your letter to the attention of my colleague, the minister of justice, for consideration."[27]

"The Petition of Bruno Sylvester Perzenowski, Walter Hans Wolf, Heinrich Thomas Busch, and Willy Ludwig Müeller, Requesting the Exercise of His Majesty's Royal Prerogative of Mercy" was submitted on October 31, 1946. Three weeks later, the clerk of the privy council issued a statement for the governor general in council that after carefully considering the transcript and other documents relating to the case, he "is unable to order any interference with the sentence of the court."[28]

* * *

The decision by the governor general to decline to exercise his royal prerogative did not prevent a number of people from continuing to petition the government. On December 3, a mere two weeks from the date set for what the newspapers were already calling the largest hanging in Canada since Louis Riel in 1885, Albert Weldon wrote to King and Canada's minister of justice. The seventy-four-year-old, who did not know the condemned men, begins in a folksy way that belies his residence in the Bronx, New York, and career as a lawyer. "Several boys in the Lethbridge Jail are scheduled to die very soon. Their fault is that they are good German soldiers." Weldon speaks of his sons, both veterans of the Second World War (one now a commander in the U.S. Navy and the other a Harvard-educated engineer) and asks, "Had they been taken P.O.W. and the enemy won, God knows what might have been meted out to them. Can we make a wrong right doing wrong?" The American suggests, "Perhaps by giving these boys mercy (what a beautiful attribute) we will someday obtain mercy." He then invokes Ecclesiastes 11: "I know by casting our bread upon the waters, it has never returned to us void. If this is so individually, it must be so nationally."[29]

As promised in early December, the YMCA's Boeschenstein again wrote Ottawa. The letter, addressed to the new minister of justice, James L. Ilseley, K.C., reached Ottawa on December 16. Dr. Tracy Strong, general secretary of the world's committee of the YMCA, had authorized Boeschenstein to convey his "deep approval of my plea, submitted to the minister of justice, for commutation of the death sentences." Strong also expressed his agreement with Boeschenstein's belief that the men were "product[s] of a shockingly brutal political education which they were unable to evaluate or to recognize as such, at least... until they became involved in a horrible crime."[30]

Pleas for mercy from church leaders and relatives of the condemned were to be expected. More surprising was the petition sent along with a letter from Paul R. Hediger, a United Church of Canada minister from Medicine Hat. It contained 1,134 "signature[s] of your loyal Canadian citizens of Medicine Hat and vicinity." For Hediger and those denizens of the city in which the killing occurred, the fact that the murder "was committed under circumstances that made it on their part an obligation under the oath of allegiance to the supreme commander of the German army and to a national policy that now no longer exists," was a mitigating factor. The petition, which includes the names of many veterans, was inspired by pure "Christian and humanitarian motives." Should his own German-sounding name raise a doubt about his background, the minister avers that he is "a loyal Canadian of Swiss origin" and that his only son served in the RCAF for three years.[31] Hediger ends his letter by expressing the hope that his prayers and those of the men and women who signed the petition will lead to a commutation of the sentence.

On December 17, the last full day that Perzenowski, Busch, Wolf, and Müller were slated to live, a letter from John Fedist of Edmonton arrived in Ottawa. In addition to claiming that the four prisoners had an "unreasonable trial," he made a number of legal arguments, albeit expressed in an amateur's language. First, he said that "they did not know much of our Canadian law." Second, "by right they should of went to a military trial, not a civilian trial." Since "they were not brought here as civilians... they did not commit a crime under civilian life." The killings "happened in time of war" and, thus, should not be viewed as murder. He plead for them to "get a break."[32]

Even as the ministry of justice in Ottawa continued to receive pleas for mercy, officials moved forward with the last bureaucratic details to the coming executions. On December 16 W. P. J. O'Meara, the acting under-secretary of state telegraphed the sheriff in Lethbridge: "I am commanded to inform you that His Excellency the Governor General in Council is unable to order any interference with the sentence of the court in the capital case of Bruno Perzenowski." Identical telegrams were sent for each of the other men. Each telegram ordered the sheriff to "repeat back this telegram without fail immediately after its receipt."[33]

That same afternoon, the POWs were told that all legal avenues had been exhausted and that they were going to hang early on December 18. Three of the POWs, proud members of what had been the Luftwaffe and the Afrika Korps, were so disgusted to learn that they would not be shot as soldiers but, rather, would hang—and at the same time as a confessed child-killer, Donald Sherman Staley, to boot—they tried to kill themselves. On the evening of December 17, the three slashed their arms and wrists using razor blades probably smuggled to them in books sent by other POWs. A guard spotted the blood and they were rushed to the hospital where their wounds were dressed. The condemned men were then transported back to the Lethbridge jail to await their fate.

CHAPTER 12

The Executions of Bruno Perzenowski, Heinrich Busch, Walter Wolf, and Willy Müeller

December 18, 1946

AN EXECUTION JURY OF six men was appointed to witness the last moments of the four German POWs convicted of killing Dr. Karl Lehmann in Medicine Hat POW Camp 132 in July 1944. The six, dressed in business suits, arrived at the jail late in the evening of December 17, 1946, but did not expect all the Germans to die as scheduled. They were "waiting for a telegram" recalled former RCMP Sergeant William Westgate, "at least for Müeller."[1]

Westgate shared the hope, which for him was based on equal measures of personal feelings and professional judgment. While guarding the POWs during their trials, he had gotten to know the prisoners. He disliked the Prussian manners of the one with which he had most in common,

THE EXECUTIONS

Bruno Perzenowski, who before joining the Luftwaffe had been a member of Germany's national police force. But Westlake had become friends with the outgoing pugilist, Müeller. "I don't want to go into court with a scruffy looking policeman," Müeller would tease (showing his command of idiomatic English) before offering to shine both the boots and Sam Browne belt of the RCMP officer he called "Wilhelm."[2]

After Müeller's conviction, when RCMP business brought Westgate to the penitentiary in Lethbridge, the warden would rib the Mountie by saying, "your buddy up on death row wants to see you."[3] The warden gave Westgate permission to visit the condemned man, who had made him a watch strap. A veteran investigator of hundreds of cases, many of which he prosecuted, Westgate believed that the Canadian legal system should and would redeem the implied promise it made to Müeller when he agreed to testify for the crown.

Westgate had been invited by RCMP Staff Sergeant Harvey to attend the hangings. And, though he was in Lethbridge that night, Westgate demurred. As the clock ticked down toward midnight, however, in his mind's eye he saw the room that would serve as the gallows. He knew how the unstained wood of the scaffold contrasted with the polished, dark wood paneling of the room that had originally been meant for a less grisly purpose. He had seen the thirteen steps that led up to the platform and knew that the hangman, known only by a pseudonym, Camille Branchaud, had prepared five ropes. The length of each was determined by the prisoner's weight as indicated on the "Official Table of Drops," so that when the body stopped falling the drop energy would be about 1,000 pounds, enough to break the prisoner's neck and bring about a "humane" death.

As midnight approached, the men who had survived the cauldron of battle and were now about to die on a cold winter's night almost

8,000 kilometres from home waited in silence. The bandages on the left wrists of all but Müeller were signs of their failed attempt to follow Hermann Göring's example and cheat the Allies of another few pounds of German flesh.

Shortly before midnight Bruno Perzenowski and Heinrich Busch climbed up the thirteen steps. Once there, Branchaud led each man, his final stride placing him above one of the two steel trapdoors.

As December 17 ended and the new day began, the hangman still waited, but no telegram arrived with a reprieve. At 12:10 a.m., the hangman with practiced hand "pinion[ed] their legs, dropped the hoods [over their faces], adjusted the ropes and pulled the lever."[4] Twenty minutes later, Perzenowski's and Busch's bodies were cut down, examined by the coroner, pronounced dead, and carried directly to the common grave they had been forced to dig the previous day. At 12:45, Walter Wolf and Willy Müeller were executed. Their bodies too were brought to the common grave.

The child murderer, Donald Sherman Staley, was hanged at 1:30 p.m., bringing an end to what would be the last mass hanging in Canadian history.

The headline of the *Edmonton Journal* for December 18, 1946, conflated the executions of the child murderer and the POWs: "Staley, 4 German Prisoners Hanged." As the editors of the *Medicine Hat News* were writing their own caption: "Suicide Attempt Fails; Four Nazi POWs Hanged," the off-duty William "Wilhelm" Westgate found himself in the wee hours standing in a bar downing several shots of whisky.

EPILOGUE

Executing Justice

We can be exceedingly proud of the protection that we give to every accused person, and it makes no difference who the accused may be; it makes no difference what his nationality, his race, his colour or his beliefs, he gets the same protection in Canada as do the Canadians....

I would just like to add this, that anyone who lives in Canada and who thinks he can find a better country where he will get more justice, ought to go there and go quickly and stay there.

—Chief Justice Howson's Charge to the Jury in Sergeant Werner Schwalb's trial

JUSTICE HOWSON'S WORDS (ABOVE) notwithstanding, there are several questions raised by these two sets of trials. The first is the decision to try the POWs in the supreme judicial court of Alberta and not in military court.

When faced with similar cases, as per the Geneva Convention, the Americans tried POWs in military court, which the Canadian government knew. Canada, too, had signed the convention and was generally punctilious in following it, if only in hopes that Germany and Italy would follow the same provisions in the treatment of Canadian soldiers held in those countries.

Canada's War Measures Act is also relevant here. It directed that if a district military officer in Lethbridge was unable to administer a summary sentence or otherwise dispose of a case, "he shall take steps to bring the accused to trial before a military court." As George Rice, who defended the men accused of killing Karl Lehmann, admitted in court, the War Measures Act also gave the district military officer the authority to "communicate with civil powers in order that the accused may be dealt with by a civil court or criminal jurisdiction." The question then becomes whether such a communication with the civil powers actually occurred. Rice insisted that there was no evidence the district military officer ever requested that the Plaszek and Lehmann murder trials be assigned to the criminal courts—and the extant record would seem to bear him out.

For the crown and the judges, the mere calling in of the RCMP and the Medicine Hat city coroner to investigate the murders constituted proof that the district military officer had turned the cases over to civilian authorities. The position of the crown and the decisions of both Judge Howson and the appeals court is consistent with the May 17, 1945, intelligence report. Written soon after the murder of Karl Lehmann, the report said, "The RCMP are working with the camp staff in an endeavour to clear up the murders at Camp 132. Some information has been obtained and turned over to the police as the matter is one for the civil [criminal] courts and is being taken care of [by] the civil authorities." But, neither the crown nor the judges and, especially, not the defence were aware of this report which had Top Secret stamped on it. Unfortunately, there is nothing in Justice Minister St. Laurent's papers nor cabinet documents that explains the government's reasons for allowing the POWs to be tried in civilian court.

The government's intention and the appeals court's decisions may have settled the matter in 1946 but they do not do so today. The violation of the Geneva Convention and the War Measures Act may seem to be technical legal points. They are not. For, by trying the POWs in civilian court, Canadian authorities deprived them of something vitally important: jurors of their peers, that is jurors who understood military ethos.

In the trials of the men accused of killing August Plaszek, defence attorney Louis C. Turcotte argued almost in passing what Rice argued in detail in the trials of the men accused of killing Lehmann: their status as accused prisoners of war in Canada did not alter these soldiers' duty under German military law to kill traitors. As such, Hitler's order to "liquidate traitors" after the failure of the Hitler bomb plot in late July 1944 merely amplified existing military law.

Judge Howson was a veteran of the First World War, having served in France between 1916 and 1918, and the thirty-six men who made up six all-male juries who heard the Plaszek and Lehmann cases likely included a number who had also served in that war. No jury, however, appears to have had a majority of veterans and some may have had none. Certainly, no juror was a serving military officer. Accordingly, unlike the panel of between three or five military officers in a court martial, the men who judged the evidence and rendered the verdicts, had (at best) an incomplete or outdated understanding of military culture, a lack which bears directly on how the requirement to follow orders is understood.

Today, perhaps the most famous achievement of the Nuremberg trials was the (International Military Tribunal's (IMT) rejection of the "I was only following orders" defence. At the time, however, with the Nuremberg court still in session, this defence was more nuanced, especially in Grand Admiral Karl Dönitz's trial, the verdict of which was handed down in October 1946 (i.e., while the Medicine Hat verdicts were being appealed).

The charge sheet against Germany's last leader, Grand Admiral Karl Dönitz, listed three counts:

1. conspiracy to commit crimes against peace and war crime and crimes against humanity;
2. planning, initiating and waging wars of aggression;
3. crimes against the laws of war.

The first two of these counts were identical to those made against most other members of the Nazi high command and government. And, like them, Dönitz was found guilty on those charges. Yet, even as IMT found him guilty of the second charge, it noted that the admiral was not so-much a "planner" as a "line officer performing strictly tactical duties." In this, the tribunal came rather close to sanctioning the "*Befehl ist Befehl*" (an order is an order) defence.[1] Evidence against the only defendant allowed to wear his uniform—the Kriegsmarine uniform—into court appeared more concrete because it included unrestricted submarine warfare, which Dönitz oversaw, breaching the Second London Naval Treaty (1936).

Yet, it was on this third charge that Dönitz was exonerated. "The tribunal," read the French judge, Henri Donnedieu de Vabres, "is of the opinion that the evidence does not establish with the certainty required that Dönitz deliberately ordered the killing of shipwrecked survivors."[3] In so deciding, the IMT ignored the so-called *Laconia Order*. (On September 12, 1942, after U-156 torpedoed R.M.S *Laconia*, the U-boat surfaced to aid the survivors. It was soon attacked by an American plane. In response, Dönitz ordered that, "No attempt of any kind must be made at rescuing members of ships sunk, and this includes picking up persons in the water and putting them in life boats, righting capsized lifeboats and handing over food and water.

The grand admiral had his defence lawyer, Otto Kranzbühler, to thank for the court's reticence and likely for the votes of the American and British judges to acquit Dönitz on this count.

Since no one would have believed the argument that Dönitz had not issued the orders attributed to him, Kranzbühler argued that both the British and American navies had conducted similar campaigns. He even coaxed U.S. Admiral Chester Nimitz to sign an affidavit saying that from the day after the attack on Pearl Harbor, the U.S. Navy had waged a campaign of unrestricted submarine warfare against Japan, despite the American's signature on the Second London Navy Treaty. When Kranzbühler presented this document to the court, he said, no doubt with a smirk, "I in no way wish to prove or even maintain that the American admiralty in its U-boat warfare against Japan broke international law. On the contrary, I am of the opinion that it acted strictly in accordance with international law."[4] Kranzbühler won his point. The judges of the IMT accepted that the exigencies of war affected their judgement about the legitimacy of orders that might otherwise have led Dönitz to the gallows. Instead, he was sentenced to ten years in prison.

Had the judges on the Alberta appeals court followed the way the IMT judged Dönitz on the second count and the nuanced understanding of the guilty verdict on the third count, they might very well have accepted the *Befehl ist Befehl* defence Rice constructed.

* * *

Howson's opinion "that the land comprised in the prisoner of war camp, No. 132, at Medicine Hat, is part of the Dominion of Canada," that it is "merely an area of land fenced in for the safe-keeping of German prisoners of war" ignored the fact that the world within the wire was more contested. Geneva recognized that even as they were subject to the laws of the country in which they were prisoners, POWs remained subject to their army's laws. Thus, for example, Canadians could punish attempts to escape, but had to recognize that such attempts were legal because German military law required men who could to try to escape; the same dichotomy existed in German POW camps holding Canadian POWs. Geneva stipulated that the POWs choose their own leaders—hence the elections in Camp 132. Canadian law authorized the camp leadership to deal out punishments for infractions. Indeed, the level of infraction, being not saluting or violating the German military's code against homosexual behaviour does not really matter. What matters is that the recognition of the camp leadership's right (even duty) to police its own.

Nor does Howson's opinion (and the appeals decisions that accepted it) accord with precedent set in the South African case involving POWs Paul Wallet and Walter Warner. The South African judge who heard the evidence that they had murdered a POW named Haensel in a South African POW camp did not doubt they had killed the man. But, unlike Howson, the judge recognized the unnatural nature of the world within the wire: they feared for their lives if they did not carry out the order to kill Haensel, just as several of the men accused of murdering Lehmann had feared for their lives. As noted above, the South African judge said, "The circumstances surrounding the death of Haensel were thus such as to exterminate the offence committed by Wallet and Warner and it was for this reason that the case did not call for the infliction of the death penalty."

There is no question that the Canadian government was aware of the case against Wallet and Warner. Ottawa would have had to authorize the investigation that took place in Canada and would have been party to the transfer agreement that sent them and an unknown number of witnesses first to the United Kingdom and then on to South Africa. The MI7 note makes clear that the results of the investigation were sent to external affairs in Ottawa.

Had the crown been apprised of this case, it is possible that it would not have sought the death penalty. Had the juries known that another common law jurisdiction had more or less accepted the argument that a POW was not free to refuse an order, the juries might have recommended mercy for all of the accused, as the jury that tried Kratz did. Finally, had Howson and the appeals court known of this case, they, too, might have viewed the question of *mens rea* differently.

Two other cases, one involving a Canadian, Inouye Kano, who was found guilty of High Treason for war crimes committed in Hong Kong, and two German soldiers who defected to the Canadians in the last days of the war, also have bearing on whether justice was served in Judge Howson's court.

Inouye's trial highlights the limits of being "in the King's peace." Inouye was a Nisei (first generation born in North America of Japanese parents). After graduating from Vancouver Technical High School in 1936, he studied in Tokyo at Waseda University for two years before transferring to an agricultural college. Inouye was still studying in Japan when Japan bombed Pearl Harbor and invaded British possessions, including Hong Kong in December 1941. Under Japanese law, as the son of a Japanese father, Inouye was considered Japanese, and thus was drafted into the army in early 1942. Because of his fluency in English, he was made an interpreter for the *Kempeitai* (the Japanese equivalent of the Gestapo) and sent to a POW camp in Hong Kong, which held some 1,750 Canadians who had been sent to defend the island and who had surrendered the previous Christmas Day. (Another 250 Canadians had died in the seventeen-day battle and a like number would die because of maltreatment and diseases caused by their starvation diet.)

Inouye quickly developed a reputation for brutality, earning the sobriquets "Slap Happy" and the "Kamloops Kid." He ordered two guards to hold Royal Rifleman Henry Lyons so that Inouye could punch away at him. When, after the beating ended, with more guts than tact, Lyons said, "They've never made a Jap in Tokyo who could knock me off my feet," Inouye swung his rifle like a club so that the butt hit Lyons squarely in his collar bone, breaking it.[5] Inouye also tied Winnipeg Grenadier Jim Murray, one of the few Indigenous Canadians in what was called C-Force, to a pole and beat him with his fists. Afterwards, Inouye taped Murray's mouth closed and put burning cigarettes up his nostrils so he had to breathe through them.

Canadian Major George Puddicomb's investigators filed three counts against Inouye: two of beating and insulting officers while on parade, and another of causing the death and physical suffering of several victims.[6] Lawyers at Canada's department of external affairs argued that since Inouye was a British subject (as all Canadians were until the 1948 Citizenship Act), he should be returned to Canada and tried for treason. Mackenzie King's cabinet demurred, and Inouye was tried as a Japanese national in the International Military Tribunal for the Far East.

Inouye was convicted on May 27, 1946, and sentenced to hang. However, on November 19 the commander of the military district ruled that because Inouye was a British subject he should not have been tried as a foreigner. At first, Canadian authorities did not want to accept that Inouye was their responsibility, arguing that he had renounced his British citizenship. After it was established that Inouye was, indeed, a British subject—and a Canadian one at that—the decision was made to try him as a Canadian.

Inouye's second trial took place in 1947, too late to have any bearing on the fate of the men convicted of killing Lehmann. The law Inouye was tried under, which dated to 1321, is also important. He was accused of "high treason by adhering to the King's Enemies elsewhere than in the King's Realm, to wit, in the Colony of Hong Kong and its Dependencies."[7] In other words, even in Japanese-occupied Hong Kong, the prosecution argued, Inouye owed fealty to King George VI.

Perzenowski, Busch, Wolf, and Müeller were in an analogous situation. Like every German soldier (after Hitler combined the offices of chancellor and Reich president), they had sworn an oath of personal allegiance to the führer, not the Canadian monarch. Though transferred to Canadian custody by Britain, they had never consented to be within the King's peace in Canada, nor did they consider themselves within it, especially within the wire.

It is worth pausing a moment to consider that in neither the Plaszek nor Lehmann case did the German POWs kill a Canadian soldier or civilian; nor did they commit any act of violence outside the enclosure. One does not have to go as far as Rice did, arguing that the "King should laugh with glee if the whole of them were killed, they are all his enemies," to grasp the potential legal difference between an escaping German POW on the run killing a Canadian soldier or civilian, and a POW acting on their shared understanding of the military code of the army to which he owes allegiance. If Inouye's presumed allegiance to King George VI trumped the metropolitan law that assigned his allegiance to Emperor Hirohito, then for the POWs within the enclosure, the German military code and Hitler's order to exterminate traitors should have trumped the metropolitan law of the criminal code of Canada.[8]

None of the attorneys, judges, or jurors involved in the Medicine Hat trials knew about the strange perseverance of German military law five days after Germany's unconditional surrender (on May 7, 1945) and the extinguishment of the German state. Oddly, a Wehrmacht military court continued to function with the active support of the Canadian army.

To be sure, the situation was abnormal. At war's end, the First Canadian Army in Holland suddenly found itself accepting the surrender of tens of thousands of German soldiers. The Canadians did not see surrendering Germans as possessing the status of POWs, which would have meant that their food and supplies were Canada's responsibility. They assigned the Germans the status of "surrendered enemy personnel," as distinct from POWs, which stretched the letter of the Geneva Convention but made the management of the German units far easier for the Canadians. For one thing, it left the Germans responsible for their own communications networks, among other matters (in a manner not unlike the world within the wire).[9]

As this was going on, the Dutch Resistance on May 12 handed two German naval deserters, Bruno Dorfer and Rainer Beck, to the Canadians for safekeeping; the two had deserted to the Dutch before the end of hostilities. Even though the Allies, including Canada, had used propaganda to entice Germans to defect during the war, the Canadian army took a more jaundiced view of deserters when the fighting stopped. Within hours of accepting Dorfer and Beck from the Dutch, Canadian major J. Dennis Pierce passed the two German deserters back to the Wehrmacht. The next day, May 13, Pierce informed his superior that the deserters were "being tried this morning. German commander intends [to] shoot them." But first, the German commander arranged a court martial with a team of military lawyers and a presiding judge. It was witnessed by all 1,817 marines in the German camp. The court was not swayed by Beck's explanation that he deserted when he realized "that any further fighting by us against the Canadians would be senseless bloodshed."[10]

The German military court the Canadians allowed to operate saw desertion not merely as a crime against the military code. Even in the final days of the war, German military law and German officers viewed desertion as *Wehrkraftzersetzung*, subversion of the "will to fight." This was a crime against the *Volksgemeinschaft*, the "people's community." An individual who failed to adhere to the Nazi ideals at the heart of the *Volksgemeinschaft* was not simply cast out; rather, such miscreants warranted destruction in what amounted to a "purification procedure" under the "principles of the National Socialists community." The result was a sentence of death by firing squad for Dorfer and Beck.[11]

Since the Canadians had disarmed the Germans, the Canadians had the ability to stop the executions, and the law under which the Canadian army operated gave it the power to intervene. The Geneva Convention places POWs under the laws of both their home army and the detaining power, and there was no question that for a short time Dorfer and Beck were prisoners of war. Had they been deserters from the Canadian army, Canadian military law would have required not only the protection of liberties and the presumption of innocence but also the creation of a court martial board of three disinterested officers, for a death sentence to have been carried out. But Pierce allowed the German court martial to operate and accommodated the subsequent executions by arranging truck transport, giving the Germans eight rifles and sixteen rounds for each, and sending his second in command "to ensure the Germans got back safely" to their position.[12]

Canadian general Charles Foulkes was blasé about the incident: "I personally was much more concerned with the safety of Canadian soldiers and the welfare of Dutch citizens than with Germans." Two days after the executions, an order from Foulkes and Field Marshall Bernard Montgomery's headquarters restricted the German military courts, requiring that death sentences be "referred, through military government channels, to Montgomery's headquarters," but it did not suspend them.[13] At least twelve more deserters were handed over to German authorities, very likely leading to their deaths, before the policy changed on May 18, 1945.

The executions of Dorfer and Beck violated the Geneva Convention, under which death sentences "shall not be executed before the expiration of a period of at least three months" after communication with the protecting power.[14] By ignoring this international requirement, or perhaps because of his ignorance of it, Pierce and his superiors inadvertently stole a march on the lawyers in Ottawa.

Again, none of the judges or jurors involved in the Plaszek or Lehmann cases could have known about the events in Holland in the first half of May 1945. Nor is it likely that either the minister of justice or the minister of national defence were aware that the First Canadian Army was behaving in this manner in the days after Germany's unconditional surrender. The Nazi state and many of its institutional structures may have been dissolved, but for a few days, thanks to Major Pierce and his superiors, its military enjoyed a special ontological status beyond the life of the German state.

Had they known of it, Rice and his clients would have made something of the fact that the Canadians allowed German military law to operate among prisoners. The crown would have found it problematic, at best, to argue that the accused murderers at Camp 132, men who acted according to their military consciences in 1944, were acting outside the law as they understood it.

* * *

The governor general's decision to refrain from exercising his royal prerogative is also questionable. There is a document in Wolf's file at Library and Archives Canada that clearly states that the minister of justice, (Louis

St. Laurent at the time), recommended that Wolf's death sentence be "commuted to a term of life imprisonment in the Saskatchewan Penitentiary." The absence of a similar document in the other condemned men's files should not be taken as proof that in their cases the minister made no such recommendation. The clerk of the privy council, in documents he prepared on November 23, noted the existence of "the report of the acting minister of justice adverse to the commutation of the sentence."[15] Without recommendations for commutations from St. Laurent for Perzenowski, Busch, and Müeller, as well as Wolf, there would have been nothing for the acting minister of justice to be "adverse to." Accordingly, it is reasonable to assume that at some point St. Laurent issued documents similar to the one in Wolf's file for each of the condemned.

Unfortunately for the four, as they awaited the gallows in late November 1946, Louis St. Laurent was on Long Island. He was representing Canada at the general assembly of the United Nations, housed at the time in the village of Lake Success, New York. St. Laurent would be replaced as justice minister by James L. Ilsley on December 9. The records of the department of justice and newspaper accounts do not indicate who was acting for St. Laurent before then when he was already out of town. The most likely candidate is deputy justice minister Frederick P. Varcoe. While acting ministers have all the powers of sitting ministers, save for times of emergency, they are to behave in a caretaker fashion. But not here. "The decision by the acting minister of justice was certainly legal," says University of Ottawa law professor Michel W. Drapeau, Col. (retired). "Yet, in such a unique case, at least from our perspective, it does look curious."[16]

There is no known document that explains the reason for the change in the ministry of justice's advice to the governor general. Nor is it known if the governor general knew that St. Laurent's opinion differed.

The privy council document, however, makes clear that the advice not to use the royal prerogative was essential to the decision to let the executions go ahead as scheduled.

* * *

The vast majority of Medicine Hatters believed any accused German POW was guilty—the jurors who acquitted Wittinger were taunted as "Nazi lovers"—and it is a safe bet that most other Canadians would have thought the same. But did the Mounties, in this case, get their man?

In one sense, yes. The thousands of hours of investigation chronicled in RCMP reports, only a fraction of which are mentioned above, led inexorably to the three POWs charged with killing August Plaszek and the execution of one of these men, just as the investigation into the killing of Karl Lehmann lead to the arrests, trials and executions of the four other German soldiers.

In a larger sense, however, the Mounties only get their man if the entire justice system correctly identifies the criminal, charges him/her properly, proves the charges beyond a reasonable doubt in the right court and, in the end, metes out a just sentence. The killings of Plaszek and Lehmann required trials. Had the accused been tried in military court, Canadian officers would likely have been more understanding than civilians of the plight of the accused POWs. "If a Canadian in a German prison camp had an honest belief that one of their group was a traitor and, in a melee, this Canadian was killed, surely the government of Canada would not execute Canadian soldiers who had taken part in the melee," argued Turcotte.

And Canada would not have been responsible for the fact that five more men were dangling from the ends of ropes in 1946.

Acknowledgments

ONE OF THE SAD realities of having started to research this book a decade and a half ago is that several of the people I interviewed are no longer here for me to send inscribed copies to. Chief among the "absent" is Joyce Reesor Keating. I thank her both for her time on the phone and for sending me her high-school essay, without which the opening of the book would be much less human. Joyce's husband, James was an invaluable resource in understanding what "the Hat" was like in the 1930s and 1940s. Also gone is William Westlake, the retired RCMP constable who walked me through the investigation and his "friendship" with the condemned murderer, Willie Müeller. Nor is Howard Millen with us, but his words have remained.

While I was finishing my research, in the days of the Covid pandemic, I had the great honour to interview retired Col. Michel Drapeau who was an invaluable legal resource. So, too, was the retired Supreme Court of Canada justice, the Honourable Louise Charron, who read the text and saved me from a number of rookie errors.

The archivists at Library and Archives Canada, the Medicine Hat Archives, the Glenbow Museum, the Provincial Archives of Alberta, and the Department of History and Heritage (of the Department of National Defense) have, as they always have, worked wonders.

My agent, David Johnston, has believed in the project these long years, and for that, and making sure the t's are crossed and the i's are dotted, I thank him.

Ken Whyte, whom I've worked with in a number of different venues, welcomed me into Sutherland House warmly, while keeping his editor's blue pencil handy. He has wielded it lightly, so lightly, in fact, that I have not found myself tearing my hair out.

I would also like to thank Jennifer Westaway, the editor to whom Ken handed the manuscript off when his eyes had become all-too-familiar with it. She made helpful suggestions and caught a number of faux pas and for that I thank her.

Notes

ALL INVESTIGATIVE REPORTS ARE indicated below by their RCMP, Military Intelligence, or Department of National Defence number (when readable) and by date (when readable). Unless otherwise indicated, by reference such as DHH (Department of History and Heritage), Glenbow (Glenbow Museum at the University of Calgary) or Provincial Archives of Alberta, references to official documents originate at Library and Archives Canada. The reference numbers or websites are indicated in the Bibliography.

PROLOGUE

1. Army Intelligence officer, sergeant James "Jim" Papsdorf's young children attended at least one Christmas concert put on by the POWs in the camp.
2. Joyce Reesor, Interview with the author.
3. Barry Broadfoot, *Six War Years: Memories of Canadians at Home and Abroad* (Toronto: Paperjacks, 1976), p. 61ff.
4. Reesor, Interview with the author.
5. William McDougall (1822–1905) attended all three Confederation conferences, and was Lieutenant Governor of Rupert's Land and the North-Western Territory, which encompassed Medicine Hat before Alberta was made a province. He joined the party that met with U.S. President Abraham Lincoln in 1863 to renegotiate the Reciprocity Treaty. Lincoln later invited McDougall to accompany him to Gettysburg, PA, where he heard what became known as the Gettysburg Address. Another of Joyce Reesor's

ancestors was David Reesor (1823–1902), who served in the parliament of the Upper Canada prior to Confederation, and later sat in the Canadian Senate.
6. *Medicine Hat News*, February 25, 1946, 3; February 26, 1946, 2; March 2, 1946, 2.
7. All quotes from Reesor's essay come from a copy in the author's possession.
8. James Keating, Interview with the Author. When the Hatters boasted that no matter how hard the wind blew, the street lights still burned, they meant it. The large natural gas deposits nearby meant that unlike most other cities in Canada, the streets Joyce and Jim walked were lit by gas lamps.
9. *Medicine Hat News*, August 2, 1937, 6.

CHAPTER 1

1. Christopher Pugsley, *A Bloody Road Home: World War Two and New Zealand's Heroic Second Division* (Auckland: Penguin Books, 2014), 221.
2. Sidney Bradshaw Fay, "German Prisoners of War," *Current History* 8, no. 43 (1945): 193.
3. John Melady, *Escape from Canada!: The Untold Story of German POWs in Canada 1939–1945* (Toronto: Macmillan of Canada, 1986), 24.
4. Robin Warren Stotz, "Camp 132: A German prisoner of war camp in a Canadian Prairie Community during World War Two" (Masters diss., University of Saskatchewan, 1992), 8.
5. Stotz, 28.
6. Essentially, this debt was never settled. Britain repaid only a fraction of its war debt to Canada.

CHAPTER 2

1. In total, there were 26 POW and Internment camps in Canada during the Second World War. Some held specific groups: Camp 30 at Bowmanville, Ontario held captured U-boat men. One Quebec camp was in Hull, across the river from Ottawa, and another was on St. Helen's Island, the future site of Expo 67. The Medicine Hat and Lethbridge camps were the largest.
2. David J. Carter, *POW, behind Canadian Barbed Wire: Alien, Refugee and Prisoner of War Camps in Canada, 1914–1946* (Elkwater AB: Eagle Butte Press, 1998), 71.
3. Stotz, 42.
4. Carter, 74.
5. Stotz, 80.
6. Stotz, 63f.
7. Stotz, 60.
8. Melady, 76.

NOTES

9. Stotz, 58.
10. By 1944, of the 31,000 prisoners in Canada, 5,000 worked in logging, 8,000 on farms in Ontario and Quebec and others in canneries. Materials for their handicrafts came from wood scraps and shavings from the woodshop, razor blades, and even tin toothpaste tubes.
11. Martin F. Auger, *Prisoners of the Home Front: German POWs and "Enemy Aliens" in Southern Quebec, 1940–46* (Vancouver: UBC Press, 2005), 64f.
12. Letter from Anneliese Grubb, postmarked June 16, 1943.
13. Letter from Liesel, postmarked July 19, 1943.
14. "Puppa" had no way of knowing that by the time she sat down to write this letter, her beloved uncle had been dead for almost three weeks.
15. Kratz letter, January 1943.
16. Lehmann Letters, on page with September 22, 1944.
17. This not entirely translatable word, *Heimat*, means much more than "home" or "homeland." It is bound up with ideas of German culture, itself linked to the German Romanticism of such writers as Johann W. Goethe and Friedrich Schiller, as well as with notions of German nationalism and the people's links to German soil.
18. John J. Kelly, "Intelligence and Counter-Intelligence in German Prisoner of War Camps in Canada During World War II," *Dalhousie Review* 58, no. 2 (1978): 287.
19. Stotz, 83.
20. Auger, 56f.
21. Auger, 53.
22. Auger, 53.
23. Auger, 53.
24. Herbert W. Tustin, *Escaping from the Kaiser* (Barnsley, UK: Pen and Sword Books, 2014): 25.
25. While researching my first book, *The Battle of the St. Lawrence: The Second World War in Canada* (2005), I came across a picture of a graduation ceremony in 1942 or 1943 at Queen's University in Kingston, Ontario, in which a Waffen *SS* officer in full uniform marches proudly across the stage holding his diploma in his hand.
26. Robert Prouse, *A Ticket to Hell Via Dieppe: From a Prisoner's Wartime Log, 1942–1945* (New York: Van Nostrand Reinhold, 1982): 44.
27. Auger, 54.
    Yves Bernard and Caroline Bergeron, *Trop loin de Berlin des Prisonniers Allemands au Canada (1939–1946)* (Quebec City: Septentrion, 1995): 298.
28. Paul Jackson, "The Enemy Within the Enemy Within," *Left History* 9, no. 2 (2004): 65.
29. Jackson, 66.
30. Not long after the first POWs arrived in Canada, Under-Secretary of State for External Affairs, Norman Robertson, authorized the taking of pictures of the prisoners while engaged in sports that were then distributed to Canadian and American newspapers. This was done for two reasons. First, the government hoped that word of them would get back to Germany and might lead to an improvement in the conditions of Canadians held by the Germans, and second that it might make it easier for

Germans to surrender in the future. The same logic undergirded John Grierson's decision in 1944 to have the National Film Board produce a film intended to be seen in neutral countries that showed the POWs living in what amounted to vacation camps. It is unknown whether German authorities ever saw the film or photos.

31. Stotz, 76.
32. Stotz, 79.
33. Favoured for decades by writers and artists, these fine pencils "were not admitted into the compound, nor was bismuth, since the zinc could be extracted from it and used to make excellent secret ink." Kelly, "Intelligence and Counter-Intelligence," 291. Any POW awaiting a shipment of marzipan was destined to be disappointed since it was always confiscated; it had the same elasticity as solid ink.
34. Carter, 125.
35. Stotz, 48.
36. George Yackulic, "Prisoners of War in Canada," *Canadian Business* (November 1944): 51.
37. Carter, 76.
38. Carter, 113.
39. Kelly, 288.
40. Auger, 56.
41. Jackson, 69.
42. Jackson, 69.
43. Jackson, 70.
44. Prior to taking command of Camp 132, R. O Bull was commandant of Camp M in Mimico (New Toronto, later Camp 22). At Camp M, Major Bull argued for employing POWs in the nearby agricultural sector. In 1941 he wrote his superiors, "It is the writer's opinion that with farmers dangerously short-handed and rough labourers at a premium, a work programme could be instituted without appreciable lowering of security." (Major R.O. Bull, "Appreciation of the Treatment of German P/W in Internment Camps," August 26, 1941, HQS 7236; Policy, Treatment of Enemy Aliens, C-5368, RG24, LAC)
45. Jackson, 70.
46. The irony of a Canadian criminal court and military authorities acting to protect a homosexual man at a time when homosexuals faced being drummed out of the Canadian army and when men were prosecuted for committing homosexual acts was apparently missed by the court and other officials.

CHAPTER 3

1. This account is based on the narrative contained in the report of the Court of Inquiry held into the death of POW August Plaszek dated July 24, 1943. ("Court of Inquiry")
2. Army Intelligence Report, No. 132-T-3/4, July 27, 1943, 1.

NOTES

3. Court of Inquiry, 1.
4. F. Jones, "German POW's tale of terror," *Toronto Star*, March 15, 1981, A13.
5. The common law legal systems of Canada, Britain, Australia, New Zealand and the United States are adversarial, meaning the prosecutor has to first demonstrate that there exists a prima facie case; in Canada, this is done before a judge in what's called a "preliminary hearing," during which the prosecution can call witnesses to corroborate the charge. Equally importantly, during the preliminary hearing, the defence sees the evidence against the accused, which allows defence lawyers to structure their argument. If the case goes to trial, the prosecution's evidence is tested in open court. By contrast, the civil law system, which has its roots in Roman law, is more inquisitorial, with the prosecutor and judge working closely together. Witnesses are rarely called to testify. Instead, the judge's decision about guilt is made from a thorough review of written material presented to the court by the prosecution and the defence.
6. Jones, A13.
7. Army Intelligence Report into the murder of POW August Plaszek, August 21, 1943, 1.
8. Court of Inquiry, (Second set of pages), 2.
9. Court of Inquiry, 2.
10. RCMP Report, Lieutenant W. A. Dawe Re: the Disturbance in the Enclosure of Internment Camp, Medicine Hat, Alta., July 22, 1943, 1.
11. Court of Inquiry, 2.
12. RCMP Report, Corporal A. R. Bull, No. ZK 636/4 5, August 28, 1943, 2.
13. RCMP Report, Corporal A. R. Bull, August 21, 1943, 2.
14. RCMP Report, August 28, 1943, 7.
15. RCMP Report, August 28, 1943, 7.
16. RCMP Report, August 28, 1943, 6.
17. Court of Inquiry, 4.
18. Army Intelligence Report, RCMP Corporal A. R. Bull interview with POW Bernhard Kafka, 132-T-3/4, July 27, 1943, 1f.
19. Carter, *POW, behind Canadian Barbed Wire*, 156.

CHAPTER 4

1. Department of National Defence Report, RCMP Corporal A. R. Bull, No. 132-/P/6-0, July 23, 1943, 2,3.
2. RCMP Report, Corporal A. R. Bull, September 15, 1943, 2.
3. Report, 1.
4. By July 27, requests for protection were fairly flying in to Commandant Bull's office. He heard that men who had sought or wanted to seek protection feared reprisals would be "taken upon their relatives in Germany." Elstermann was said to be transmitting the names of these men to Germany via a Swiss consul. Bull asked his

superiors to consider "preventing the transmission of such information to Germany" RCMP Report, Constable A. F Bull, August 21, 1943, 5.

5. Army Intelligence Report, July 27, 1943, 1.
6. RCMP Report, Corporal A. R. Bull, August 21, 1943, 1.
7. RCMP Report, Corporal A. R. Bull, August 21, 1943, 2.
8. Extracts and Precis from RCMP File 43K 636/45, d/Sept. 15th, Statement by Hega Johannes, July 22, 1943, 2.
9. RCMP Report, Corporal A. R. Bull, No 43K 636 4 5, September 17, 1943, POW Ludwig Beck, 1.
10. RCMP Report, Corporal A. R. Bull, September 17, 1943, 2.
11. RCMP Report, Corporal A. R. Bull, No 43K 636/ 4 5, September 20, 1943, 2.
12. RCMP Report, Corporal A. R. Bull, September 20, 1943, 3.
13. RCMP Report, Corporal A. R. Bull, September 20, 1943, 3.
14. Stolte was so worried, in fact, that before beginning to speak to the court of inquiry, he stripped off all his clothes and threatened to kill himself if he were returned to the enclosure. After being calmed by Camp Commandant Bull and assured that he would be taken into protection, Stolte put on his clothes and his interview commenced.
15. Department of National Defence, Request for Protection by Hugh Stolte, No. 132-P-Pers., August 20, 1943, 1.
16. DND, Request for Protection, August 20, 1943, 1.
17. Extracts and Precis from RCMP File, 1945, Interviews Conducted in 1943 and 1944, Statement by Georg Friedrich, July 24, 1943, 2.
18. RCMP Report, Corporal A. R. Bull, No. 43K 636/ 4 5, September 1, 1943, 1.
19. Precis taken from D. F. G. W Frile HQS 7236, Interview with Paul Kasmierczak, Court of Inquiry, np.
20. Extracts and Precis from RCMP File, Interview with Adam Jansen, 1.
21. RCMP Report, Corporal A. R. Bull, No. ZK 636 4 5, August 28, 1943, 13.
22. RCMP Report, Constable George G. Krause, No. 4ZK 636/4-5, October 12, 1943, 2.
23. RCMP Report, Krause, October 12, 1943, 2.
24. RCMP Report, Constable George G. Krause, No. 4ZK 636/ 4-5, October 13, 1943, 1.
25. Department of National Defence, Army Internment Camp, R. O. Bull, Commandant to Director, Prisoners of War, "P/W Reaction to surrender of Italy," September 13, 1943.
26. RCMP Report, Krause, October 13, 1943, 2.
27. Canadian Naval Intelligence had cracked codes telling of the impending breakout. Instead of ordering the RCMP into the camp to search for tunnels, the navy planned to use the escapees to lure a U-boat into the Baie de Chaleurs where it could be captured.
28. Nathan M. Greenfield, *The Battle of the St. Lawrence: The Second World War in Canada* (Toronto: HarperCollins Canada, 2005), 211.
29. RCMP Report, Corporal A. R. Bull, 43K 636/4-5, September 11, 1943, Interview with Severin Fries, 1.

NOTES

30. RCMP Report, Corporal A. R. Bull, September 11, 1943, Int with Fries, 2.
31. Extracts and Precis from RCMP File, 2.
32. Walter Kohle, POW, letter to his wife, December 14, 1943, 3.
33. RCMP Report, September 17, 1943, 2. Edward Everett Hale's "Man Without a Country" tells the story of U.S. lieutenant Philip Nolan who, after cursing the United States, is condemned to live out his life on U.S. naval ships, never hearing of the country again. It was published in *The Atlantic* in 1863 and quickly became a staple of high school readers and compendiums of short stories.
34. RCMP Report, Corporal A. R. Bull, December 17, 1943, 2,3.
35. The prisoners did not only eat well on Christmas. Some weeks later, a shipment of 2,883 pounds of chocolate ordered by the International Committee of the Red Cross from the Fry-Cadbury Co. in Montreal arrived in Medicine Hat. The receipt of so much chocolate for the POW canteen was problematic because their Canadian guards' canteen was "sold out of this commodity" (Bull, R. O. Commandant, Department of National Defence, Army, Letter to Major A. H. Norrington, Internment Staff Officer, Headquarters, Military District, 13, Calgary, Alberta, February 7, 1944). Canadian officials, worried that the disparity would be made public, could not agree on how to solve the problem. In Ottawa's time-honored fashion, they referred it to an interdepartmental committee.
36. RCMP Report, E. G. Frere, Supt. Commanding "A" Division, Ottawa, Narrative about Captain Dr. M. Nolte, March 16, 1944, 1.
37. RCMP Report, Frere, 2.
38. RCMP Report, Frere, 3.
39. This would become a major issue in Kratz's trial, though, interestingly enough, neither Dornseif nor Zehpfund were called to testify on this.
40. RCMP Report, Frere, 3, 4.
41. RCMP Report, Frere, 4.
42. RCMP Report, Frere, 4, 5.
43. RCMP Report, Corporal A. R. Bull, January 14, 1944, 1.
44. The seven PERHUDA subjects were: Political leanings, Education, Religion, attitude toward Hitler, Usefulness (i.e. willingness to work), Dependability, and whether the POW as pro-Allies or anti-Allies.
45. RCMP Report, Corporal A. R. Bull, February 11, 1944, 2.
46. Ron T. Robin, *The Barbed-Wire College: Reeducating German POWS in the United States During World War II* (Princeton: Princeton University Press, 1995), 21.
47. Arnold Krammer, *Nazi Prisoners of War in America* (New York: Stein and Day, 1979), 161.
48. *Medicine Hat News*, February 15, February 25, and April 18, 1944.
49. Robin, 18.
50. Also see Adam Tooze, *The Wages of Destruction: The Making and Breaking of the Nazi Economy* (London: Allan Lane, 2006).
51. Additionally, Schmidt ordered that, if forced to work, little work was to be done and sabotage was to be undertaken. Further, all disciplinary power, the general ordered, rested in the hands of the camp leader.

52. RCMP Report, Corporal A. R. Bull, August 21, 1944, 2.
53. RCMP Report, Staff Sergeant G. Harvey, July 15, 1944, 4f.
54. RCMP Report, Corporal A. R. Bull, August 21, 1944, 3.
55. RCMP Report, Corporal A. R. Bull, August 21, 1944, 3.
56. RCMP Report, Corporal A. R. Bull, August 21, 1944, 1.

CHAPTER 5

1. *Winnipeg Tribune*, July 21, 1944, 1, 8.
2. Ian Kershaw, *Hitler: 1936-1945 Nemesis* (London: Penguin Books, 2000), 684.
3. Department of National Defence, Army. November 24, 1945, 4.
4. RCMP Report, Detective/Corporal J.W. Stanton, Interview with POW Werner Glasesing, November 10, 1944, 2. The Canadians appear to have become aware of this *aktion* three days after Lehmann's murder during Glasesing's interview.
5. Historian Judith Gansberg writes that the arrival of thousands of Normandy POWs who realized the war was lost broke the back of the Gestapo in many U.S. camps. For reasons that remain unclear, the arrival of Normandy POWs appears to have had no impact on the Gestapo in Canadian camps.
6. RCMP Report, Staff Sergeant G. A. Renton, Interview with POW Robert Stoehr, Oct 2, 1944, 3. Several other men made similar statements to the RCMP, which indicates either (1) Lehmann was rather vocal about his sexual preferences or (2) the Nazis in the camp engaged in coordinated character assassination.
7. RCMP Report, Renton, 3.
8. RCMP Report, Detective/Corporal J. W. Stanton, Narrative, September 18, 1944, 6.
9. RCMP Report, Stanton, Interview with POW Karl Gassner, September 23, 1944, 2.
10. RCMP Report, Stanton, September 18, 1944, 8.
11. RCMP Report, Stanton, September 18, 1944, 1.
12. Department of National Defence, Directorate of Censorship, Letter of September 14, 1944 by POW Karl Grabhandt, Translated by Captain E.G. Gerridzen on November 2, 1944.
13. Extract of Major P. Lieven's interrogation of POWs T. Hohnelohe, Walter Falk, Rudlof Altmeir and Alfred Jaeger on September 25, 1944.
14. Karl Grabhandt, letter to Lisa, September 14, 1944.
15. RCMP Report, Stanton, September 18, 1944, 11.
16. RCMP Report, Stanton, September 18, 1944, 9.
17. September 27, 1944. Department of National Defence, Internment Camp, Medicine Hat, Alta., Sept. 27, 1944, 132-F-1/0. Department of History and Heritage.
18. Report Camp 132, 2nd Lieutenant George Ferguson to Camp Commandant, Search of Orderly Room, Camp Spokesman's [Leader's] Office, Hospital and Certain Quarters, 1.

NOTES

19. Report Camp 132, Ferguson, 2. Given the similarity between these documents and others found in a POW camp in Gravenhurst, Ontario, it is likely that the instructions were for the "Stern Code," which involved a key word, such as "Hasenkopf," which indicated that every letter of the alphabet save for "J" was assigned a numeric value. Though time consuming, the system allowed for detailed messages to be sent and received in what appeared to be completely innocuous messages. See Yves Bernard and Caroline Bergeron, *Trop Loin de Berlin: Des Prisonniers Allemands au Canada, 1939-46*.
20. Department of National Defence, Army Report, Captain L. B. Yule, October 16, 1944, (3 pages) 2.
21. Karl Grabhandt, letter to Lisa, September 14, 1944.
22. Department of National Defence, Army Report, Captain L. B. Yule, October 16, 1944, (1 page) 1.
23. Judith M. Gansberg, *Stalag, USA: The Remarkable Story of German POWs in America* (New York: Thomas Y. Crowell, 1977), 54.
24. RCMP Report, Narrative of Letter found in Search at Nyes, Ontario on November 1, 1944, 1.
25. RCMP Report, Letter found at Nyes, November 1, 1944, 1,2.
26. Canadian National Telegram, October 10, 1944.
27. Proceedings of 'Court of Inquiry," September 26, 1944, Testimony by Lance Corporal J. W. Stewart, 8.
28. Presumably, this is where Lehmann's hut mates assumed he was when they thought he had been out drinking beer.
29. Testimony by Lieutenant M. W. English, 4.
30. Testimony by Major W. C. H. Pinkham, 9f.
31. Pinkham, 10.
32. Army Intelligence Report, Lieutenant L.C. Thornton-Prehn, Narrative of POW Ewald Kruppa, October 17, 1944.
33. Von Helmel: Letter and "Scrap-book" delivered to the Scouts and intended for Lieutenant Bohn at Internment Camp 133 (Lethbridge), November 4, 1944, POW Hans Friedrich von Helmel (von Helmel letter), 3,5.
34. Von Helmel, 5.
35. Department of National Defence, Army Report, Captain L. B. Yule, November 22, 1944.
36. Department of War Services, Prisoner of War Mail, "Complaint RE Treatment by Guard" in letter of February 2, 1945 (February 24, 1945).
37. Internment Camp Censorship, Intercepted letter, Neys, Ontario. February 15, 1945, 2.
38. RCMP Report, Narrative by Corporal A. R. Bull, POW Robert Schufart, February 20, 1945, 2.
39. RCMP Report, Bull, February 20, 1945, 3.
40. RCMP Report, Bull, February 20, 1945, 3.
41. RCMP Report, Bull, February 20, 1945, 3.

HANGED IN MEDICINE HAT

42. RCMP Report, Corporal A. R. Bull, Interview with POW August Siegel, March 27, 1945, 1.
43. Department of National Defence, Report RE: POW Heinrich Weiler, April 4, 1945.
44. Auger, *Prisoners of the Home Front*, 82.
45. Department of National Defence, Army Internment Camp, Report by Captain and Intelligence Officer H. Smith, May 4, 1945.

CHAPTER 6

1. *P.O.W. WOW: Internment Camp, Medicine Hat, Alberta*, Vol. 2, No. 9, March 2, 1946.
2. *Medicine Hat News*, May 9, 1945, 1.
3. A. Rettig A, "De-programming Curriculum: Allied Reeducation and the Canadian-American Psychological Warfare Program for German POWs, 1943–47," *American Review of Canadian Studies* 29 no. 4 (1999), 597.
4. Department of National Defence, Army Internment Camp. POW Anonymous Letter Found at Neys POW Camp 13, June 19, 1945 (translation July 13, 1945), 1.
5. DND, Anonymous letter found at Neys, 1.
6. DND, Anonymous letter found at Neys, 1.
7. In October 1944, according to Canadian reports, Wolf brought charges of "illegal actions" (presumably homosexuality) against Sergeant Hermann Koerber. Under the authority given by (Lt.) General Schmidt, Koerber was made to stand on the parade ground while Sergeant Major Waechtar, the so-called "Minister of Punishments," reduced him in rank (October 29, 1945 Report; see also October 20, 1944 Report). Koerber presented himself to Canadian authorities and was taken into protection.
8. DND, Anonymous letter found at Neys, 2.
9. RCMP Report, August 30, 1945.
10. Department of National Defence, Army Intelligence Report, August 27, 1945.
11. Information and Complaint, 11 October 1945, 1.
12. *Medicine Hat News*, October 15, 1945, 1, 10.
13. *Lethbridge Herald*, October 15, 1945, 3.
14. This decision will become a major issue in both the subsequent trials of the men accused of killing August Plaszek and Dr. Karl Lehmann and in the appeals of the death sentences.
15. Department of National Defence, Army Intelligence, September 17, 1945.
16. Department of National Defence, Army Intelligence, Interview with POW Gunther Pabst, October 15, 1945, 2.
17. DND, Interview with Pabst, 2.
18. DND, Interview with Pabst, 3.
19. DND, Interview with Pabst, 4.
20. Auger, *Prisoners of the Home Front*, 53.

NOTES

21. Department of National Defence, Army, Narrative and Analysis by Lieutenant Colonel W.C.H. Pinkham, October 30, 1945, 4,7.
22. DND, Pinkham, October 30, 1945, 7, 8 7.
23. DND, Pinkham, October 30, 1945, 10.
24. DND, Pinkham, October 30, 1945, 11.
25. DND, Pinkham, October 30, 1945, 10.
26. DND, Pinkham, October 30, 1945, 19.
27. DND, Pinkham, October 30, 1945, 20, 21, 21, 21.
28. Department of National Defence, Army Intelligence, Lieutenant Paul F.O. Black (I.O.), Statement by POW Otto Krueger, November 24, 1945, 3.
29. DND, Statement by Krueger, 4.
30. DND, Statement by Krueger, 5.
31. Department of National Defence, Army Intelligence, Statement by POW George Herdel, November 24, 1945, 1.
32. DND, Statement by Herdel, 2.
33. DND, Statement by Herdel, 2.
34. DND, Statement by Herdel, 3.
35. Department of National Defence, Army Intelligence, Statement by POW Helmut Porcher, November 24, 1945, 1,2.
36. Intent, also known as *Mens rea*, is the mental state of the accused when the purported criminal act occurs. In this case, Wolf assumes that the Canadian courts will view his actions as that of a soldier merely following orders.
37. DND, Statement by Porcher, 3.
38. RCMP Report, G. Miller, Intelligence Branch, Interview with POW Otto Work, November 31, 1945, 4.
39. RCMP Report, Interview with Otto Work, 4.
40. Department of National Defence, Army Intelligence, Lieutenant Paul P.O. Black (I.O.), Interview with POW Hermann Schweizer, 8 December 1945.
41. Carter, *POW, behind Canadian Barbed Wire, 147.*
42. After immigrating to Canada in 1910 and working at the Molson's bank in Montreal, von Ribbentrop started a champagne importing business in Ottawa. He was part of Ottawa's Minto ice-skating team that competed for the Ellis Memorial tournament in Boston in February 1914. As a member of Ottawa "society," he would have crossed paths with Prime Minister Robert Borden and the future prime minister, William Lyon Mackenzie King. Ribbentrop slipped out of Canada to the neutral United States in the hours after the beginning of the First World War and made his way back to Germany.
43. Patrick Brode, *Casual Slaughters and Accidental Judgements: Canadian War Crimes Prosecutions, 1944-1948* (Toronto: University of Toronto Press, 1997), 231.
44. *Winnipeg Tribune*, December 11, 1945.
45. *Calgary Herald*, December 13, 1945.
46. Canadian Major-General Christopher Vokes commuted Meyer's death sentence to life imprisonment. In the end, he served six years in Dorchester prison in Halifax

and another three in a West German prison before being released in 1954. Upon leaving prison, he became active in the Mutual Aid Association of former Waffen-SS Soldiers and campaigned for their rehabilitation.
47. RCMP Report, Detective Corporal George Krause, Interview with POW Wilhelm Müeller, January 24, 1946, 3.
48. RCMP Report, Interview with Müeller, 3.
49. RCMP Report, Detective Corporal George Krause, Interview with POW Bruno Kroell February 2, 1946, 1.
50. RCMP Report, Detective Corporal George Krause, Interview with POW Robert Stuffert, February 2, 1946, 2.
51. RCMP Report, Detective Corporal George Krause, Interview with POW Interview with (Camp Leader) POW Wilhelm Wendt, 2f.
52. RCMP Report, Interview with Wendt, 3, 4.
53. *Calgary Herald*, February 11, 1946, 2.
54. *Calgary Herald*, February 11, 1946, 2.

CHAPTER 7

1. By attending court a day earlier, these men and the others summoned to be part of the jury pool did more than discharge their "civic duty;" they avoided a fine of $50 and/or imprisonment for 30 days.
2. Turcotte also represented the Hutterites before a commission of the Alberta Legislature which ultimately recommended a 40-mile distance between Hutterite communities.
3. Rex v. Werner Schwalb, Trial Transcript, LAC (Shwalb), 7, 6, 12, 19.
4. *Rex v. Schwalb*, 22.
5. *Rex v. Schwalb, 22, 23.*
6. *Rex v. Schwalb, 50.*
7. *Rex v. Schwalb, 140.*
8. Surely the oddest parole request was received several weeks after the end of the war in Europe. The camp leader gave the Canadian authorities a note from a POW that asked if his mother, Emilie Radke, who had lived in Sheboygan Falls, Wisconsin since 1923, could visit him in the POW camp. "I think have not seen my mother since she left Germany and I think there might be a good opportunity to see her in this Country," he wrote (Department of National Defence, Army, March 23, 1945). Flummoxed by the request, Colonel W.J.H. Elwood wrote to the Internment Staff Officer, Headquarters for Military District 13 in Lethbridge, Alberta. On April 4, Major General A. E. Walford responded denying the request while adding, "After the conclusion of hostilities it is possible that modifications of the regulations may permit the interview you suggest." He concluded his response by saying, "It is not considered advisable, however, that the PW should be unduly encouraged in such a hope" (Department of National Defence, Army, April 4, 1945).

NOTES

9. *Rex v. Schwalb*, 181f.
10. *Rex v. Schwalb*, 217, 202.
11. *Rex v. Schwalb*, 207.
12. *Rex v. Schwalb*, 223.
13. *Rex v. Schwalb*, 235.
14. *Rex v. Schwalb*, 270.
15. *Rex v. Schwalb*, 286.
16. Standing Orders – Camp 132, Duties of Camp Leader of Prisoners of War: April 1, 1943, 1.
17. Standing Orders, 2.
18. *Rex v. Schwalb*, 309.
19. *Rex v. Schwalb*, 331, 332, 333.
20. *Rex v. Schwalb*, 393.
21. *Rex v. Schwalb*, 352, 355.
22. *Rex v. Schwalb*, 362.
23. *Rex v. Schwalb*, 511.
24. *Rex v. Schwalb*, 511, 514.
25. *Rex v. Schwalb*, 524.
26. *Rex v. Schwalb*, 526.
27. *Rex v. Schwalb*, 526.
28. *Rex v. Schwalb*, 526.
29. *Rex v. Schwalb*, 417.
30. *Rex v. Schwalb*, 419, 420.
31. *Rex v. Schwalb*, 421.
32. *Rex v. Schwalb*, 421, 426f.
33. *Rex v. Schwalb*, 446, 451f.
34. *Rex v. Schwalb*, 456, 458.
35. *Rex v. Schwalb*, 501, 502.
36. *Rex v. Schwalb*, 506.
37. *Rex v. Schwalb*, 507f.
38. *Rex v. Schwalb*, 548.
39. *Rex v. Schwalb*, 572.
40. *Medicine Hat News*, March 2, 1946, 5.
41. *Rex v. Schwalb*, 574, 572.
42. *Rex v. Schwalb*, 583f.
43. *Rex v. Schwalb*, 584, 587.
44. *Rex v. Schwalb*, 599.
45. *Rex v. Schwalb*, 650, 653, 655, 656.
46. *Rex v. Schwalb*, 662.
47. *Rex v. Schwalb*, 661.
48. *Rex v. Schwalb*, 670.
49. *Rex v. Schwalb*, 680.
50. *Rex v. Schwalb*, 683, 684, 685, 686.

51. *Rex v. Schwalb*, 685.
52. *Rex v. Schwalb*, 691.
53. *Rex v. Schwalb*, 703.
54. *Medicine Hat News*, March 5 1946, 3.
55. *Calgary Herald*, March 6, 1946, 1.
56. In an interview conducted in 1981 by Tom Kirkham for the Glenbow Archives, Turcotte said that Nolte might have had more responsibility than the other three because he was the only officer in the camp.
57. *Calgary Herald*, March 6, 1946, 1.
58. *Rex v. Schwalb*, Charge to Jury, 1-55 at end of Second Volume, 6.
59. *Rex v. Schwalb*, Charge to Jury, 15.
60. Joyce Reesor's essay.
61. *Rex v. Schwalb*, Charge to Jury, 53.
62. Reesor essay, 8.
63. Reesor essay, 8.

CHAPTER 8

1. *Rex v. Adolf Kratz*, Trial Transcript, LAC (Kratz), 95.
2. *Rex v. Kratz*, 121, 123.
3. *Rex v. Kratz*, 163.
4. *Rex v. Kratz*, 163f.
5. *Rex v. Kratz*, 222.
6. *Rex v. Kratz*, 400.
7. *Rex v. Kratz*, 392, 393f.
8. *Rex v. Kratz*, 402, 401.
9. *Rex v. Kratz*, 416, 417, 428.
10. *Rex v. Kratz*, 442, 443.
11. *Rex v. Kratz*, 447, 448.
12. *Rex v. Kratz*, 457.
13. *Rex v. Kratz*, 459.
14. *Rex v. Kratz*, 460, 462.
15. *Rex v. Kratz*, 468.
16. Tobruk, on the Libyan coast, approximately 800 kilometres west of Cairo, was captured by General Erwin Rommel's Afrika Corps on June 21, 1942. The Germans took 80,000 British and dominion prisoners. Rommel's subsequent drive for Suez was stopped at the Second Battle of El Alamein which began on October 23. The British 8th Army, commanded by Field Marshal Bernard Montgomery, pursued Rommel as he fell back. On November 11, the German garrison at Tobruk surrendered.
17. *Rex v. Kratz*, 482.
18. *Rex v. Kratz*, 492, 498.

NOTES

19. *Rex v. Kratz*, 515.
20. *Rex v. Kratz*, 550, 560.
21. *Rex v. Kratz*, 562.
22. *Rex v. Kratz*, 562.
23. *Rex v. Kratz*, 565.
24. *Rex v. Kratz*, 566.
25. *Winnipeg Tribune*, March 16, 1946, 8.
26. *Windsor Star*, March 16, 1946, 7.
27. *Edmonton Journal*, March 16, 1946, 1.
28. *Rex v. Kratz*, Charge to the Jury, 1-69 at end of Second Volume, 66.
29. *Rex v. Kratz*, Charge to the Jury, 66.
30. *Rex v. Kratz*, Charge to the Jury, 67.

CHAPTER 9

1. *P.O.W. WOW*, 2, 4.
2. The King and Werner Shwalb, Notice of Appeal and Leave to Appeal, April 1, 1945, Appeal No. 3239, 2.
3. Report on *Rex v. Werner Schwalb* by Chief Justice Howson to The Honourable, The Secretary of State, for the information of His Excellency, The Governor General of Canada, pursuant to Section 1063 of the Criminal Code of Canada, March 11, 1946, 8.
4. Henry Jackson Wilson, Deputy Attorney General of Alberta, Letter to the Secretary of State of Canada, April 4, 1946, 1.
5. Frederick Percy Varcoe, Deputy Minister of Justice (Canada), Telegram, April 11, 1946.
6. Memo to Frederick Varcoe, April, 11, 1946.
7. Carter, *POW, Behind Canadian Barbed Wire*, 205.
8. Wilson, Memorandum For File, Re-*Rex v. Werner Schwalb*, Denial of Appeal, May 21, 1946.
9. Wilson, Memorandum For File, Re-*Rex v. Adolf Kratz*, Denial of Appeal, May 21, 1946.
10. Louis S. Turcotte, The Petition of Werner Schwalb and Adolf Kratz Requesting the Exercise of His Majesty's Royal Prerogative of Mercy, June 2, 1946, 3.
11. Turcotte, *The Petition of Werner Schwalb and Adolf Kratz*, 4.
12. Turcotte, *The Petition of Werner Schwalb and Adolf Kratz*, Part 2, 2. Turcotte is quoting from the book by George F. Arnold, *Psychology Applied to Legal Evidence*, 2nd ed. (Calcutta: Thacker, Spink & Co, 1913), 493–497.
13. Turcotte, *The Petition of Werner Schwalb and Adolf Kratz*, Part 2, 3.
14. Report on *Rex v. Johannas Wittinger* by Chief Justice Howson to The Honourable, The Secretary of State, for the information of His Excellency, The Governor General

of Canada, pursuant to Section 1063 of the Criminal Code of Canada, March 18, 1946, 4.
15. Report on *Rex v. Johannas Wittinger*, 4.
16. Report on *Rex v. Johannas Wittinger*, 4.
17. Report on *Rex v. Johannas Wittinger*, 9.
18. Report on *Rex v. Johannas Wittinger*, 10.
19. Report on *Rex v. Johannas Wittinger*, 10.
20. Report on *Rex v. Johannas Wittinger*, 12.
21. Report on *Rex v. Johannas Wittinger*, 18.
22. Report on *Rex v. Johannas Wittinger*, 26.
23. Carter, 167.
24. Carter, 168.
25. Gottfried Dukes, the POW who received twenty-two letters in one day at Camp 132, got to know Wittinger well in the 1980s. He says "Wittinger was an active Nazi" and part of the illegal "underground S.A. Hitler's storm troopers in Austria before the Germans invaded and annexed Austria."
26. *Edmonton Journal*, June 22, 1946, 1.
27. Interview with the author.
28. Carter, 168.
29. Interview with the author.
20. Douglas Sagi, "My Fuehrer, I Follow Thee." *The London Free Press. The Canadian Magazine*" January 4, 1975, 6.

CHAPTER 10

1. As he had in the Plaszek murder trials, Howson said that even if the accused chose to be tried by a judge alone, he would have still directed a jury trial. Because of the seriousness of the charge, he would not accept responsibility for conducting the trial and judging the evidence.
2. RCMP Report, Corporal A. R. Bull, Interview with POWs Wolf, Perzenowski, Müeller and Busch, May 8, 1946, 1. (Glenbow Museum)
3. Walter D. Gow, K.C., Letter to RCMP Inspector H. A. Maxted, May 7, 1946. (Glenbow Museum)
4. Gow, letter to Maxted.
5. RCMP Report, Bull's Interview with POWs, 2.
6. *Rex v. Bruno Perzenowski*, Trial Transcript, LAC, 2
7. *Rex v. Perzenowski*, 3.
8. *Rex v. Perzenowski*, 3.
9. *Rex v. Perzenowski*, 6.
10. *Rex v. Perzenowski*, 57.
11. *Rex v. Perzenowski*, 78.

NOTES

12. *Rex v. Perzenowski*, 80.
13. *Rex v. Perzenowski*, 80.
14. *Rex v. Perzenowski*, 81f.
15. *Rex v. Perzenowski*, 101.
16. *Rex v. Perzenowski*, 101. This *pas de deux* would be repeated in each of the subsequent trials.
17. *Rex v. Perzenowski*, 114.
18. *Rex v. Perzenowski*, 114.
19. *Rex v. Perzenowski*, 127.
20. In this second set of trials, homosexuality in the Medicine Hat POW camp was raised at least eight times in Perzenowski's trial, six in Bush's, five in Wolf's, and five in Müeller's.
21. *Rex v. Perzenowski*, 127.
22. *Rex v. Perzenowski*, 128.
23. *Rex v. Perzenowski*, 128.
24. *Rex v. Perzenowski*, 128.
25. Harsh punishment of suspected traitors was not rare in German ranks. In February 1944, in Amiens, France an army private was declared by a court to be an "inferior human being" for *Wehrkraftzersetzung* (subversion of the will to fight) and sentenced to death. He had commented that "National Socialism would be forced to go." See Manfred Messerschmidt, "German Military Law in the Second World War," in *The German Military in the Age of Total War*, ed. Wilhelm Deist (Dover, N.H.: Berg. Pub. Ltd., 1985), *331*.
26. *Rex v. Perzenowski*, 128.
27. *Rex v. Perzenowski*, 120.
28. *Rex v. Perzenowski*, 132.
29. *Rex v. Perzenowski*, 133.
30. *Rex v. Perzenowski*, 133, 134.
31. *Rex v. Walter Wolf*, Trial Transcript, LAC, 150.
32. *Rex v. Perzenowski*, 137.
33. *Rex v. Perzenowski*, 139.
34. *Rex v. Perzenowski*, 140.
35. *Rex v. Perzenowski*, 148.
36. *Rex v. Perzenowski*, 148.
37. *Rex v. Perzenowski*, 149.
38. *Rex v. Perzenowski*, 155.
39. *Rex v. Perzenowski*, 155.
40. *Rex v. Perzenowski*, 156.
41. Walter Benjamin, *The Origin of German Tragic Drama*, trans. John Osborne (London: New Left Books, 1977), 65.
42. Canada's diplomatic relations with the Third Reich were handled by the British, but Canada maintained a trade office in Berlin until the outbreak of war. Prime Minister Mackenzie King did not question the legitimacy of Hitler's

government. In what was surely not King's finest hour, on June 29, 1937, while on a several-days trip to Germany, in his diary King compared Hitler to a modern-day "Joan of Arc." (https://www.junobeach.org/canada-in-wwii/articles/aggression-and-impunity/w-l-mackenzie-kings-diary-june-29-1937/)

43. *Rex v. Perzenowski*, 158, 159, 160, 340, 356, 357.
44. *Rex v. Perzenowski*, 167.
45. *Rex v. Perzenowski*, 192.
46. *Rex v. Perzenowski*, 193.
47. *Rex v. Perzenowski*, 193.
48. *Rex v. Perzenowski*, 202.
49. *Rex v. Perzenowski*, 203.
50. *Rex v. Perzenowski*, 205, 207.
51. *Rex v. Perzenowski*, 207.
52. *Rex v. Perzenowski*, 213, 216.
53. *Rex v. Perzenowski*, 224, 219.
54. Jackson, 64.
55. *Rex v. Perzenowski*, 235.
56. *Rex v. Perzenowski*, 235.
57. *Rex v. Perzenowski*, 238.
58. *Rex v. Perzenowski*, 239f.
59. *Rex v. Perzenowski*, 241.
60. *Rex v. Perzenowski*, 216.
61. Ian Kershaw, *Hitler: 1889-1936* (London: Alan Lane, Penguin Press, 1998), 527.
62. *Rex v. Perzenowski*, 262.
63. *Rex v. Perzenowski*, 265.
64. *Rex v. Perzenowski*, 267.
65. *Rex v. Perzenowski*, 267.
66. *Rex v. Perzenowski*, 269, 270.
67. *Rex v. Perzenowski*, 272.
68. *Rex v. Perzenowski*, 272.
69. *Rex v. Perzenowski*, 273.
70. *Rex v. Perzenowski*, 273.
71. *Rex v. Heinrich Busch*, Trial Transcript, LAC, 198.
72. *Rex v. Wilhelm Müeller*, Trial Transcript, LAC, 165.
73. *Rex v. Müeller*, 165f.
74. *Rex v. Perzenowski*, 280.
75. *Rex v. Perzenowski*, 283f.
76. *Rex v. Perzenowski*, 285.
77. *Rex v. Perzenowski*, 285.
78. Messerschmidt, "German military law," *The German Military*, 330.
79. *Rex v. Perzenowski*, 288.
80. *Rex v. Perzenowski*, 289.
81. *Rex v. Perzenowski*, 289.

NOTES

82. *Rex v. Perzenowski*, 289.
83. *Rex v. Perzenowski*, 289.
84. *Rex v. Perzenowski*, 289. In each of the subsequent trials, Miller recounts the POWs as saying the same thing in similar idiomatic expressions. In Wolf's trial, for example, the court heard him say, "Well, I have decided to burn my bridges behind me" (*Rex v. Wolf*, 296).
85. *Rex v. Perzenowski*, 290.
86. *Rex v. Perzenowski*, 291.
87. *Rex v. Perzenowski*, 292.
88. *Rex v. Perzenowski*, 295f.
89. *Rex v. Perzenowski*, 297.
90. *Rex v. Perzenowski*, 311.
91. *Rex v. Perzenowski*, 311.
92. *Rex v. Perzenowski*, 312.
93. *Rex v. Wolf*, 358.
94. https://ihl-databases.icrc.org/applic/ihl/ihl.nsf/ART/305-430010?OpenDocument
95. *Rex v. Perzenowski*, 330.
96. *Rex v. Perzenowski*, 363, 364.
97. *Rex v. Perzenowski*, 366.
98. *Rex v. Perzenowski*, 371f.
99. *Rex v. Perzenowski*, 374f.
100. *Rex v. Perzenowski*, 375f.
101. *Rex v. Perzenowski*, 373.
102. *Rex v. Perzenowski*, 378f.
103. *Rex v. Perzenowski*, 384.
104. *Rex v. Perzenowski*, 387f.
105. *Rex v. Perzenowski*, 387.
106. *Rex v. Perzenowski*, 388, 391.
107. *Rex v. Perzenowski*, 390.
108. *Rex v. Perzenowski*, 401f.
109. *Rex v. Perzenowski*, 404.
110. *Rex v. Perzenowski*, 408f.
111. *Medicine Hat News*, July 2, 1946, 3.
112. *Rex v. Perzenowski*, 423f.

CHAPTER 11

1. Hermann Boeschenstein, letter from The War Prisoners' Aid of the Young Men's Christian Association to Louis St. Laurent, Minister of Justice, In the Matter of POWs Perzanowski (sic), Müeller, Wolf and Busch, September 6, 1946, 2.
2. W. R. Howson, Chief Justice of the Trial Division, Alberta, letter to Elizabeth Lehmann, Bergen-Enkheim, Germany, August 9, 1946, 1f.

3. Elizabeth Lehmann (no relation to victim Karl Lehmann), sister of POW Heinrich Busch, letter to Judge Howson asking for mercy, August 9, 1946, (Sent through the Red Cross, August 24, 1946), 1, 2.
4. Elisabeth Busch, mother of POW Heinrich Busch, letter to Judge Howson asking for mercy, July 22, 1946. (Sent through the Red Cross, August 24, 1946).
5. K. Wessendorft, Pastor and spokesman for the Confessional Church in the Synod Hanau-City, August, 8, 1946 (Sent through the Red Cross, August 24, 1946).
6. Because the post-trial records of the four convicted men are more complete for Walter Wolf, the arguments listed in text come from the appeal Rice filed on his behalf.
7. George Rice, Counsel for the Appellant Bruno Perzenowski, September 20, 1946, In the Appellate Division of the Supreme Court of Alberta: *His Majesty the King and Walter Wolf*, 2.
8. *His Majesty the King and Walter Wolf*, 3.
9. *His Majesty the King and Walter Wolf*, 5.
10. *His Majesty the King and Walter Wolf*, 5.
11. *His Majesty the King and Walter Wolf*, 6.
12. Lieutenant Colonel A. G. Wygard, MI7. Note covering the submission of Despatch No. 266 from the High Commissioner for Canada in Pretoria to the Secretary of State for External Affairs, November 12, 1946.
13. Unfortunately, the extant record does not make clear whether this trial took place in civilian court or was court martial. For our purposes, it does not matter which legal system the POWs were tried and convicted in. The important point is the South African judge's recognition that the POWs were not free actors but constrained by German military law.
14. Author unknown, to Office of the High Commission for Canada, Pretoria, Letter No. 266, Pertaining to Murder Trials of German POWs in South African POW Camps, October 8, 1946 (C-8437).
15. Reinard, Walter Wolf's teacher, translation of letter, October 2, 1946.
16. Walter, a parson with the Evangelical Parish of Crumstadt and Philippshospital, Certificate given by the parish: Re: Walter Wolf, October 2, 1946.
17. Au Lic, Hans v.d., Dr Philosophy, Pastor and Professor, Office of the Protestant Parson, Darmstadt-Eberstadt, "Petition for pardon on behalf of the prisoner of war, Walter Wolf, domiciled at Goddelau," October 2, 1946.
18. *Calgary Herald*, October 16, 1946, 1.
19. *Calgary Herald*, October 17, 1946, 1. The Crown was represented by C. S. Blanchard, K.C., who countered with this argument: "the fact that the war was over and Germany had no *de facto* government but was occupied by other powers, nullified provisions of the Geneva Convention requiring information on such cases being handed to the protecting power to be forwarded to the government of the country from which the men had come."
20. *Saskatoon Star Phoenix*, October 16, 1946, 1.
21. *Calgary Herald*, October 17, 1946, 19.

NOTES

22. *Vancouver Province*, October 17, 1946, 15.
23. *Saskatoon Star Phoenix*, October 17, 1946, 5.
24. Müeller, Dr., Rev. Petition to Rev. John Duplanil, Patrick's Rectory, Lethbridge, Alberta, Canada: "On behalf of the prisoner of war Walter Wolf, native of Goddelau, now imprisoned at Lethbridge, Alberta, Canada," October 3, 1946.
25. Francis P. Carroll, letter to The Right Honourable Mackenzie King, Prime Minister of Canada, October 18, 1946.
26. Carroll letter to King.
27. William Lyon Mackenzie King, letter to "The Most Reverend Francis P. Carroll, D.D., Bishop of Calgary, October 21, 1946.
28. Privy Council, 4825, His Excellency The Governor General in Council, November 23, 1946.
29. Albert Weldon, letter to the Prime Minister of Canada and the Minister of Justice, December 3, 1946.
30. Hermann Boeschenstein, The War Prisoners' Aid of the Young Men's Christian Association to The Honourable James Lorimer Illsely, K.C., Minister of Justice and Attorney General of Canada, In the Matter of POWs Perzanowski (sic), Müeller, Wolf and Busch, 1, December 14, 1946.
31. Paul Hediger, Reverend, The United Church of Canada, Medicine Hat, Alberta, Covering Letter and Petition for Mercy, December 4, 1946.
32. John Fedis, letter to the Minister of Justice, In the Matter of POWs Perzanowski (sic), Müeller, Wolf and Busch, December 12, 1946.
33. W. P. J. Omera, Acting Under-Secretary of State, Telegram, December 16, 1946 at 2:51 p.m. (Ottawa time).

CHAPTER 12

1. William Westgate, interview with the author.
2. Westgate interview.
3. Westgate interview.
4. Carter, *POW, Behind Canadian Barbed Wire*, 189.

EPILOGUE

1. Telford Taylor, in his memoir *The Anatomy of the Nuremberg Trials* (New York: Alfred A. Knopf, 1992), 594.
2. http://lawcrimehistory.org/journal/vol.1%20issue1%202011/Bennett.pdf, accessed March 26, 2022, 16.
3. Norbert Ehrenfreund, *The Nuremberg Legacy: How the Nazi War Crimes Trials Changed The Course of History (*New York: St. Martin's Press, 2007), 62.

4. Ehrenfreund, 61.
5. Nathan M. Greenfield, *The Damned: The Canadians at the Battle of Hong Kong and the POW Experience, 1941-45,* (New York: Harpercollins Publisher, 2010), 281.
6. https://hkwctc.lib.hku.hk/exhibits/show/hkwctc/documents/item/88, accessed March 26, 2022.
7. Greenfield, 378.
8. Kanao was found guilty of treason and was again sentenced to hang. On August 25, 1947 he was executed. His last word was the Japanese battle cry "*Banzaï*"(For the Emperor).
9. Chris Madsen, "Victims of Circumstance: the Execution of German Deserters by Surrendered German Troops Under Canadian Control in Amsterdam, May 1945," *Canadian Military History* 2, no. 1 (1993): 4.
10. Madsen, 8.
11. Messerschmidt, 1985, 328.
12. Madsen, 12.
13. Madsen, 11.
14. Madsen, 13.
15. Clerk of the Privy Council, Assistant. The Governor General in Council, November 23, 1946.
16. Interview with Colonel Michel Drapeau, retired.

Bibliography

BOOKS AND ARTICLES

Auger, Martin F. *Prisoners of the Home Front: German POWs and 'Enemy Aliens' in Southern Quebec, 1940-46.* Vancouver: University of British Columbia Press, 2005.

Bartov, Omer. *Hitler's Army: Soldiers, Nazis and War in the Third Reich.* New York: OUP, 1991.

Beeby, Dean. *Cargo of Lies: The True Story of a Nazi Double Agent in Canada.* Toronto: University of Toronto Press, 1996.

Billinger, Robert D. Jr. *Hitler's Soldiers in the Sunshine State: German POWs in Florida.* Gainesvill, FL: 2000.

Benjamin, Walter. Trans. John Osborne. *The Origin of German Tragic Drama.* London: New Left Books, 1977.

Bernard, Yves and Caroline Bergeron. *Trop loin de Berlin: Des Prisonniers Allemands au Canada (1939-1946).* Montreal, Septenrion, 1996.

Biess, Frank. *Homecomings: Returning POWs and the Legacies of Defeat in Postwar Germany.* Princeton: Princeton UP, 2006.

Breycha-Vauthier, A.C. "Reading For Prisoners of War as Seen from Geneva." *The Library Quarterly*, Vol. XI, No. 4. October 1941, 442–447.

Broadfoot, Barry. *Six War Years: 1939-1945.* Toronto: Paperjacks, 1974.

Brode, Patrick. *Casual Slaughter and Accidental Judgements: Canadian War Crimes Prosecutions, 1944-1948.* Toronto: University of Toronto Press. 1997.

Carter, David J. *Behind Canadian Barbed Wire.* Elwater, Alberta: Eagle Butte Press, 1998.

Dancocks, Daniel. *In Enemy Hands: Canadian Prisoners of War, 1939-1945.* Toronto: McClleland and Stewart, 1990.

Doyle, Peter. *Prisoners of War in Germany.* Oxford, UK: Shire Publications, 2008.

Ehrenfreund, Norbert. *The Nuremberg Legacy: How the Nazi War Crimes Trials Changed the Course of History.* New York: Palgrave MacMillan, 2007.

Erichsne, Heino R. *The Reluctant Warrior: Former German POW finds Peace in Texas.* Austin, Texas: Eakin Press, 2001.

Fay, Sidney B. "German Prisoners of War." *Current History* 8, no. 43 (March 1945): 193–199.

Feltman, Brian K. *The Stigma of Surrender: German Prisoners, British Captors, and Manhood in the Great War and Beyond.* Chapel Hill, NC: University of North Carolina Press, 2015.

Fooks, Georgia Green. *Prairie Prisoners: POWs in Lethbridge During Two World Conflicts.* Lethbridge, AB: Lethbridge Historical Society, 2003.

Gansberg, Judith M. *Stalag: U.S.A. The Remarkable Story of German POWS in America.* New York: Thomas Y Crowell, 1977.

Gilbert, Adrian. *POW: Allied Prisoners of War in Europe, 1939–1945.* London: John Murray, 2006.

Goodlet, Kirk W. " 'When suitable arrangements could be made' The Geneva Convention, Medical Treatment, and the Repatriation of German POWs in Ontario, 1940-46." *Canadian Military History* 21, no. 3 (Summer 2012): 3–15.

Green, Vincent. *Extreme Justice.* New York: Pocket Books, 1995.

Greenfield, Nathan M. *The Battle of the St. Lawrence: The Second World War in Canada.* Toronto: HarperCollins, 2004.

Greenfield, Nathan M. *The Damned: The Canadians at the Battle of Hong Kong and the POW Experience, 1941–45.* Toronto: HarperCollins, 2010.

Greenfield, Nathan M. *The Forgotten: Canadian POWs, Escapers and Evaders in Europe, 1939–45.* Toronto: HarperCollins, 2013.

Greenfield, Nathan M. *The Reckoning: Canadian Prisoners of War in the Great War.* Toronto: HarperCollins, 2016.

Hirsch, Francine. *Soviet Judgement at Nuremberg: A New History of the Internation Military Tribunal After World War II.* Oxford, UK: Oxford University Press, 2020.

Hodgson, Lynn P. and Alan Paul. *Word of Honour-Camp 30, Bowmanville.* Port Perry, ON: Blake Books, 2003.

Hoffman, Daniel. *"Erhenwort" A German Prisoner-of-War Camp in Bowmanville 1941–1945.* Bowmanville, ON: Mothersill Printing, 1988.

Iacobelli, Teresa. *Death or Deliverance: Canadian Courts Martial in the Great War.* Vancouver: University of British Columbia Press, 2013.

Jackson, Paul. *One of the Boys: Homosexuality in the Military During World War II.* Montreal: McGill-Queen's University Press, 2004.

Jackson, Paul. "The Enemy Within the Enemy Within The Canadian Army and Internment Operations during the Second World War." *Left History* 9, no. 2 (Spring/Summer 2004).

Kershaw, Ian. *Hitler: 1889–1936, Hubris.* New York: Penguin, 1998.

Keyserlingk, Robert H. "Political Warefare Illusions: Otto Strasser and Britain's World War Two Strategy of National Revolts Against Hitler." *Dalhousie Review* 61, (1981), 71–92. https://dalspace.library.dal.ca/bitstream/handle/10222/63099/dalrev_vol61_iss1_pp71_91.pdf accessed April 7, 2020.

Krammer, Arnold. *Nazie Prisoners of War in America.* New York: Stein and Day, 1979.

Levinas, Emmanuel. *Carnets de captivité suivi Écrits sur la captivité et Notes philosophiques diverses.* Paris: Bernard Grasset, 2009.

BIBLIOGRAPHY

Madsen, Chris. "Victims of Circumstance: the Execution of German Deserters by Surrendered German Troops Under Canadian Control in Amsterdam, May 1945." Canadian Military History 2, 1 (1993). https://scholars.wlu.ca/cgi/viewcontent.cgi?article=1121&context=cmh accessed April 7, 2022.

Makepeace, Clare. *Captives of War: British Prisoners of War in Europe in the Second World War.* Cambridge: Cambridge University Press, 2017.

Melady, John. *Escape from Canada!: The Untold Story of German POWs in Canada, 1939–1945.* Toronto: Macmillan, 1981.

Messerchmidt, Manfred. "The Wehrmacht and the Volksgemeinschft." Trans. Anthony Wells. *Journal of Contemporary History* 18, 1983, 719–744.

Messerchmidt, Manfred. "German Military Law in the Second World War". In *The German Military in the Age of Total War*, ed. Wilhelm Deist. Dover, N.H.: Berg Publishers, 1985, 323–335.

Moore, Bob and Kent Fedorowich, eds. *Prisoners of War and Their Captors in World War II.* Oxford: Berg Press, 1996.

Priebe, Eckhart J. *Thank You, Canada: From Messerschmitt Pilot to Canadian Citizen.* West Vancouver, BC: Condor Publishing, 1990.

Prouse, Robert A. *A Ticket to Hell Via Dieppe: From a Prisoner's Wartime Log, 1942–1945.* New York: Van Nostrand Reinhold, 1982.

Pugsley, C. *A Bloody Road Home: World War Two and New Zealand's Heroic Second Division.* New York: Penguin Books, 2014.

Rettig, A. "A De-programming Curriculum: Allied Reeducation and the Canadian-American Psychology Warfare Program for German POWs, 1943–1947". *The American Review of Canadian Studies*, (Winter, 1999): 593–619.

Robin, Ron. *The Barbed-Wire College: Reeducating German POWS in the United States During World War II.* Princeton, NJ: Princeton University Press, 1995.

Rundell, Walter Jr. "Paying the POW in World War II". *Military Affairs* 22, no. 3 (Autumn, 1958): 121–134.

Sagi, Douglas. "My Fuehrer, I Follow Thee." *The London Free Press.* "The Canadian Magazine," January 4, 1975, 1–6.

Sihls, Edward A. and Morris Janowitz. "Cohesion and Disintegration in the Wehrmacht in World War II," in *Public Opinion*, Summer 1948.

Smith, Beverly. "The Afrika Korps Comes to America." *American* 136, no. 2, August 1944, 27–30.

Stotz, Robin W. "Camp 132: A German Prisoner of War Camp In a Canadian Prairie Community During World War Two" PhD Thesis, Saskatoon, University of Saskatchewan, 1992.

Stanzel, Franz-Karl. "German Prisoners of War in Canada, 1940-1946: An Autobiography-Based Essay," *Canadian Military History* 27, no. 2., Article 19.

Yarnall, John. *Barbed Wire Disease: British & German Prisoners of War, 1914-1919.* Stroud, Gloucestshire, UK: The History Press, 2011.

Tooze, Adam. *The Wages of Destruction: The Making and Breaking of the Nazi Economy.* London: Allan Lane, 2006.

Tustin, Herbert W. *Escaping from the Kaiser.* Barnsley, UK.: Pen and Sword Books, 2014.
Whittingham, Richard. *Martial Justice: The Last Mass Execution in the United States.* Annapolis, MD: Naval Institute Press, 1997.
Wright, H. Millard. *Otto Strasser in Paradise: A Nazi in Nova Scotia.* Lawrencetown Beach, NS: Pottersfield Press, 2011.
Yackulic, G. A. "Prisoners of War in Canada." *Canadian Business*, 51 (November 1944).
Zimmermann, Ernest R. *The Little Reich on Lake Superior: A History of Canadian Internment Camp R.* Edmonton: University of Alberta Press, 2015.

TRIAL TRANSCRIPTS (LIBRARY AND ARCHIVES CANADA)

Busch, Heinrich: "Transcript of Heinrich Busch's Trial". RG 13, Vol. 1658, File No. cc608. Pt. 1.
Busch, Heinrich: "Transcript of Heinrich Busch's Trial". RG 13, Vol. 1658, File No. Pt 2.
Kratz, Adolf: "Transcript of Adolf Kratz's Trial, Vol. 1 and Vol. 2". RG 13, Vol. 1657. File No. cc601, Part 1 and Part 2.
Mueller, Willi. "Transcript of Willi Mueller's Trial." RG 13-B-1, Vol. 1659, File No. cc609
Perzenowsky, Bruno: "Transcript of Bruno Perzenowsky's Trial, RG 13, Vol. 1658, Pt 1.
Perzenowsky, Bruno: "Transcript of Bruno Perzenowsky's Trial, RG 13, Vol. 1658, Pt 2.
Perzenowsky, Bruno: "Transcript of Bruno Perzenowsky's Trial, RG 13, Vol. 1658, Pt 3.
Schwalb, Werner: "Transcript of Warner Schwalb's Trial, Pts 1 and 2". RG 13C-1, Vol. 1655 75367.
Wolf, Walter: "Transcript of Walter Wolf's Trial." RG 13-B-1. Vol. 1658, File No. cc 607.

INVESTIGATION REPORTS (LIBRARY AND ARCHIVES CANADA)

Death of Prisoner of War August Plaszek
RG 25-A-3-b, Volume number: 2784, File number: 621-LW-40, File part: 1
1944/08/08-1945/11/30

Plaszek, August (file parts 1 to 4)
RG 24-C-5, Volume number: 1594, File number: POW-1026-23, File part: 1
1943-1960

Secret and Confidential Subject Files, Army - Plaszek, August. - Prisoner of War
RG 24-C-1, Microfilm reel number: C-8437, File number: 9139-P-794
Microfilm reel number: C-8437

Secret and Confidential Subject Files, Army - Lehmann, Karl - Prisoner of War
RG 24-C-1, Microfilm reel number: C-8437, File number: 9139-L-51
Microfilm reel number: C-8437

Lehmann, Karl (file parts 1 & 2)
RG 24-C-5, Volume number: 1592, File number: POW-1026-18, File part: 1
Date: 1943-1960

BIBLIOGRAPHY

Lehmann, J. Karl
RG 117-A-3, Volume number: 1049, File number: 39577
1946/07-1946/09
117-15

Investigation Reports, Camp 132, 1943-1946
RG 24m ewwk C-5416, File HQS 7236-94-6-132

Schwalb, Werner.
RG 24. Reel C-8117, File 9139

INTERVIEWS

Joyce Keating, neè Reesor
James "Jim" Keating
Howard Millin
William Westage, RCMP (retired)

OTHER MUSEUMS AND ARCHIVES

Department of History and Heritage (DHH) Department of National Defence, Canada
Kardex File Nos.
169.000 (D134)
329.009 (D2), (D3) and D4)

Glenbow Museum
https://glenbow.ucalgary.ca/wp-content/uploads/2019/06/m-2124-3-pt2.pdf
Medicine Hat Archives
Provincial Archives of Alberta
Accession Number GR1983.0323 Box 1.

NEWSPAPERS

Calgary Herald
Edmonton Journal
Lethbridge Herald
London Free Press
Medicine Hat Daily News
Saskatoon Star Phoenix
Toronto Star
Windsor Star
Winnipeg Free Press
Winnipeg Journal
Vancouver Province

Prisoner of War Camp 132, Medicine Hat